CW01376236

JANE AUSTEN'S LOVERS AND OTHER STUDIES IN FICTION AND HISTORY FROM AUSTEN TO LE CARRÉ

Jane Austen's Lovers
and Other Studies in Fiction and History from Austen to le Carré

John Halperin

Centennial Professor of English
Vanderbilt University

MACMILLAN
PRESS

First published 1988

Published by
THE MACMILLAN PRESS LTD
Houndmills, Basingstoke, Hampshire RG21 2XS
and London
Companies and representatives
throughout the world

Typeset by Wessex Typesetters
(Division of The Eastern Press Ltd)
Frome, Somerset

Printed in Hong Kong

British Library Cataloguing in Publication Data
Halperin, John
Jane Austen's Lovers and Other Studies in Fiction and
History from Austen to le Carré
1. English fiction – 19th century –
History and criticism   2. English fiction –
20th century – History and criticism
I. Title
823'.009   PR861
ISBN 0–333–43443–9

In Memoriam
Gordon N. Ray, 1915–1986
and
Donald R. Howard, 1927–1987

Contents

Acknowledgments

I am grateful to the following for kind permission to reprint the essays which appear in this volume: the editors of *Studies in English Literature* for "Jane Austen's Lovers" (vol. 25, Autumn 1985, 719–36); the editors of *Modern Language Quarterly* for "The Novelist as Heroine in *Mansfield Park*: A Study in Autobiography" (vol. 44, June 1983, 136–56); the Oxford University Press for "On *The Ordeal of Richard Feverel*," from the World's Classics edition of *The Ordeal of Richard Feverel* by George Meredith, edited by John Halperin (1984, pp. vii–xviii); Duke University Press for "Trollope's Conservatism," *South Atlantic Quarterly* (vol. 82, Winter 1983, 56–78); the editors of *English Studies* for "Trollope's *Phineas Finn* and History" (vol. 59, Spring 1978, 121–37); the Modern Humanities Research Association and the editors of the *Yearbook of English Studies* for "Trollope, James, and the International Theme" (vol. 7, January 1977, 141–7); the New American Library for "On *The Golden Bowl*," from the Meridian and New American Library edition of *The Golden Bowl* by Henry James, edited by John Halperin (1972, 1973, 1975, pp. 549–60); the Modern Humanities Research Association and the editors of *Modern Language Review* for "Leslie Stephen, Thomas Hardy, and *A Pair of Blue Eyes*" (vol. 75, October 1980, 738–45); Duke University Press for "How Gissing Read Dickens," *South Atlantic Quarterly* (vol. 83, Summer 1984, 312–22); the editors of the *Virginia Quarterly Review* for "*Eminent Victorians* and History" (vol. 56, Summer 1980, 433–54); the editors of the *Dalhousie Review* for "Bloomsbury and Virginia Woolf: Another View" (vol. 59, Autumn 1979, 426–42); Louisiana State University Press for "Elizabeth Bowen and Henry James," *Henry James Review* (vol. 7, Autumn 1986, 45–8); Macmillan Press Ltd for "Barbara Pym and the War of the Sexes," from *The Life and Work of Barbara Pym*, ed. Dale Salwak (London and Iowa City, 1987, pp. 88–100); Duke University Press for "Between Two Worlds: The Novels of John le Carré," *South Atlantic Quarterly* (vol. 79, Winter 1980, 17–37).

I should also like to thank the following for encouragement, advice, or help in preparing the present volume and its contents for publication: Frances Arnold, Edith Baras, Joanne Ferguson, Oliver Ferguson, Roma Gill, Donald Greene, Elaine P. Halperin,

Diana Hobby, Glenda Hudson, Alberta Martin, Douglas Matthews, Mary Sue McAlister, Florence Muncy, Ira B. Nadel, Hershel Parker, Heddy Richter, Valery Rose, Dale Salwak, and Virginia Shaefer.

J.H.

Introduction

We murder to dissect.
– Wordsworth

These essays were written between 1971 and 1985, and published between 1972 and 1987. With only a few exceptions they reflect my interest in historical and biographical studies, and any reader who may be hoping to find in this volume a dazzling display of critical virtuosity is going to be disappointed. One might perhaps detect a vaguely structuralist approach in the essay on *The Golden Bowl*, written in 1971 as the introduction to a paperback edition of the novel; like most students of literature who came of age in the 1960s, I read the structuralists as they published, and there is some concern in that essay with figurative language and with the relation of the novel's operative metaphors to each other and to the wider issues of the text in which they appear. In the essay on Barbara Pym, the latest of those in this volume to be written, there are, admittedly, similar concerns – and I must confess that I found that piece, written in 1985, the most difficult of this group to compose; by the time of its submission I had largely lost interest in the approach it had to take, which is that of a "pure" reading of several novels. For, as structuralism gave way to deconstruction and worse, the new movements in textual criticism struck me as increasingly faddish and irrelevant. By the 1980s I was absorbed by the only concern which now seems to me to justify the profession of criticism, a concern which can, at times, enable the critic to make a contribution to contemporary, "relevant" elucidation of classic literature – not so much the relation of the component parts of a text to one another, but rather the illumination of the historical and biographical milieux in which texts are brought into being and by which their nature is determined: the relation, to put it bluntly, of art to "real" life. For the last fifteen years, as most of these essays may testify, my overriding interest has been in the connections between literature and the cultural moment at which it is composed and by which its shape is molded.

This may seem to some an ossified approach to artistic endeavor at a time when the new schools of criticism are trumpeting forth

1

their discoveries about the "science" of linguistics, the revelatory properties of syntax, the impossibility of finding bedrock "meaning" or of articulating it. I confess to having little interest in criticism which reveals to us what the text is composed of without attempting to explain *why* it has been composed in that fashion. For me, every artistic act appears to have its origin in the confluence of the artist and the moment; and, while texts can be ingeniously deconstructed to yield up their component parts and to show the relation of these to each other, such a critical approach strikes me as contingent, limited, and ultimately amoral. It's the new naturalism: it lays bare, but draws no conclusions.

I don't believe that "meaning" is necessarily inaccessible or undiscoverable. Different critics may indeed find different meanings in the same text, and each of these meanings may be mutually inclusive; that is, each interpretation or reading, different though it may be from all of the others, might be "right" (or at least plausible) in the sense that it can be supported in some way by the manner in which we apprehend the text. But the abandonment by the deconstructionists of the primary function of literary criticism – that is, the attempt to illuminate meaning, or meanings – seems to me to be a retreat into nihilism. It may be good exercise, but it develops useless muscles. It is finally a throwing up of the hands and saying, "Well, it could mean *anything*, depending on how we read it." While any work of art can certainly mean simultaneously any number of things, I don't believe that it must always mean nothing in particular. Which possible meaning or meanings seem most congruent with what the artist, on the face of it at least, actually seems to be saying? I think that this question is more important to pose and to answer than the question of how he or she says what is said, how the words are arranged on the page, what the nature of the sentence structure is, and so on. True, we cannot separate what is said from how it is said; but we ought not to be so exclusively concerned with the latter (how) that we forget to address the former (what; not to mention why).

For the words on the page are only one possible route to meaning. The chief task of the critic is to discover, if possible, why *these* words, rather than other words, are there. And if you believe this, as I do, then inevitably you come back again and again not to the reader but to the author as the paramount and most reliable source of "meaning," for it is within his or her personality and his or her point of view, shaped by forces not always undiscoverable, that keys to "meaning" can be found; whereas each reader will bring to the text a highly personal perspective. By focusing on the reader's collision with the text as a source of potential meaning, the new schools have turned literary criticism into a highly subjective act, with "meaning" to be found not in the text, where it exists if it exists anywhere, but within the critic or the critical methodology itself. Thus criticism becomes its own end, and the critic rather than the text or the author becomes the focus and the subject of criticism. The critical act becomes so subjective that it requires us to study the critic and what he or she does rather than the author and what he or she does. Literature gets lost in the search for the critic. The critic turns into his or her own subject, the author dies, and courses in critical theory replace courses in literature, while criticism itself becomes little more than intellectualized phenomenology.

To ignore the author, as if he or she were not responsible for the words on the page – as if the madness of art overtakes him or her every time he or she picks up a pen, and goes into a Lacanian trance during which words no conscious thought has been given to magically appear – is naive and onanistic. How can we separate the dancer from the dance? All artists, even bad ones, are to some degree conscious of what they do. Nor can any writer, even if it occurred to him or her to try to do so, escape from the historical moment or the envelope of personality out of which creativity emerges.

Trollope writes in the Palliser novels about contemporary politicians because he was fascinated by the politics of his day, held strong political prejudices, even stood for Parliament late in his life. Two of the three essays on Trollope in this volume attempt to tackle him through historical analysis, and precisely for these reasons. You don't need to deconstruct *Phineas Finn* or *The Prime Minister* to detect in their pages cartoons of political leaders of his time (such as Disraeli, Bright, and Derby), with many of whom Trollope was personally acquainted. Even some of John le Carré's novels, beyond being immensely entertaining, can be seen as founded in particular historical moments and arising out of public events very specific indeed. It is only when the historical apparatus disappears altogether that you can have biographies as demonstrably unreliable, or indeed as fictionalized, as those by Lytton Strachey in *Eminent Victorians*. In the same way, literary criticism can become "fictionalized" – simply made up, a game with no rules – when attention to biographical and historical fact is deliberately excluded from it. Does it assist us as readers to know that the love stories in Jane Austen's novels are conditioned by events in her own life which shaped her views on marriage? Such knowledge may or may not help us to read the novels intelligently; what is certain is that to ignore the facts – by which I mean both the story of her life, and the historical and social nature of marriage and the position of undowried, unmarried women in the late eighteenth century in England – prevents us from reaching some of the possible "meanings" the new textual critics profess themselves so anxious to find. If they really want a multiplicity of meanings in literary texts, why is their approach to literature so deliberately narrow and exclusive?

Several of the essays in this volume touch upon matters of literary influence, an approach which by its very nature must include a study of both history and biography. Questions of influence are perhaps the most slippery and difficult of all of those the critic may choose to grapple with. Like circumstantial evidence in a trial, you never *see* "influence" happening; you can only infer or guess, intelligently or badly as the case may be. Influence can never be proven beyond the shadow of a doubt. But just as no man or woman can write as if outside the borders of his or her historical and psychic reality, so no writer who reads – and I take it that all writers read – can remain utterly beyond the reaches of what he or she reads. Consciously or not, the writer becomes, as a writer, the sum of what he or she thinks writers are and do; he or she acquires this knowledge from reading other writers; he or she learns, as all of us in every walk of life learn, by example, positive or negative. John le Carré has made no secret of his debt to Kipling and Conrad; Elizabeth Bowen actually worried about writing too much like the later Henry James; due to his own complex personality, Gissing found in Dickens what he wished to find there; Thomas Hardy was not beyond appropriating silently for his own use ideas, situations, and themes he excavated in other writers; Trollope and James at one point in their careers found themselves writing about the same things, whether by accident or design. These are facts. Some members of my profession will therefore find them, *a priori*, irrelevant.

There is in each of these essays at some level the assumption that no writer writes without reference to self, consciously or not.

Mansfield Park, which has often been considered a "sport" among Jane Austen's novels – the least "characteristic" of them and of her, the least "Janeite" of them all – may be seen, read as I read it, as immensely autobiographical, in this sense the most "characteristic" of her novels after all. Gissing's account of what he thinks Dickens said in his novels is virtually a transcript of everything he himself believed about fiction. Strachey's picture of the Victorians could have been written only by a Georgian who blamed his grandfathers for the catastrophe of the Great War – it could have been written, that is, only by a man who, at a particular juncture, and due to history itself, of which at Cambridge he was a poor student, found himself with a particular axe to grind. In the same way, perhaps, my account of Bloomsbury may be seen as an exercise in Stracheyesque historiography, written by someone living later and no less prone to grinding personal axes. The most superficial investigation into the matter reveals that in her own life Barbara Pym had a talent for disastrous romances, for obsessions with selfish men. It adds something to our reading of her novels if we are able to see the relation of the sexes, temporarily one hopes, as she saw them.

It is soothing to think that one becomes a more perceptive critic and a more skillful writer as one gets older, whether it is true or not. Accordingly, I have made in these essays a few changes, mostly stylistic, and in two or three instances substantive. Young men write more words than older men do, both because they have less sense of style through the crucible of practice, and also because they have more energy. But for the most part, and for better or worse, these essays are reprinted more or less as they first appeared. They are arranged (loosely) in order of their subjects rather than in order of their composition. Whether they will be seen as the last croak of an outmoded method, as the reassertion of critical values now sometimes forgotten, or as the expression of interests men and woman always take in literature they enjoy – or as none of these – remains, as they say, to be seen.

1

Jane Austen's Lovers

*Jane Austen . . . seemed to have as shrewd an
eye as anyone could who didn't really know
what sexual feeling was.* – C. P. Snow

But Miss Austen has no romance – none at all.
– John Henry Newman

A discussion of sex in Jane Austen's novels need not be brief.
For what it may be worth, there is more sex in the Big Six than in
the fifteen novels of Charles Dickens, whose heroes and heroines
are uniformly insipid in comparison to Jane Austen's.

What, after all, finally brings Elizabeth and Darcy together in
Pride and Prejudice? It is Elizabeth's fifteen-year-old sister Lydia
running away with the professional seducer Wickham, who had
earlier very nearly made a similar conquest of Darcy's teenaged
sister Georgiana. (One remembers Mrs. Bennet's famous response
to Darcy's ill-natured comment on the dullness of country life: "I
assure you there is as much of *that* going on in the country as in
town.") In *Sense and Sensibility*, the nominal hero, Colonel
Brandon, is prevented at the last minute from going off with his
own sister-in-law; her husband, we are told, "had no regard for
her; his pleasures were not what they ought to have been" – more
than a suggestion that he has no interest in women. Brandon's
sister-in-law, tired of waiting for her husband to cultivate such an
interest, turns promiscuous and produces an illegitimate daughter
who, as still another teenager, falls prey to the seducer Willoughby
and later produces yet another illegitimate child. The climax of
Mansfield Park comes when the silver-tongued Henry Crawford
goes off with Maria Bertram, who has just married another man –
thus precipitating a nasty divorce. And there is the mysterious
illegitimacy of Harriet Smith in *Emma*, and Mr. Elliot's long liaison
with a mistress in *Persuasion*; and so on.

"I am proud to say that I have a very good eye for an adulteress,"
Jane Austen wrote in a letter at the age of twenty-five, after seeing

7

one in the flesh, and adultery flourishes as successfully in her novels as it has always done everywhere else. The later years of her life were lived during the Regency, years during which the Prince Regent was flaunting his pack of high-placed mistresses – of whom Jane Austen in her letters keeps careful track – and long separated from his wife, Princess Caroline, who led an equally raffish life on the Continent. Their divorce case, though it took place after Jane Austen's death, was one of the greatest scandals in the already scandalous history of the House of Hanover. It is ironic that the Prince (as we shall see) was a great admirer of Jane Austen's novels; perhaps he saw more in them than many modern readers do. At any rate, it is pleasant to think of the future George IV reading Jane Austen in his various royal residences when he was not occupied with his mistresses. Jane Austen was on Princess Caroline's side in the great debate between the Prince Regent and his wife; and (as we shall also see) it was only after being bullied by the Prince's chaplain that Jane Austen agreed to dedicate *Emma* to the future George IV.

Jane Austen was a Georgian, and brought up in the frank atmosphere of the age. The forms of Regency society were among other things a screen for adulteries, fornications, seductions, illegitimacies and the occasional acts of incest and inversion; and Jane Austen, alert, curious, and perceptive as she was, did not miss (as it were) a trick. George Moore said of her novels,

> We do not go into society for the pleasure of conversation, but for the pleasure of sex, direct or indirect. Everything is arranged for this end: the dresses, the dances, the food, the wine, the music! Of this truth we are all conscious now, but should we have discovered it without Jane Austen's help? It was certainly she who perceived it, and her books are permeated with it.

Well: this could have been my subject – but, alas, it is not. I am concerned here, as I have been elsewhere, with the novelist's own life and with the men in that life rather than the men in her books. But, contrary to the popular conception, that life was not dull or uneventful – though admittedly it was not quite as spectacular and salacious as that of her exact contemporary, the Marquis de Sade.

"I remember [a colleague] when we once got on the subject of Jane Austen – [she] apparently wrote her M.A. thesis on Jane

Austen, God help us – asking me in accents of the deepest seriousness, 'Do you think Jane Austen was a virgin?', as though it mattered," the distinguished eighteenth-century scholar Donald Greene once remarked. "Well," he went on, "God knows [my colleague] isn't [a virgin], but that hasn't made her a great novelist, or even a very good scholar."[1]

That Jane Austen died a virgin is probably both true and irrelevant, as Greene suggests. For her literary genius, her instinctive understanding of how people function, could not be affected by a momentary physiological experience, a series of them, or even an addiction to them. This does not mean, however – despite the conventional wisdom to the contrary – that Jane Austen was uninformed in matters emotional and amatory; indeed, despite what most people believe, she had a succession of admirers, a number of chances to marry, and several disastrous romantic disappointments. One would never know this from reading the standard sources.

In the *Memoir* of his aunt published more than half a century after her death, James Edward Austen-Leigh made a series of solemn pronouncements which have often been accepted as gospel truth. "Of events her life was singularly barren: few changes and no great crisis ever broke the smooth current of its course," Jane Austen's clergyman nephew declared. And he added, "I have no reason to think that she ever felt any attachment by which the happiness of her life was at all affected."[2] The evidence was there, had James Edward Austen-Leigh (and his successors in the field) chosen to consider it, that none of this was true; and unfortunately this view of Jane Austen has remained largely unquestioned by those who wish to see the novelist as a serene, untroubled woman at home in her world.

But the truth is less easy and more sharp-edged. Events, changes, crises, attachments – Jane Austen's life was full of them. Could it possibly have been otherwise? Could this woman to whom nothing ever happened be the same woman whose ironic moral vision the world has been celebrating for nearly two centuries? That there were a number of "attachments" to men, and a number of men who were attached to her, and that this "affected" her "happiness," was inevitable.

Jane Austen's first romantic interest was Tom Lefroy, the nephew of the Rev. Isaac Lefroy and his wife Anna. During the novelist's first twenty-five years, the Austens lived at Steventon

Rectory in Hampshire, and the Lefroys at nearby Ashe Rectory (they were neighbors). In January 1796, a month after Jane Austen's twentieth birthday, Tom Lefroy, having just come down from Trinity College, Dublin, visited his uncle and aunt. He was a month younger than Jane.

The opening paragraph of the novelist's earliest extant letter – written to her sister Cassandra – mentions that it is Tom Lefroy's birthday. He "has but one fault, which time will, I trust, entirely remove," Jane Austen declares. "It is that his morning coat is . . . too light." She surmises that he dresses in imitation of his namesake Tom Jones. She dares not tell Cassandra how badly she and Tom have been behaving: "Imagine to yourself everything most profligate and shocking in the way of dancing and sitting down together." She describes Tom as "a very gentlemanlike, good looking, pleasant young man." Her only complaint is that he is lazy when it comes to making calls – or dropping by, as we might say today: they seem to meet only at dances. He is her "friend," and no doubt on those grounds Cassandra must, Jane assumes, be "impatient to hear something about him."[3] Five days later she writes again. In the course of a party the next evening she expects "to receive an offer from my friend. . . . I shall refuse him, however, unless he promises to give away his white coat." She plans "to confine myself in future to Mr. Tom Lefroy, for whom I don't care sixpence," and give up all other admirers. The next morning Jane writes again: "The day is come on which I am to flirt my last with Tom Lefroy, and when you receive this it will be over. My tears flow as I write at the melancholy idea."[4]

We must not take the novelist's flippancy at face value. The tone here is similar to that of her juvenilia, some of which was composed during this same period of her life and most of which is devoted to burlesque and parody of sentimental and romantic excesses in the literature of her day. The Lefroy "affair" took on more meaning for her in later years – because of its abrupt termination, because the novelist was genuinely attached to him (as these excerpts from her letters clearly indicate), and because Jane Austen had difficulty (with one exception, as we shall see) finding anyone else she liked quite so well as Tom Lefroy. What happened was this. Tom's aunt Mrs. Lefroy decided to send her Irish nephew packing before his visit had reached its projected length – "that no more mischief might be done," according to Jane Austen's niece Caroline.[5] The two young people between them commanded nothing to live on – and that was that. Ironically, Tom Lefroy, had he been allowed to remain in the neighborhood and make the expected declaration, would have found no difficulty in supporting a wife, for he turned out to be one of the most distinguished lawyers of his generation. He was called to the Irish bar in the following year, 1797, quickly advanced in his profession, and ultimately became Lord Chief Justice of Ireland (1852–66). In 1798 he engaged himself to a wealthy Irish girl, and married her in 1799. He and Jane Austen never saw one another again after that hectic month of January 1796.

Years later the old Chief Justice told his nephew that he had once been in love with the famous Jane Austen, but "he qualified his concession by saying that it was a boyish love." The available evidence suggests that he recovered more quickly than she from whatever disappointment there may have been; Tom, after all, had all the world before him, while Jane lived with her brothers and sister in a quiet country rectory. One of the novelist's nieces recalled later that if there was any "heartlessness" in the matter it was undoubtedly on the gentleman's side, not the lady's.[6] A major theme of *Persuasion*, Jane Austen's last completed novel, is that woman's love is more enduring than man's; it is likely that she never entirely forgot Tom Lefroy. "Our tears are always young, the saltwater stays the same from cradle . . . to grave."[7]

Jane Austen's surviving letters – those left to posterity by the vigilant, scissors-happy Cassandra Austen – contain only one other reference to Tom. In November 1798, nearly three years after his visit to Hampshire, Jane's feelings were still smoldering. Informing Cassandra that Mrs. Lefroy had called, the novelist remarks that her neighbor "did not once mention the name" of her Irish nephew "to *me*, and I was too proud to make any enquiries."[8] These are not the accents of indifference. Jane Austen's feelings had been touched; this is clear. Tom Lefroy brought the first bit of romance into her life; the outcome, for her, was not fortunate.

That she had romance on her mind during the 1790s is plain enough. One sees it everywhere in the juvenilia, despite the debunking there of sentimental romances.[9] Her first three novels, all of which concern themselves with the search by provincial girls for husbands, were initially drafted during this decade. And in her clergyman father's parish register, under the Entry of Publication of Banns, she forged one day the announcement of a proposed marriage between "Henry Frederick Howard Fitzwilliam

of London and Jane Austen of Steventon." As Elizabeth Jenkins
has pointed out, the hypothetical gentleman whose banns were to
be published bore the names afterwards given to Henry Crawford
(*Mansfield Park*), Frederick Wentworth (*Persuasion*), the Mr. Howard
who was to marry Emma Watson ("The Watsons"), and Fitzwilliam
Darcy (*Pride and Prejudice*). In the Entry of Marriage register itself
there is an account in the novelist's hand of a supposed marriage
between Jane Austen of Steventon and one Arthur William
Mortimer of Liverpool.[10]

On her way to visit her elder brother Edward and his family in
Kent in the autumn of 1796, Jane Austen passed a house she
knew. We find her writing to Cassandra, "We went by Bifrons,
and I contemplated with a melancholy pleasure, the abode of
Him, on whom I once fondly doated."[11] While the fulsomeness
of the language may seem suspicious, especially when invoked by
this writer, the fact is that there was a real gentleman in the case.
Bifrons, in Kent, was the home of the Rev. Mr. Taylor, who had
five sons. One of them, Edward, is the subject of Jane Austen's
reference here. When or where she met him, or how serious their
relationship ever became, remains tantalizingly mysterious. Four
years later, in the autumn of 1800, the novelist refers in a letter to
the news that Edward Taylor is to marry his cousin Charlotte:
"Those beautiful dark Eyes will then adorn another Generation at
least in all their purity," she remarks.[12] Since she did not know
the lady, the "beautiful dark Eyes" must be the gentleman's.
Edward Taylor, though we know little else of him, touched the
novelist's heart, however briefly.

About Jane Austen's next suitor there is more information,
though much of what follows here is the result largely of
guesswork and deduction; his name is not mentioned in any
surviving letters written by Jane Austen. During the Christmas
festivities at Steventon in 1797, just after the novelist's twenty-
second birthday, she met the Rev. Samuel Blackall, a Cambridge
don who was then paying a visit to the Lefroys. He seems to have
fallen in love with Jane Austen – or managed to convince himself
that he had done so. Four years older than she, Blackall, great-
grandson of the Bishop of Exeter in the time of Queen Anne,
became a Fellow of Emmanuel College, and was ordained in 1794.
In later years (from 1812 onwards) he was Rector of North (not
"Great," as Jane has it in a letter) Cadbury in Somerset.

In the autumn of 1798, nine months after meeting the novelist in Hampshire, Blackall wrote to Mrs. Lefroy that he wished to improve his acquaintance with the Austens, and especially with Jane – "with a hope of creating to myself a nearer interest. But at present I cannot indulge my expectation of it."[13] Mrs. Lefroy showed Blackall's letter to Jane, who wrote of it to Cassandra: "This is rational enough; there is less love and more sense in it than sometimes appeared before, and I am very well satisfied. It will all go on exceedingly well, and decline away in a very reasonable manner." It is clear from this that Blackall had made his feelings known to her the previous year, and that she had made it equally clear to him that his feelings were not reciprocated. It was less than three years since lively Tom Lefroy had disappeared, and the ponderous Blackall was hardly the man to take his place in Jane Austen's affections. Jane tells Cassandra that Blackall will not come into Hampshire this Christmas (1798), "and it is therefore most probable that our indifference will soon be mutual, unless his regard, which appeared to spring from knowing nothing of me at first, is best supported by never seeing me."[14] This was a one-sided romance. Blackall's name is never given; he is referred to by the novelist only as a "friend."

As Jane predicted, Blackall soon ceased his attentions. Years later, in 1813, he married. Hearing of this, and of his acquiring the Somerset living, the novelist wrote complacently to Cassandra of Blackall's "succeeding . . . to the very Living, which we remembered his talking of and wishing for." She adds, "He was a piece of Perfection, noisy Perfection himself whom I always recollect with regard." "Pictures of perfection," Jane Austen told one of her nieces a few months before her death, "make me sick and wicked"; her characterization of Blackall here should be seen in that light. She could never summon up more than "regard" for him; indeed, she seems to have found him pompous and didactic. When she goes on in her 1813 letter to Cassandra to describe what she hopes for in Blackall's wife, we may see a little more of what he might have been like: "I would wish Miss Lewis to be of a silent turn and rather ignorant, but naturally intelligent and wishing to learn; – fond of cold veal pies, green tea in the afternoon, and a green window blind at night."[15] So much for Blackall. It would seem from this that he was not seeking intellectual companionship in a wife, and this may have been another reason why Jane Austen could not bring herself to accept him.

The next three men to be mentioned here passed quickly through the novelist's life and her consciousness, but they are nonetheless part of the picture. In the autumn of 1800, Cassandra again being away from Steventon, Jane and her friend, neighbor, and future sister-in-law Mary Lloyd, were invited to dine at Ashe Park by the man who was then renting it. This was a Mr. Holder. In conformity with a truth universally acknowledged – having made a good fortune in the East Indies, he was in want of a wife. Here is part of Jane's description of the evening.

> a sudden invitation & an own postchaise took us to Ash[e] Park, to dine tete a tete with Mr Holder, Mr Gauntlett, & James Digweed; but our tete a tete was cruelly reduced by non-attendance of the two latter. – We had a very quiet evening, I beleive [sic] Mary found it dull, but I thought it very pleasant. To sit in idleness over a good fire in a well-proportioned room is a luxurious sensation. – Sometimes we talked & sometimes we were quite silent; I said two or three amusing things, & Mr Holder made a few infamous puns.[16]

She apparently liked Mr. Holder. One notes the declaration, "To sit in idleness over a good fire in a well-proportioned room is a luxurious sensation." Jane Austen, now nearly twenty-five, had had little enough opportunity for this sort of luxury, but she never forgot its advantages. For her, such indulgences could come only with marriage. Though comfortable at Steventon, the Austens were not wealthy, and the novelist's father had no fortune to bequeath his daughters. In *Pride and Prejudice*, the first draft of which had been completed several years before this evening at Ashe Park, Lydia Bennet, it may be worth recalling, taunts her sister Jane about being still a spinster at twenty-three.

In January 1801, a few months later, Jane Austen's friendship with Mr. Holder arrived at a notable anti-climax. On another visit to Ashe Park she found herself shut up in the drawing-room alone with Mr. Holder for ten minutes. "Nothing," she told Cassandra, "could prevail on me to move two steps from the door, on the lock of which I kept one hand constantly fixed." Despite this "betrayal . . . into a situation of the utmost cruelty," as Jane characterizes it, no proposal of marriage was made – and the novelist left Ashe Park, she told her sister, "*very* cross."[17] She had expected a proposal. To expect and not to get, even should you intend not to take, may be annoying and humiliating.

In 1800 the Austens decided to move from Steventon to Bath in the following year. The novelist's father, now sixty-nine, was retiring; and undoubtedly he and Mrs. Austen rated Bath a more propitious place for their two unmarried daughters to find husbands. Both sisters were now well into their twenties (Cassandra was Jane's senior by two and a half years). A tradition persists that the family's decision to leave Steventon was part of a resolve to put some distance between the sisters and the Digweed family, residents of Steventon Manor House. From time to time Jane suggested that one of the Digweed brothers, James, was in love with Cassandra, and some of the other Austens may have suspected that James's brother Harry Francis Digweed, who was a year or two younger than Jane, was in love with her. There is no evidence to support any of this; it goes little beyond speculation on the part of some early biographers. Indeed, such a state of affairs would have provided a good reason for the Austens to remain in their comfortable home of many years, for the Digweed brothers would have been good catches, and the sisters apparently liked them. The Digweed theory of the Austens' departure from Steventon is anything but convincing;[18] it is more likely that the family left because Jane and Cassandra had too few suitors than that they did so because they had too many.

A letter written by Jane to Cassandra early in 1801 helps explain how the Digweed story may have begun. It concludes,

> I get more & more reconciled to the idea of our removal. We have lived long enough in this Neighbourhood, the Basingstoke Balls are certainly on the decline. . . . It must not be generally known however that I am not sacrificing a great deal in quitting the Country – or I can expect to inspire no tenderness, no interest, in those we leave behind.[19]

Only a reader utterly devoid of a sense of humor could take any of this seriously.

Once in Bath, the family was squired about by Mrs. Austen's wealthy brother and his wife, Mr. and Mrs. James Leigh Perrot. The Leigh Perrots gave evening parties, and invited to them as many of the eligible bachelors of Bath as they knew. At one such gathering, Jane was reintroduced to a gentleman she had once thought she disliked, but about whom she was now forced to change her mind. This was a Mr. Evelyn, a friend of her brother Edward's. The novelist had first met Mr. Evelyn when she was visiting the Leigh Perrots in Bath in 1799. At that time she was put off by his passion for horses. He had got her brother Edward to buy some, and was always talking of them himself. Jane, who detested field sports (though she liked to ride), had written to Cassandra in June 1799, "if the judgment of a Yahoo can ever be depended on, I suppose it may now, for I believe Mr. Evelyn has all his life thought more of Horses than of anything else."[20] Two years later, in May 1801, she again met Mr. Evelyn in Bath, and began to form a better opinion of him. She complains in a letter to Cassandra that she has seen little of him despite his promise to take her out for a drive in his phaeton – and goes on, "whether it will come to anything must remain with him. – I really beleive [*sic*] he is very harmless." Her aunt, she says, has been trying to think up a pretext for visiting Mr. Evelyn, but so far has utterly failed in this endeavor. "She ought to be particularly scrupulous in such matters & she says so herself," Jane declares, "but nevertheless. . . ."[21] The sentence is left sadly unfinished; the novelist seemed to have her fingers crossed. The day after writing this she was taken out by Mr. Evelyn for a ride in his phaeton; but the gentleman, simply making good on a promise, offered no other declaration. That was that.

We come now to two of the most important events in this account of Jane Austen's romantic history. They occurred within a year and a half of one another.

The Austens spent the summer of 1801 in Devon, by the sea – probably either at Newtown or Sidmouth. It was at this time that a most mysterious event in the novelist's life took place – mysterious because so little is known about it, because Cassandra ultimately destroyed all of Jane's letters written during the next three years, and because many second- and third-hand versions of what happened have been given to posterity via family gossip: nieces and nephews and great-nieces and -nephews reporting what they were told their Aunt Cassandra told their mama or papa.

What is certain is this. While on holiday, the Austen party became intimate with two brothers – a physician resident in Devon, and his clergyman brother visiting him there. The latter, a youngish, intelligent, charming, and handsome man, by all accounts, found himself greatly attracted to Jane Austen. Indeed, he apparently fell in love with her. After three weeks he seemed to be on the verge of a proposal – but the holiday then came to an end. The Austens and the two brothers planned to meet again soon – before the following summer – and they also agreed to take their holidays together the next year.

It was fully expected by the Austen family that at the first opportunity the clergyman would offer marriage, and that Jane would accept him. He was considered "worthy" of the novelist's hand by both sisters, who were exacting judges – of this there is no doubt. The summer ended, and the happy group broke up. Instead of an early reunion with her would-be fiancé, Jane Austen, according to Cassandra, received soon afterward from his brother notice of his death.[22]

The bitterness of Anne Elliot in *Persuasion* on the subject of happiness delayed may be a rare clue to Jane Austen's own bitterness of spirit during the years between 1801 and 1804 – a period for which, as we have seen, no letters of hers survive. Jane's prospects of marriage were few enough; here was another, the most promising, snuffed out. And in this instance she had, apparently, *loved*. At a time when they could not go to university or enter the professions, single women not in possession of a good fortune could find security only in marriage. A man one could genuinely love, with the means to support a wife in comfort, was what most women situated as Jane Austen was had to hope for. She had finally discovered the husband she wanted, which undoubtedly made all previous disappointments and frustrations seem irrelevant – and then, suddenly, she lost him. The clergyman may well have died, as tradition has it; or he may, like Tom Lefroy five and a half years earlier (under duress), simply have decamped, leaving his brother to pick up the pieces. Cassandra's story to the family would have been the same in either circumstance. There is nothing concrete to suggest the second possibility. But Cassandra's failure to provide a name, or indeed any more detail than is given here, as well as her destruction of any relevant letters, has made it unlikely that anything more will ever be known about the business. This, of course, was her intention. In itself such secretiveness is suggestive; plenty of information is available, for example, about Cassandra's own fiancé, Thomas Fowle, who died shortly before they were to

be married. Why is not similar information extant about Jane
Austen's lost lover? Without a name, no death can be substantiated;
equally true, and perhaps more to the point: no death can be
disproven. The family's attempt to flatten the mystery has only,
over the years, broadened it.

In the following year, 1802, perhaps the most bizarre of these
romantic tales unfolded itself. The Bigg Wither family of
Manydown, in Hampshire, were friends and neighbors of the
Austens in Steventon days. Late in November of this year Jane
and Cassandra stopped off at Manydown House for a visit. On 3
December the sisters suddenly and without prior warning
appeared at Steventon Rectory, where their eldest brother, the
Rev. James Austen, who had succeeded his father as Rector of
Steventon, now lived with his family and his second wife, the
former Mary Lloyd. Jane and Cassandra got out of the Manydown
carriage with their friends the three Bigg sisters, and "a tender
scene of embraces and tears and distressing farewells took place
in the hall" of the Rectory, according to Mary Lloyd Austen. Jane
was highly upset, and close to tears. Having hurriedly left
Manydown, Jane and Cassandra demanded without further
explanation that James Austen drive them back to Bath in his own
carriage the next day, which was a Saturday. This meant that
James would not get back to Steventon in time to preach on the
Sunday, and that a stand-in would have to be found for the
faithful who would gather at the parish Church of St. Nicholas.
The sisters nonetheless insisted. They wanted to leave the
neighborhood as quickly as possible; under no circumstance, they
declared, would they wait until the Monday, as their brother
suggested. He took them back to Bath.

Here is what happened. Harris Bigg Wither, twenty-one years
old and preparing to take orders, had proposed to Jane on the
evening of 2 December 1802. Now just a few weeks short of
her twenty-seventh birthday, disappointed in love and still
unpublished, the novelist had accepted him. Materially, at least,
this would have been a good match for her. Her father had little
money to give her, as we know; Harris Bigg Wither was in a
position to help the Austen family. The lot of a penurious spinster
was of course not a happy one; and Jane Austen was the only
member of her large family who, before her novels began to
appear, had no private income whatever from any source, and
thus remained utterly dependent upon the *largesse* of her relations,

her brothers especially. To such a spirit as hers, this must have been both galling and humiliating. Further, Harris Bigg Wither's sisters were old and good friends of Jane and Cassandra; the families were close. And such a marriage offered the novelist a chance to return to her native Hampshire from Bath, which she persistently detested. "For a . . . woman in Jane Austen's financial position," Joan Rees has commented, "the opportunity of marriage, motherhood, and eventually becoming the mistress of . . . an establishment [such as] . . . Manydown house, situated in the part of the country she regarded as home . . . [and] where one day she might be able to offer her sister a comfortable home, was not an offer to be turned down lightly."[23]

Jane Austen did not take it lightly. But she could not act the role so convincingly played by her own Charlotte Lucas in *Pride and Prejudice* when she accepts Mr. Collins. Jane would not, after all, marry a man she did not love in order to acquire an establishment. Having had second thoughts during that night at Manydown, she changed her mind, and the next morning announced to them all that she had done so. She had been tempted – and then vexed by the embarrassment caused on both sides by her ambivalence. And so, with Cassandra and the Bigg sisters, Jane Austen executed an instant and unceremonious retreat from Manydown House, which she made a point of never visiting again.[24]

The reaction of the Austen family to this misadventure of Jane's has never been told. If it was anything like that of the Bertrams when Fanny Price refuses Henry Crawford in *Mansfield Park*, life must have been unpleasant for the novelist when she got back to Bath and had to tell her story. Sir Thomas Bertram, we remember, lectures Fanny severely on the lack of consideration for her unprosperous relations suggested by her rejection of a suit from so wealthy and eligible a man. She should, he argues, put her own feelings behind her, and act for others. Whether or not anybody said this to Jane Austen after the Bigg Wither affair, we shall never know. But *Mansfield Park* makes a point of showing Fanny to have been right (and the Bertrams wrong) in her treatment of Henry Crawford. It is interesting to note that correspondence only recently come to light reveals that Jane and Cassandra squabbled over the ending of *Mansfield Park*, Cassandra arguing that Fanny should be allowed to marry Henry after all, Jane remaining unmoved by this suggestion.[25] It is one of the few disagreements between the sisters indisputably on record. Also on record is the fact that Jane Austen's mother liked all of her novels except *Mansfield Park*. Whether there exists any connection between the events of December 1802 and the plot of *Mansfield Park* remains unclear, but the circumstances are suggestive.

Years later the novelist's niece Caroline, James Austen's younger daughter, reconstructed in these terms what may have gone through her aunt's mind on that fateful December evening when Harris Bigg Wither proposed to Jane Austen:

> I conjecture that the advantages he could offer, and her gratitude for his love, and her long friendship with his family, induced my aunt to decide that she would marry him . . . but that having accepted him she found she was miserable. To be sure, she should not have said 'Yes' overnight; but I have always respected her for her courage in cancelling that 'Yes' the next morning; all worldly advantages would have been [hers], and she was of an age to know this quite well. . . . On their father's death, [my aunts] and their mother would be, they were aware, but poorly off. I believe most . . . women so circumstanced would have gone on trusting to love after marriage.[26]

Many women in Jane Austen's position would indeed have gone on, trusting to love after marriage if it had not come before. Few had the luxury of avoiding such an experiment. Though it is at the age of twenty-seven that Anne Elliot recovers both her old bloom and her lost lover, for Jane Austen it could not be. As Douglas Bush reminds us, "she had a very high ideal of the love that should unite a husband and wife. . . . All her heroines . . . know, in proportion to their maturity, the meaning of ardent love."[27] In *Sense and Sensibility* we find Elinor pondering that "worst and most irremediable of all evils, a connection for life" with the wrong man. In her later years, the novelist wrote long letters to her favorite niece, Fanny Knight, full of dire warnings about the consequences of marrying without love. The experience in Devon during the summer of 1801 had shown Jane Austen what it was to be in love, and she had no intention of settling for an imitation of life. She knew, at any rate, that she was not in love with the frail Harris Bigg Wither, a mean-tempered recluse with a stammer.[28] Two years later that gentleman consoled himself at the altar with another lady.

And now we move on five and a half years to June 1808, and Jane Austen, aged thirty-two, is visiting her affluent brother Edward and his family at Godmersham Park in Kent. Edward's brother-in-law Edward Bridges was (yet another) clergyman, four years younger than the novelist. During Jane's visit to Godmersham, Edward Bridges proposed marriage to her, and she declined the honor. There is some evidence to suggest that, after besieging Jane in the summer of 1808, he lay in wait for the elder sister and tried his luck with Cassandra in the autumn.[29] Cassandra also refused him. There must have been some giggles between the sisters about this Collins-like operation. *Pride and Prejudice* had already been drafted, though it was later revised; perhaps Edward Bridges sat for the portrait of Captain Benwick in *Persuasion*. At any rate, after her experience at Manydown in 1802, the novelist knew more about handling proposals from eligible young men with whom she was not in love.

Five more years must now be allowed to go by – the opportunities for marriage of course becoming scarcer as Jane grew older. Again we find the novelist staying with her brother Edward's family in Kent. It is October 1813, and she is two months shy of her thirty-eighth birthday. She has published, anonymously, *Sense and Sensibility* and *Pride and Prejudice*, and is now revising the manuscript of *Mansfield Park* whenever she can escape into the Godmersham study from relations and visitors. One of the visitors, however, she has come to like. This is Stephen Rumbold Lushington, who sat in the House of Commons for nearly thirty years as M.P. first for Rye and then for Canterbury. In later years he served as a privy councillor, and was appointed Governor of Madras.

When she first heard that an M.P. was coming to Godmersham, Jane Austen looked forward only to using his frank on the letters she was dispatching to Cassandra at Chawton, the large "cottage" in Hampshire, now their home, given by Edward to his mother and two sisters in 1809. Having met Lushington – he was a year younger than she – Jane was quite taken. He speaks well, and is fond of Milton, the novelist reports to Cassandra. "I am rather in love with him. – I dare say he is ambitious and Insincere."[30] This may appear innocuous – unless one reads it to mean, not unreasonably, that, as the novelist saw it, some of the men she had liked over the years abandoned her because, being excessively ambitious, they desired more influential wives, or because they had never meant anything by their attentions in the first place. Several of the men in whom Jane Austen took an interest found solace elsewhere with unnerving celerity. But Mr. Lushington was not around long enough to become a major disappointment. He simply appears – and then disappears. Obviously he did not reciprocate Jane's partiality for him. He is not mentioned again.

Two years later, during the autumn of 1815, Jane Austen travelled to London to negotiate publishing terms for *Emma*. She stayed in the house of her banker brother Henry in Hans Place, Knightsbridge; and while she was in town the last two men with whom she can be said in any way to be romantically linked touched her existence. She was now nearly forty (*Emma*, as a matter of fact, was published on her fortieth birthday), and would soon begin to suffer from the adrenal tuberculosis that was to kill her less than two years later.

In the midst of the negotiations with John Murray, who was publishing *Emma* (it is interesting to note than Jane Austen's publisher was also Byron's), Henry Austen, who acted as Jane's literary agent, took to his bed with an attack of bilious fever. The novelist found herself dining *tête-à-tête* several nights running with Henry's elderly business associate Mr. Seymour – with the inevitable result. Jane termed this proposal of marriage, the last she would receive, "a comical consequence" of her brother's absence, and she never took it seriously. Nothing else is known of this affair.[31]

Henry's condition alarmed her enough to call in a well-respected physician from Sloane Street. This was Charles Thomas Haden, then just twenty-nine, who was to introduce to English medicine a French innovation called the stethoscope. At this time he was physician to the Brompton Dispensary, a signal honor for so young a man. Haden came to the house in Hans Place at first as a doctor – and later, as he and the novelist became more intimate, as a valued friend. During the last days of November and the early days of December 1815, Haden was constantly in Hans Place. It was through him that Jane Austen was introduced to the Rev. James Stanier Clarke, the Prince Regent's librarian and chaplain. Clarke, in turn, was responsible for the dedication of *Emma* to the Prince Regent, who was said to be fond of Jane

Austen's fiction and to keep a set of her books in each of his royal residences. The novelist had always been appalled by the behavior of the future George IV, and the dedication was appended to *Emma* only after she discovered that Clarke's "permission" to dedicate the volume to the Prince was in fact, despite Clarke's later disclaimer, a command which she dared not disobey. And so *Emma*, of all English novels, was dedicated to George IV, of all English monarchs. But Jane Austen took her revenge. Clarke's own literary ambitions and ideas, contained in a series of highly presumptuous letters to the novelist, became the direct source of "Plan of a Novel" – a hilarious sketch, drawn up in 1816, of the sort of tale which might have been the result of her taking seriously the egregious and gratuitous literary advice Clarke was in the habit of offering. So in fact the influence of Charles Thomas Haden on the last years of Jane Austen had literary as well as personal ramifications.

It is clear from the surviving correspondence that the novelist was infatuated with her brother's physician, that Haden did not reciprocate her feelings, and that she ultimately recognized this and resigned herself, reluctantly, to friendship rather than love. She was eleven years older than he. The letters nonetheless give us a picture of Jane Austen, by now a veteran of potentially romantic encounters, being knocked over by the advent of this sexy new playmate. "Tomorrow Mr. Haden is to dine with us," she tells Cassandra in one letter. "There's Happiness! – We really grow so fond of Mr. Haden that I do not know what to expect." Whatever she may have been "expecting" of Haden, that gentleman, following the line so often taken by the men Jane Austen hoped might fall in love with her, proceeded to marry another lady soon afterwards. Of course the novelist could not know this in November 1815. She begrudges the visits of others when Haden has been asked to the house. Such occasions she calls evenings "spoilt" and "disappointing"; she wanted him all to herself. She goes out of her way to "foil" the attempts of others to call on them; she wishes to see "nobody but our Precious" Haden. The two of them did manage to dine alone together several evenings running. Jane Austen found herself impressed yet again by Haden's "good Manners & clever conversation"; she characterizes these occasions as utterly "agreable" [*sic*].

Cassandra Austen was alarmed by the letters she was receiving from her smitten sister, and wrote to her accordingly. In those days physicians were sometimes looked upon as little better than superior tradesmen – only marginally genteel. The tenor of Cassandra's (lost) letters can be gauged by Jane's response. Haden, the novelist hastens to inform her sister, is not just an apothecary: "he is a Haden, nothing but a Haden, a sort of wonderful nondescript creature on two legs, something between a Man and an Angel – but without the least spice of an Apothecary. – He is perhaps the only Person *not* an Apothecary hereabouts."[32] This sounds like a woman in love. Jane must have suspected that the younger man would find a younger wife; and perhaps the bitterness of the early chapters of *Persuasion*, then being written in Henry Austen's back room at Hans Place, take their autumnal tone in part from her certainty – in Anne Elliot, who is still in her twenties, it is no more than a fear – that time has passed her by, the bloom of youth being too far gone ever again to attract a man who might love her.

Jane Austen seems to have had a tendency to attract men younger than herself, and on occasion to be attracted to younger men. Yet "maternal" is an adjective one is unlikely to apply to her, and she was hardly the type to interest herself in the Regency equivalent of male go-go dancers. But we should never forget that her novels, without exception, are about country girls looking for husbands. Her fiction, like all fiction, is the product of experience as well as imagination. Freud suggests that art largely is the result of daydreaming, and that daydreaming often follows the paths of wish-fulfillment.[33] But what is daydreaming, what indeed is art, if not a merging of the imagination – what *might* happen – and experience – what the dreamer believes, based on understanding, is most *likely* to happen? Jane Austen's fictional subjects must in part be the subject of her fantasy life: true enough. But they are also the inevitable results of her knowledge of the world – knowledge which, despite the great weight of uninformed opinion to the contrary, continued to expand during the last two decades of her life.

James Edward Austen-Leigh's characterization of his aunt may now be seen, perhaps, in its proper light: "Of events her life was singularly barren: few changes and no great crisis ever broke the smooth current of its course . . . I have no reason to think that she ever felt any attachment by which the happiness of her life was at all affected." This might well have been true – were it not for Tom Lefroy, Edward Taylor of Bifrons, the Rev. Samuel

Blackall, Mr. Holder of Ashe Park, Harry Francis Digweed, Mr. Evelyn of Bath, the unnamed clergyman encountered in Devon in 1801, Harris Bigg Wither of Manydown, the Rev. Edward Bridges, Stephen Rumbold Lushington, M.P., Mr. Seymour of London, and Dr. Charles Thomas Haden.

NOTES

1. Letter to the present writer, 22 May 1983.
2. See J. E. Austen-Leigh, *A Memoir of Jane Austen* (London, 1870; 1871), pp. 2 and 46–7.
3. *Jane Austen's Letters to Her Sister Cassandra and Others*, ed. R. W. Chapman (London, 1932; rev. edn., 1952; 1959); the letter of 9 January 1796 is quoted from pp. 2–4.
4. *Letters*, 14 January 1796, pp. 4–6.
5. See Douglas Bush, *Jane Austen*, (New York, 1975), p. 26.
6. See R. W. Chapman (quoting Caroline Austen and T. E. Lefroy), *Jane Austen: Facts and Problems* (Oxford, 1978), pp. 57–8.
7. John Updike, *Rabbit Is Rich* (New York, 1981), p. 422.
8. *Letters*, 17 November 1798, p. 27.
9, See, for example, John Halperin, "Unengaged Laughter: Jane Austen's Juvenilia," *South Atlantic Quarterly*, 81, no. 3 (Summer 1982), 286–99.
10. See Elizabeth Jenkins, address given at the Annual General Meeting of the Jane Austen Society, *Report for the Year 1965*; and Joan Rees, *Jane Austen: Woman and Writer* (London and New York, 1976), pp. 45–6.
11. *Letters*, 15 September 1796, pp. 14–15.
12. *Letters*, 8 November 1800, p. 87.
13. Chapman, *Facts and Problems*, p. 59.
14. *Letters*, 17 November 1798, p. 28.
15. *Letters*, 3 July 1813, pp. 313–18; see also the letter of 23 March 1817.
16. *Letters*, 8 November 1800, pp. 84–5.
17. *Letters*, 8 January 1801, pp. 104–5.
18. On the Digweeds, see Rees, *Woman and Writer*, p. 80.
19. *Letters*, 3 January 1801, pp. 102–3.
20. *Letters*, 19 June 1799, p. 73.
21. *Letters*, 26 May 1801, pp. 136–7.
22. The mysterious summer romance of 1801 is also described by Elizabeth Jenkins, *Jane Austen* (London, 1938; 1949), pp. 129–30; David Cecil, *A Portrait of Jane Austen* (New York, 1980); and Marghanita Laski, *Jane Austen and Her World* (London, 1969; rev. edn., New York, 1975), p. 53.
23. Rees, *Woman and Writer*, p. 90.
24. Cassandra did not hesitate to go back to Manydown, however. The Bigg Wither affair of 1802 is also described in Chapman, *Facts and Problems*, pp. 61–2; Rees, *Woman and Writer*, p. 90; and Laski, *Jane Austen and Her World*, p. 54.

25. Elizabeth Jenkins, "Some Notes on Background," address given at the Annual General Meeting of the Jane Austen Society, *Report for the Year 1980*.

26. William and Richard Arthur Austen-Leigh, *Jane Austen: Her Life and Letters* (London, 1913), p. 93.

27. On Anne Elliot in this connection, see Jane Aiken Hodge, *Only a Novel: The Double Life of Jane Austen* (London, 1971), p. 82. See Bush, *Jane Austen*, p. 27.

28. See Reginald F. Bigg Wither, *Materials for a History of the Wither Family* (Winchester, 1907).

29. Edward Bridges and his possible suits are also discussed by Hodge in *The Double Life*, pp. 100 and 103.

30. *Letters*, 14 October 1813, p. 353.

31. On Mr. Seymour, see *Letters*, Chapman's note to letter 111.

32. Jane Austen on Haden is quoted from *Letters*, 24 and 26 November and 2 December 1815, pp. 433–41, *passim*.

33. See, for example, Geoffrey Green, "The Nightmarish Quest of Jerzy Kosinski," in *The Anxious Subject: Nightmares and Daymares in Literature and Film*, ed. Moshe Lazar (Los Angeles, 1982), p. 51.

2

The Novelist as Heroine in *Mansfield Park*: A Study in Autobiography

Mansfield Park is Jane Austen's *Vanity Fair*. Almost everyone in it is selfish: self-absorbed, self-indulgent, and vain. This helps make it her most unpleasant novel – and her most controversial. For years critics have exercised themselves trying to explain, justify, expound, or attack its moral slant. Misreadings of the book by otherwise sensible men and women are legion: *Mansfield Park* "continually and essentially holds up the vicious as admirable," says Kingsley Amis.[1] Commentators complacently discuss the expulsion of wit and scourging of irony in *Mansfield Park*, pronounce Fanny Price a failure, and conclude that the novel as a whole must be one too. The book is supposed somehow to be "different" – not at all, really, Jane Austen's sort of thing, and thus requiring a good deal of explanation.

This is nonsense. *Mansfield Park* is very much of a piece with her other books, and in fact it is one of the best of them. It is also, as we shall see, one of her most autobiographical volumes. No doubt because of its apparent complexity, more has been written about it than about any of the other works.

Like *Pride and Prejudice*, which preceded it into print by only a year, *Mansfield Park* (1814) is largely about true and false values, right and wrong ways of looking at things – how to live, in short. "Selfishness must always be forgiven you know, because there is no hope of a cure," declares Mary Crawford.[2] In this, as in everything else she says and does, Mary (as well as her brother Henry) is wrong. Like Becky Sharp (and Milton's Satan), she is more lively and amusing than many of her fellow players. But, as in Thackeray's novel (and Milton's poem), the author's moral perspective on false values never wavers. "Miss Crawford, in spite of some amiable sensations, and much personal kindness, had still been Miss Crawford, still shewn a mind led astray and

27

bewildered, and without any suspicion of being so; darkened, yet fancying itself light" (p. 367), the narrator remarks late in the story; Edmund observes of Mary, ultimately, that she lacks "the most valuable knowledge we could any of us acquire – the knowledge of ourselves" (p. 459). "Her mind was entirely self-engrossed" (p. 358), the narrator says of Mary. It is indicative that, when Fanny remarks to Mary, "One cannot fix one's eyes on the commonest natural production without finding food for a rambling fancy," Mary should reply, "To say the truth . . . I see no wonder in [nature] equal to seeing myself in it" (pp. 209–10). Henry Crawford is described as subject to "the freaks of a cold-blooded vanity" (p. 467); "entangled by his own vanity" (p. 468); a victim of "the temptation of immediate pleasure"; and "unused to make any sacrifice to right" (p. 467). Dr. Grant's great fault, it is obvious, is lack of self-knowledge. Everyone at Mansfield is, to quote a well-known passage in the novel, "shut up, or wholly occupied each with the person . . . dependent on them . . . for everything" (p. 449).

Of course vice is alluring; it is supposed to be. But we perceive Mary as odious throughout. She and her brother may be more interesting than Fanny Price and Edmund Bertram – more fun at a dinner party – but we know that immorality can be more seductive and fascinating than virtue. And certainly it is easier, often enough, to mock propriety than attempt to understand it, as Stuart Tave has said in what is perhaps the best essay on *Mansfield Park*.[3] He goes on to remind us that what the Crawfords really represent is "liveliness without life";[4] they are foils to the less "lively," but more virtuous, protagonists. That virtue may be duller than vice need not require us to be vicious. Jane Austen hints at something like this in the final chapter, when the narrator comments that "the public punishment of disgrace . . . is . . . not one of the barriers, which society gives to virtue. In this world, the penalty is less equal than could be wished" (p. 468).

Mansfield Park is not nearly so complicated a book as many have thought. Fanny Price, looking on and listening, "not unamused to observe the selfishness which, more or less disguised, seemed to govern them all, and wondering how it would end" (p. 131), stands in for Jane Austen here. True, the light and bright and sparkling Elizabeth Bennet has gone away. Too much time has passed; the novelist cannot possibly be the same person. Her view of things inevitably is different from what it was in the relatively cheerful 1790s, when *Pride and Prejudice* (then called "First Impressions") was initially drafted. But Fanny Price is as much a part of Jane Austen's personality as Elizabeth Bennet; and it is this, perhaps, that many critics have not wanted to see or admit. A few have recognized that *Mansfield Park* is no "sport" among the books. "Can we doubt that [Fanny's] is Jane Austen's own position, that even when the self is alone and unsupported by human example of approval, it must still imperatively act in accordance with what is 'right,' must still support what is valid in its moral inheritance?" Alistair M. Duckworth asks.[5] "There can be no stability of life, no certainty of conduct, without principles of action, a matter of continual importance to Dr. Johnson as to Jane Austen," Tave reminds us.[6] It is always Fanny who sees what the others are up to when they themselves do not understand their own actions. It is she who has the strength of character here – dull or not. "The novel . . . is designed to vindicate Fanny Price and the values for which she stands," as Bernard J. Paris rightly says.[7] Fanny's "judgment may be quite . . . safely trusted" (p. 147), Edmund declares. We need not love her in order to see that her moral perspective is the most strictly focused one in *Mansfield Park*. "If you are against me, I ought to distrust myself" (p. 155), Edmund remarks to Fanny over the business of the theatricals. Indeed he should. Later he tells his father: "Fanny is the only one who has judged rightly throughout, who has been consistent" (p. 187).

Those who believe that "there is no clearly discernible irony hedging off what [the characters] say from what their author is apparently saying"[8] are surely wrong. And, because so many readers have felt this way, the point here about the consistency and clarity of the novel's moral slant must be all the more emphatically made. Nor is *Mansfield Park* in any way a falling-off from the high standard set by preceding works. Newman, incidentally, is known to have read this book once a year "to preserve his style."[9]

Fanny's moral focus is so consistently before us because it is that of Jane Austen. Let us consider the autobiographical resonances of a novel so often said to be uncharacteristic of its author.

Fanny Price has a sailor brother who, after some impatient delay, is promoted through family connections – and who brings her a present of jewelry from abroad. Jane Austen's younger brother Charles is the apparent model here; and he actually brought back for his sister, from one of his ocean journeys in 1801, a topaz cross on a gold chain. Like Charles Austen, William Price loves to dance. William tends to write long, chatty letters to Fanny; both of Jane Austen's sailor brothers, Charles and Francis, wrote to her, but not as often as she would have liked – there may be some wish-fulfillment here. "I cannot rate so very highly the love or good nature of a brother, who will not give himself the trouble of writing any thing worth reading, to his sisters, when they are separated" (p. 64), Fanny declares. William is also more generous about distributing his prize money to his relations than either of Jane Austen's sailor brothers ever was; the unspoken reproach may be inferred. Much is said in this book about the advantages "for a lad who, before he was twenty, had gone through . . . bodily hardships, and given . . . proofs of mind" (p. 236). *Mansfield Park* extols the virtues "of heroism, of usefulness, of exertion, of endurance" (p. 236). In the course of the book the names of several of Francis Austen's ships are used in passing (e.g., the *Endymion*, the *Elephant*, the *Cleopatra*). The novelist wrote to her brother to ask his permission to use these names; he replied that she was welcome to do so, though he thought this might endanger her anonymity as a novelist.[10] Mr. Price's description of exactly how the *Thrush* lies in harbor at Spithead (p. 380) is so technical and nautically exact that we may be certain it was drafted for Jane Austen by her brother Francis, who was staying at Chawton when this section of *Mansfield Park* was written.

Between the sisters (Maria and Julia) there is sibling rivalry in love matters more spectacular than that in any of the earlier works (with the possible exception of the youthful "Three Sisters"). *Sense and Sensibility*, *Pride and Prejudice*, and *Persuasion* bristle with rivalry between sisters. The love between siblings, *Mansfield Park* pointedly reminds us, which is "sometimes almost every thing, is at others worse than nothing" (p. 235). Jane Austen was two years younger than her sister Cassandra; and, though the contrary is generally believed, the fact is that they did not always get along. A careful reading of some of the surviving letters Jane wrote to her elder sister makes this plain enough. Indeed, the sisters had a disagreement over the ending of this very novel.

Also we have one mother here (Lady Bertram) who is selfishly heartless, and uninterested in her children – and in everything that does not directly concern herself; and another (Mrs. Price) who virtually ignores a grown-up daughter. Can this be a coincidence? While there may be little of Jane Austen's mother in Lady Bertram, the fact remains that, in refusing to "go into public with her daughters" and being "too indolent even to accept a mother's gratification in witnessing their success and enjoyment at the expense of any personal trouble" (p. 35), Lady Bertram undoubtedly recapitulates the reclusive side of Mrs. Austen, who became disinclined while still a healthy woman to leave home for any reason. Of Lady Bertram it is said: "Every thing that a considerate parent *ought* to feel was advanced for her use; and every thing that an affectionate mother *must* feel in promoting her children's enjoyment, was attributed to her nature" (p. 285) – falsely, of course, for she feels nothing. The phrasing here is vivid and probably reflects an aspect of Jane Austen's view of her mother. Lady Bertram's "playing at being frightened" (p. 427) in emergencies may represent Mrs. Austen's lifelong hypochondria, which always infuriated her novelist daughter. The mortification of Fanny at her mother's indifference to her is described by Jane Austen with equally striking vividness: "She had probably alienated Love by the helplessness and fretfulness of a fearful temper, or been unreasonable in wanting a larger share than any one among so many could deserve" (p. 371). The last part of this statement sounds distinctly personal; the Austens, like the Prices, were a large family, and probably there was not enough time for a busy mother laden with household cares to tend to all the needs and desires of a younger daughter. Mrs. Price's "heart and her time were . . . quite full; she had neither leisure nor affection to bestow on Fanny. Her daughters never had been much to her. She was fond of her sons . . . her time was given chiefly to her house and her servants" (p. 389). The Austens had six boys and two girls, and throughout her early and middle years Mrs. Austen would have been chiefly concerned with household management. Nor can there be any doubt that she doted on her sons. In *Mansfield Park* Fanny reflects bitterly that her mother had "no curiosity to know her better, no desire of her friendship, and no inclination for her company" (p. 390). Should we still fail to get the point, the novel makes it plain for us: "Mothers certainly have not yet got quite the right way of managing their daughters. . . . To be neglected before one's time, must be very vexatious. . . . [it is] entirely the mother's fault" (pp. 50–1). Probably Jane Austen was "neglected before [her] time" by her mother; it may go far to explain her hostile nature as an adolescent, her lifelong penchant for satire, and the number of silly and insipid mothers who populate her books. Other instances of her impatience with and resentment of her mother abound in more obvious ways in the novelist's letters; mother and daughter even fought over household expenses. These feelings are articulated here in sublimated ways, but without much artifice. Surely it is indicative that Mrs. Austen, who enjoyed the Dashwood sisters and admired Elizabeth Bennet, is on record as detesting Fanny Price.[11]

And it should be equally clear, though critics have not noticed this, that Fanny's aunt Norris is a highly unflattering likeness of Mrs. Leigh Perrot, the woman who married Jane Austen's mother's brother. Mrs. Norris is a tightfisted aunt who torments a saintly niece – and steals. Mrs. Leigh Perrot was accused of, tried for, and eventually acquitted of stealing some lace from a shop in Bath. There is some evidence to suggest a strain of kleptomania in her, though no particular offense was ever positively proven.[12] In any case, she was no favorite with her husband's family during Jane Austen's lifetime. The Austen ladies were infuriated, after the death of the novelist's father and during subsequent years, by the prosperous Leigh Perrots' refusal to help any member of the family except the already comfortable James Austen, Jane's eldest brother. Since James Leigh Perrot was both a blood relative and perceived as affectionate and likable, his wife was blamed by the Austens, and considered parsimonious. Jane Austen would never know this, but after her husband's death in 1817 Mrs. Leigh Perrot dealt more generously with the Austen family than he had ever done. That Mrs. Norris is a malicious portrait of the resented aunt of the Austens is obvious. Mrs. Norris on two occasions steals baize from Mansfield Park, eventually winding up with the whole curtain bought for the theatricals secreted away in her own house. After the ball at Mansfield she makes off with "all the supernumerary jellies" (p. 283). As for her impoverished nieces in Portsmouth – Mrs. Price's verdict on her sister undoubtedly reflects the feelings of Mrs. Leigh Perrot's nieces at Bath, Southampton, and Chawton: "Aunt Norris lives too far off, to think of such little people as you" (p. 387), Mrs. Price tells one of her daughters.

Other aspects of autobiography are patent here. Into every one of her novels Jane Austen tosses at least one ball, much in the manner in which Trollope would introduce a fox hunt into virtually every tale. What interests a writer will find its way into the fiction. Fanny's enjoyment of dancing reflects that of the novelist years earlier, as Jane Austen's youthful letters amply testify: "The ball . . . such an evening of pleasure before her! . . . she began to dress for it with much of the happy flutter which belongs to a ball" (p. 270). Afterwards, creeping up to bed, Fanny is still "feverish with hopes and fears, soup and negus, sore-footed and fatigued, restless and agitated, yet feeling, in spite of every thing, that a ball was indeed delightful" (p. 281).

Like Jane Austen, Fanny becomes a subscriber to a circulating library – "amazed at being any thing *in propria persona*, amazed . . . to be a renter, a chuser of books!" (p. 398). Like the novelist herself, Fanny abhors "improvements" made by gardeners and architects – it is indicative that Henry Crawford is said to be "a capital improver" (p. 244) – who tear up avenues of trees, remove walks, and fabricate ruins to recreate the "natural" through a synthetic impression. *Sense and Sensibility* and *Northanger Abbey* argue in the same vein.

In this connection, *Mansfield Park* betrays Jane Austen's love of nature, her dislike of urban life, and her growing neurasthenia and distaste for "society." "We do not look in great cities for our best morality" (p. 93), Edmund declares; it might be one of the novel's epigraphs. Even the quality of sunshine is said to be "a totally different thing in a town and in the country." In Portsmouth, "its power was only . . . a stifling, sickly glare, serving but to bring forward stains and dirt that might otherwise have slept. There was neither health nor gaiety in sun-shine in a town" (p. 439). Fanny in Portsmouth – losing, as she observes, the glories of a garden in spring – sits "in a blaze of oppressive heat, in a cloud of moving dust" (p. 439). In the country it is a different matter altogether:

> Fanny spoke her feelings. 'Here's harmony!' said she, 'here's repose! Here's what may leave all painting and all music behind, and what poetry only can attempt to describe. Here's what may tranquillize every care, and lift the heart to rapture! When I look out on such a night as this, I feel as if there could be neither wickedness nor sorrow in the world; and there

certainly would be less of both if the sublimity of Nature were more attended to, and people were carried more out of themselves by contemplating such a scene.' (p. 113)

Thus Fanny at Mansfield. The emphasis here is on the tranquilizing of care; in the city, care is stimulated rather than tranquilized. When Fanny returns home to Mansfield from Portsmouth, "Her eye fell every where on lawns and plantations of the freshest green; and the trees, though not fully clothed, were in that delightful state, when farther beauty is known to be at hand, and when, while much is actually given to the sight, more yet remains for the imagination" (pp. 446-7). Here is another indication that Jane Austen preferred nature untouched by "improvers," who left little to the "imagination."

Fanny's love of nature is underscored by her hatred of noise and disorder; and the Portsmouth chapters of *Mansfield Park* show Jane Austen's chronic neurasthenia growing to greater proportions, undoubtedly stimulated by her hatred of Godmersham, her brother Edward's house, where we know she spent several traumatic months in 1813 revising the novel. Her letters of the time show that she grew impatient to be gone from the place, where a continuous stream of visitors and an oversupply of children, as in the Price household in Portsmouth, provided a constant uproar and made life miserable for anyone who valued peace and quiet. In Portsmouth the Price boys run around and slam doors until Fanny's "temples ache" (p. 381); she is said to be "almost stunned" by the noise (p. 382). "The living in incessant noise was to a frame and temper, delicate and nervous like Fanny's, an evil which no superadded elegance or harmony could have entirely atoned for. It was the greatest misery of all" (p. 391). Here, certainly, is the neurasthenic novelist at Godmersham. It is no accident that Fanny at Portsmouth, subjected to "closeness and noise . . . confinement, bad air, bad smells" (p. 432), thinks (p. 431) of Cowper's line, "With what intense desire she wants her home" (*Tirocinium; or, A Review of Schools*, l. 565). The "ceaseless tumult of her present abode," where "every body was noisy, every voice was loud," where "the doors were in constant banging, the stairs were never at rest, nothing was done without a clatter, nobody sat still, and nobody could command attention when they spoke" (p. 392), must describe Jane Austen's life at Godmersham in 1813, unheard and "want[ing] her home." The accounts of the effects on a sensitive nature of noise and chaos cannot be wholly invented. *Mansfield Park* gives us a magnificent picture of Jane Austen's personality in her late thirties. In this way it may be seen less as a "sport" among the novels than a most characteristic and revealing performance.

Other elements of autobiography should be mentioned. There could be a carry-over of the Bigg Wither affair in the story of Fanny Price and Henry Crawford. In 1802 Jane Austen may have been put under pressure by her family to accept a proposal of marriage from Harris Bigg Wither, a young man then preparing to take orders. His sisters were close friends of the Austen girls; the families were neighbors in Hampshire. Jane Austen's refusal of Harris Bigg Wither elicted from her family some surprise and resentment, as does Fanny's of Henry Crawford. Sir Thomas petulantly declares, "The advantage or disadvantage of your family – of your parents – your brothers and sisters – never seems to have had a moment's share in your thoughts" (p. 318), and he refers to Fanny's behavior in this crisis as "a wild fit of folly, throwing away . . . such an opportunity of being settled in life, eligibly, honourably, nobly settled, as will, probably, never occur to you again" (p. 319). Something like this may have been said to the novelist by a member of her family when she turned down Harris Bigg Wither, seen by the Austens and their connections as a respectable, pleasant, prosperous man who, among other things, would have provided the novelist with a large house in her beloved Hampshire and a comfortable income at a time when she had nothing of her own, no means whatever of "being settled in life," that state so single-mindedly pursued by most of Jane Austen's heroines. Certainly we cannot know if her mother or aunt or a brother or anyone else spoke to her in this vein. But it is clear, from evidence recently come to light, that Jane's sister tried to persuade her to alter the ending of *Mansfield Park* to allow Henry Crawford to marry Fanny Price. Apparently feeling that Fanny should indeed be well "settled in life," Cassandra argued the matter gamely; Jane stood firm, and would not allow it.[13] Probably Cassandra's influence is responsible for the assertion late in the novel, by way of mitigation, that, if Crawford had "been satisfied with the conquest of one amiable woman's affections" and "persevered," Fanny must have given way to him eventually (p. 467). In the event Fanny of course is seen to be right in her resistance to Crawford. Her judgment never misleads

her; and "for the purity of her intentions she could answer"
(p. 324). She understands "how wretched, and how unpardonable,
how hopeless and how wicked it was, to marry without affection"
(p. 324). The sorely tempted novelist may well have felt something
like this during that awful, unforgettable night at Manydown, in
the course of which Harris Bigg Wither proposed marriage and
she accepted him – only to change her mind the next morning,
leaving the house in haste, tears, and embarrassment. After all, as
Fanny declares, a woman is not *required* to love a man, "let him be
ever so generally agreeable. Let him have all the perfections in the
world . . . a man [need not] be acceptable to every woman he
may happen to like himself" (p. 353). This is as passionate a
defense as we are likely to find anywhere of Jane Austen's
rejections of the half-dozen or so men who, during her lifetime,
offered her marriage. Harris Bigg Wither, according to a family
chronicler, turns out to have been a mean-tempered, frail recluse
with a stammer.[14] Fanny Price, no less than her author, may be
pardoned, even in an age of mercenary marriages, for eluding a
match she found repugnant.

The marriage question is of course at the center of *Mansfield
Park*, as it often is in the other books. "There certainly are not so
many men of large fortune in the world, as there are pretty
women to deserve them" (p. 3), the narrator complains in the
opening paragraph. And yet marriage as an institution is attacked
here with special vehemence, perhaps in part because of the
personal applications involved. Maria is said to be "prepared for
matrimony by an hatred of home, restraint, and tranquillity; by
the misery of disappointed affection, and contempt of the man
she was to marry" (p. 202). Mary Crawford tells Mrs. Grant,
"Every body is taken in . . . in marriage . . . it is, of all
transactions, the one in which people expect most from others,
and are least honest themselves. . . . it is a manœuvring business"
(p. 46). Jane Austen undoubtedly felt "taken in" by men on
several occasions – in the mid-1790s by Tom Lefroy, her first
youthful suitor, who was packed off to Ireland (later to become
Chief Justice there) when things between the impecunious young
people began to look serious to their families; by the mysterious
clergyman who courted her in Devon in 1801 and who, after
being virtually accepted by the novelist, disappeared (he may
have died, but this is unclear); by several others who proposed to
her and, after being refused, found solace elsewhere with what
seemed to the novelist spectacular celerity, in the manner of Mr.

Collins; and perhaps as well by Harris Bigg Wither, who on one evening appeared to be someone she might like to marry and by the next morning, after much reflection, turned out to be someone quite different after all.

None of this need diminish the role of marriage in giving a woman consequence. *Mansfield Park* provides a series of glimpses into the novelist's resentful perspective during the years leading up to her literary success and recognition. The most usual complaint is lack of personal consequence among others, which must have been especially galling to an intelligent and sensitive woman in her thirties who had had her chances to marry, after all, but had found marriage a "manœuvring business" and had eschewed it, thus having to give precedence, as a matter of form when in company, to married women, no matter how ignorant. We can see Jane Austen's irritation over matters such as these in *Emma*, where the insipid Mrs. Elton is given precedence over the intelligent, unmarried Emma Woodhouse merely because the silly woman happens to have a husband. The novelist's distress and impatience are evident in Fanny's feeling that she "can never be important to any one" (p. 26); in her having known, according to the narrator of *Mansfield Park*, "the pains of tyranny, of ridicule, and neglect" because "her motives had been often misunderstood, her feelings disregarded, and her comprehension under-valued" (p. 152); in Mrs. Norris's declaration to Fanny that "wherever you are, you must be the lowest and last" (p. 221); in Fanny's being "totally unused to have her pleasure consulted" (p. 280) on any matter; and in the description of her – it is Henry Crawford's – as "dependent, helpless, friendless, neglected, forgotten" (p. 297). The novelist was the only member of the large Austen family who, before her books began to appear (nothing in print until 1811), had not a single penny of private income. In all of this about Fanny there must be a touch of Jane Austen's own sensibility, though outwardly Fanny is not much like her author. But the word "neglect" echoes and reechoes through the book like a refrain. And, as we have seen, Fanny's values are almost always the novelist's.

"To be in the centre of such a [family] circle, loved by so many . . . to feel affection without fear or restraint, to feel herself the equal of those who surrounded her, to be at peace" (p. 370) – these are the things Fanny cherishes, as Jane Austen surely did. Away from Chawton – in "society" among strangers – the novelist could not be secure of them. "A well-disposed young woman, who did not marry for love, was in general but the more attached to her own family" (p. 201), *Mansfield Park* tells us. Outside the family circle she was more likely to lack consequence, certainly; and to be "neglected before one's time" is "very vexatious," as we know. Thus Fanny's sexual jealousy of all the acknowledged beauties in the book; the sight of Mary Crawford, for example, fills her "full of jealousy and agitation" (p. 159). The "necessity of self-denial and humility" (p. 463), "the advantage of early hardship and discipline," and "the consciousness of being born to struggle and endure" (p. 473)[15] are insisted upon instead; and it is precisely these qualities which Maria Bertram and Mary Crawford, so successful with men, conspicuously lack.

Another characteristic and recognizable touch here is the double vision we encounter on questions of security, comfort, and luxury. Although it is better to have these things than not to have them, it is also seen to be ridiculous to measure all life, to tote people up, purely on the basis of wealth. The attack on materialism goes on from the previous books, but it is tempered in *Mansfield Park* by some sober thought. "A large income is the best recipé for happiness I ever heard of" (p. 213), Mary declares. "It is every body's duty to do as well for themselves as they can" (p. 289). And: "Varnish and gilding hide many stains" (p. 434). Still, the moral price paid for personal comfort must not be too high; the price Mary pays is too high, and the result is loss of happiness. Jane Austen attacks the subversive side of Mary with special emphasis. "A poor honourable is no catch" (p. 394), she makes Mary say; and Fanny comments that Mary "had only learnt to think nothing of consequence but money" (p. 436). Mary's friend Mrs. Fraser "could not do otherwise than accept [her husband], for he was rich, and she had nothing" (p. 361). This is marriage as merely a stepping-stone to luxury. "Every thing is to be got with money" (p. 58), says Mary; it is one of the bitterest comments in the novel. Almost everyone in *Mansfield Park* is rated by others on the basis of how much he or she has, or can get. Fanny alone seems immune to most of these influences: "she likes to go her own way . . . she does not like to be dictated to . . . she certainly has a little spirit of secrecy, and independence," as even Mrs. Norris sees (p. 323). Throughout her life Jane Austen fiercely protected her own independence, no doubt wishing wistfully at times that she had less need of doing so.

We may see something of the Austen sisters in the amusing account of the Owen sisters, about whom Mary comments, "Their father is a clergyman and their brother is a clergyman, and they are all clergymen together" (p. 289).

And the malicious, heartless side of Jane Austen surely is in evidence when, after telling us that Lady Bertram has little to write letters about until the near-fatal illness of her elder son, the novelist comments acidly that "Lady Bertram's hour of good luck came" (p. 425) and Tom's ordeal "was of a nature to promise occupation for the pen for many days to come" (p. 426). This is Jane Austen herself – the Jane Austen of the letters – speaking, and not Lady Bertram. William Price, ravenous for promotion, is portrayed as impatiently looking forward to the death of the officer immediately superior to him in the *Thrush*. And the novelist is certainly hard on poor Dr. Grant at the end of the book. "To complete the picture of good" facing Edmund and Fanny, the narrator comments, "the acquisition of Mansfield living by the death of Dr. Grant" (due to overeating) "occurred just after they had been married long enough to begin to want an increase of income" (p. 473). There is little irony here.

Many have a fixed image of Jane Austen. People are fond of saying, for example, that Elizabeth Bennet is their idea of what the novelist must have been like. If one accepts this proposition, one is unlikely to think that Fanny Price (or Catherine Morland, or Emma Woodhouse, or Anne Elliot) is a "typical" Jane Austen heroine, or at all like her creator. But none of the heroines is in fact any more or less "typical" than any of the others; each of the novels is equally "typical" of Jane Austen, since she wrote them all. She was a person of many moods, like the rest of us. The hopeful, more playful mood in which *Pride and Prejudice* was first drafted was quite different from that in which, fifteen years or so later, *Mansfield Park* was written. Neither novel is more or less "typical" of Jane Austen than the other, though published just a year apart. One is a product of the novelist's early twenties, the other of her late thirties; and that, in addition to some understanding of how barren and disappointing the novelist's middle years were, may explain a great deal. Each book is equally a Jane Austen performance.

The personality of the novelist may be glimpsed again when we consider briefly two of the most controversial aspects of *Mansfield Park* and attempt to view them in a more autobiographical light. These are the "ordination" theme and the question of the theatricals (and "acting" in general). In fact there need be little confusion about either of these matters. Jane Austen treats them with clarity and precision – and in a highly characteristic way.

Though obviously the novel, in its final form, turned out not to be primarily about "ordination" after all, despite Jane Austen's characterization of it in these terms in a letter written before the novel had been completed or revised,[16] attitudes toward the Church, both as an institution and as a profession, are central to the story.

We should never forget that Jane Austen was the daughter of a clergyman and the sister (as it turned out) of two others. She grew up in a household in which it was taken for granted that the profession of clergyman was an important and useful one – one which society could not do without, especially in times of moral laxness. She herself was always a believing Christian, though rarely an aggressive one.

One critic, arguing that the Christianity of *Mansfield Park* is ardent, sees Fanny as the very embodiment of Christianity itself.[17] While it may be tempting for others (once again) to take the side of the vivacious and irreverent Miss Crawford, who makes fun of clergymen, against Edmund and Fanny, who are sometimes pompous and didactic on the subject of religion, one cannot for a moment suspect Jane Austen in *Mansfield Park* of any real animus against the Church. Mary Crawford's famous pronouncement, "A clergyman is nothing" (p. 92; in terms of social distinction, she means), touches off a debate in the novel on the merits of the profession. (Jane Austen's cousin and sister-in-law Eliza de Feuillide is supposed to have said something of the sort to James Austen many years earlier, when he proposed to her. She married instead his younger brother Henry, then a banker.)

Mary: "A clergyman has nothing to do but to be slovenly and selfish – read the newspaper, watch the weather, and quarrel with his wife. His curate does all the work, and the business of his own life is to dine."

Edmund: "It is impossible that your own observation can have given you much knowledge of the clergy. You can have been

personally acquainted with very few of a set of men you condemn
so conclusively."

Mary: "I speak what appears to me the general opinion; and
where an opinion is general, it is usually correct."

Edmund: "Where any one body of educated men, of whatever
denomination, are condemned indiscriminately, there must be a
deficiency of information or . . . of something else" (p. 110).

Edmund rightly surmises that Mary has got her "information"
from the example and the dinner-table conversation of the worldly
Dr. Grant. Certainly Jane Austen has no defense for *his* sort of
clergyman – or any pity either, as we have seen. But the novel
does take up the cudgels for the profession. Edmund declares
that "it is not in fine preaching only that a good clergyman will be
useful in his parish and his neighbourhood"; his "private character"
and "general conduct" provide an example for his neighbors
(p. 93). It is for this reason that Edmund plans to live in Thornton
Lacey rather than permit a curate to do "all the work." Human
nature "needs more lessons than a weekly sermon can convey,"
as Sir Thomas puts it (p. 248). If the clergyman "does not live
among his parishioners and prove himself by constant attention
their well-wisher and friend, he does very little either for their
good or his own" (p. 248). A man of social conscience himself, Sir
Thomas is not blind to the importance of the profession and
encourages Edmund in his clerical career. The assertion of self-
improvement when a clergyman does his proper duty is also
taken up by Fanny, who makes a little speech on the subject.

'A man – a sensible man like Dr. Grant, cannot be in the habit of
teaching others their duty every week, cannot go to church
twice every Sunday and preach such very good sermons in so
good a manner as he does, without being the better for it
himself. It must make him think, and I have no doubt that he
oftener endeavours to restrain himself than he would if he had
been any thing but a clergyman.' (p. 112)

The question, then, turns not so much on "ordination" as on
attitudes towards the profession of clergyman. It is no surprise
that the immoral characters in the novel have no use for the
Church, while the virtuous ones, dull or not, defend it, with Jane
Austen's unwavering blessing.

Although the question of the theatricals has been endlessly

debated, it is a much simpler matter than many readers have thought. Again a knowledge of the novelist's life is of use here. For Jane Austen there is inherently nothing wrong with putting on plays or acting in them. From the time she was a young girl, she loved the drama. Early on she relished the family theatricals at Steventon, and later the professional theater in London. All her life she was a dedicated theatergoer, sometimes attending the theater every night when she was in the metropolis. As she makes Charles Musgrove declare in *Persuasion*, "We all like a play."[18] The point here is that putting on theatricals at Mansfield Park is not in itself an evil thing. In this particular instance the occasion is used in selfish ways by several people; the situation of some of the principal characters simply makes it wrong to put on such a play as *Lovers' Vows*. For these reasons, rather than any generic ones, the theatricals can be condemned. That is to say, an activity that may be perfectly acceptable in life may be used thematically in fiction for negative purposes. As Edmund says (later) of the time of the theatricals, "we were all wrong together" (p. 349).

There were at least four adaptations of Kotzebue's *Natural Son* (originally published in Germany in 1791). In England it appeared under the title of *Lovers' Vows*, and had a great vogue between 1798 and 1802. (Interior evidence, as Chapman says, suggests that the characters in *Mansfield Park* are using Elizabeth Inchbald's text of the play.) *Lovers' Vows* was reprinted again and again; in 1799, for example, a twelfth edition was announced (the characters in Jane Austen's novel would appear to be using the fifth edition).[19] Between 1798 and 1802 *Lovers' Vows* had successful runs at Covent Garden, Bath, the Haymarket, and Drury Lane. Nathaniel Hawthorne saw a production of it in Salem, Massachusetts, in 1820;[20] it was still popular in the 1830s.

Between 1801 and 1805 *Lovers' Vows* was performed six times at the Theatre Royal in Bath; since Jane Austen lived in Bath during much of this time, it is very likely indeed that she saw it performed there. The point is that the play's concern with adultery, elopement, and an abandoned wife, its attack on the conventions of contemporary marriage, and its exaltation of feeling and impulse render it spectacularly inappropriate to the characters in *Mansfield Park* as they are placed at the time rehearsals of *Lovers' Vows* are going forward. Clearly it is dangerous for Maria to play a fallen – or falling – woman, illicitly seduced. Rushworth is cast as a foolish suitor, Mary as a free-thinking "modern" girl (Hazlitt remarked that the role of Amelia in the play was about as far as any contemporary actress was prepared to go; no wonder Edmund is horrified), and Yates as an advocate of elopement. Slated to portray a lovelorn clergyman, Edmund argues that "the man who chooses the profession" of clergyman "is, perhaps, one of the last who would wish to represent it on the stage" (p. 145) – especially when the character is presented unsympathetically. Surely a main ground of Jane Austen's disapproval is that the actors are playing exaggerated versions of themselves rather than really "acting," to which in fact she had no objection. In *Persuasion*, on several occasions, fashionable evening parties are pronounced to be less interesting and instructive experiences than nights spent at the theater, where – unlike real life – hypocrisy and insincerity are confined to the stage. Those who prefer parties to plays are that novel's most insipid characters. "*I* wanted better acting. There was no Actor worth naming," Jane Austen grumbled,[21] in the year before *Mansfield Park*'s publication, after seeing a revival of Garrick and Colman's *Clandestine Marriage* (1766) in London. Of another play in town she would comment later, "Acting seldom satisfies me."[22] No other serious reason for her disapprobation of the theatricals can exist – except, perhaps, the alteration of the house in the absence of its master. Indeed, the theme of "My father's house" is resonant.

Surely Fanny's private opinion of the goings-on once again is that of the novelist. Reading through the play, Fanny is astonished "that it could be chosen in the present instance," for she thinks that its "situation" and its "language" are unfit for "a private Theatre," for "home representation" (p. 137). This is undoubtedly true; and anyone who reads both *Mansfield Park* and *Lovers' Vows* will immediately understand the grounds of objection. As an interested follower of the fortunes of the Prince Regent and his wife, Jane Austen knew of the extraordinary condition of manners and morals at the Saxon court within the House of Brunswick in these days; inevitably she would have been suspicious of any play emanating from Germany. Needless to say, there is no blanket condemnation in *Mansfield Park* of the theater or of acting. Indeed, the novel refers enthusiastically to "a love of the theatre" and "an itch for acting . . . among young people" as being "general" and beyond reproach (p. 121). It is only this play, in these circumstances, that is objectionable. Otherwise, it is clear, Edmund would feel differently. "Nobody loves a play better than you do, or can have gone much farther to see one," Julia reminds him (p. 124). Tom Bertram "can conceive no greater harm or danger to any of us in conversing in the elegant written language of some respectable author than in chattering in words of our own" – sentiments with which, quite clearly, the novelist would concur. Tom goes on to remind the family that Sir Thomas has always been fond of promoting "the exercise of talent in young people . . . for any thing of the acting, spouting, reciting kind . . . he has always a decided taste. I am sure he encouraged it in us as boys" (p. 126) – as Jane Austen's father encouraged such activities at Steventon. Indeed, the tradition of family readings in the evening persisted long after his death. It is indicative that Sir Thomas, upon his unexpected return to the house, does not condemn the theatricals outright, but merely inquires *which play* is being rehearsed; and that Fanny, so stunned by the choice of *Lovers' Vows*, always takes great pleasure in hearing "*good* reading," to which "she had been long used" (p. 337) – like Marianne Dashwood in *Sense and Sensibility*. The fact that Henry Crawford reads well and is also a villain hardly constitutes grounds for arguing that Jane Austen hated acting and actors. Being glib and articulate, Henry reads skillfully. Mary Crawford is a brilliant conversationalist, while Fanny is not; does this mean that Jane Austen preferred dull conversation to lively? We are supposed as readers to retain our moral judgment despite any number of provocations to waver. Certainly Jane Austen's perspective never wavers.

One should see *Mansfield Park* not so much as a falling-off from *Pride and Prejudice* as simply a book in a different vein. They are different works and tell different stories by different means. Neither is any more "characteristic" of Jane Austen than the other: she is, once again, equally the author of both.

The botched ending of *Mansfield Park* is also characteristic of its author, a final piece of autobiography. Once again, in working out the conclusion of a novel, Jane Austen "uses summary rather than dramatic scene."[23] She cannot bear, it seems, to show us her characters' happiness. That goes on offstage; her interest is chiefly in their struggles.

In the last chapter of *Mansfield Park* we have, for the fourth time in four novels, a noisy authorial intrusion into the story, another retreat into cold third-person summary, and a happy resolution glimpsed only from afar. The narrative becomes pictorial rather than scenic, to use James's terminology. "Let other pens dwell on guilt and misery. I quit such odious subjects as soon as I can, impatient to restore every body, not greatly in fault themselves, to tolerable comfort, and to have done with all the rest" (p. 461). It may be tempting to see this as irony – as, that is, a burlesque of the novel in less capable hands (a *genre* to which Jane Austen often had recourse throughout her life) – this time the focus being the diet of poetic justice indiscriminately handed round at the end. But Jane Austen's "impatience" ("impatient" clearly is the key word in the passage just quoted) "to have done with" her story, once she has got everybody where she wants them, shows up too often in her fiction to be easily passed over. As in the other novels, she cannot bring herself to write the final love scene. Darcy and Elizabeth, Edward and Elinor, Henry and Catherine, all come to a final understanding out of our hearing; so will Emma and Mr. Knightley. And so here: "I . . . intreat every body to believe that exactly at the time when it was quite natural that it should be so, and not a week earlier, Edmund did cease to care about Miss Crawford, and became as anxious to marry Fanny, as Fanny herself could desire" (p. 470). We have been waiting all through the novel for this to happen; when it finally does, we are not allowed to see it, or Fanny's joy, at first hand. (One thinks of Emma's response to Mr. Knightley in the garden: "What did she say? – Just what she ought, of course. A lady always does."[24]) Jane Austen somewhat self-consciously offers a reason why she has written such an ending: "Let no one presume to give the feelings of a young woman on receiving the assurance of that affection of which she has scarcely allowed herself to entertain a hope" (p. 471). Why not? Is it because the novelist never played such a scene herself or had these "feelings" – and thus forbears to write about them? She always disliked trying to describe things of which she had no direct knowledge (nowhere in her books is there a scene between two men alone). On the other hand, there was the Bigg Wither affair. That, of course, had a different conclusion. Surely by now, at age thirty-eight, Jane Austen realized that she herself would never play such a scene as Fanny plays opposite Edmund. Perhaps, then, it was too painful for her to write. In any case, she was always more interested in her characters' distress than in their fulfillment. This is true even in *Persuasion*, where, after two drafts of the last chapters, Jane Austen came up with only half a love scene; a careful reading demonstrates that much of the climactic action and dialogue either takes place out of our sight and hearing or fails to get itself written at all.

The mood of *Mansfield Park* is more somber than that of the first three novels (though *Sense and Sensibility* runs it a close race). Now middle-aged and disappointed, Jane Austen was finding it harder to be sunny. Her anger, for example, embraces Maria Bertram, who is not forgiven at the end of *Mansfield Park*, as Lydia Bennet was in *Pride and Prejudice* for a similar offense (of course, Maria is much the guiltier of the two). The passage of time, the novelist tells us at the end of *Mansfield Park*, often undermines and revises "the plans and decisions of mortals, for their own instruction, and their neighbours' entertainment" (p. 472). No longer is detachment from the spectacle of life – seeing others as "entertainment" for oneself – treated ironically, as it was in the character of Mr. Bennet. For Jane Austen, detachment had become by 1814 less a peril to be avoided than a state of existence with which to become reconciled. Here we may see creeping in the darker shadows of the later trio of novels.

"There is nothing like employment, active, indispensable employment, for relieving sorrow. Employment . . . may dispel melancholy" (p. 443), *Mansfield Park* tells us. And so Jane Austen found "employment" in writing, and kept on writing to "dispel melancholy."

NOTES

1. Kingsley Amis, "What Became of Jane Austen? [*Mansfield Park*]," originally published in the *Spectator*, no. 6745 (4 October 1957), 339–40; quoted here from *Jane Austen: A Collection of Critical Essays*, ed. Ian Watt (Englewood Cliffs, N.J., 1963), pp. 141–2.
2. *The Novels of Jane Austen*, ed. R. W. Chapman, 3rd edn., III (London, 1934), 68. All quotations from *Mansfield Park* are from this edition; subsequent page references appear in the text.
3. Stuart Tave, "A Proper Lively Time with Fanny Price," *Some Words of Jane Austen* (Chicago and London, 1973), pp. 158–204; see especially pp. 182, 164–5, 194, and 175.
4. Tave, *Some Words of Jane Austen*, p. 165.

5. Alistair M. Duckworth, *The Improvement of the Estate: A Study of Jane Austen's Novels* (Baltimore and London, 1971), p. 76.
6. Tave, *Some Words of Jane Austen*, p. 178.
7. Bernard J. Paris, *Character and Conflict in Jane Austen's Novels: A Psychological Approach* (Detroit, 1978), p. 22.
8. Darrel Mansell, *The Novels of Jane Austen: An Interpretation* (New York, 1973), p. 110.
9. Reported in Park Honan, *Matthew Arnold: A Life* (New York, 1981), p. 60.
10. Jane Austen to Francis Austen, 3 July and 25 September 1813, in *Jane Austen's Letters to Her Sister Cassandra and Others*, ed. R. W. Chapman (London, 1932; rev. edn 1952, 1959), pp. 317 and 340.
11. Mrs. Austen found Fanny "insipid." See "Opinions of *Mansfield Park* Collected and Transcribed by Jane Austen," in *Jane Austen: The Critical Heritage*, ed. B. C. Southam (London, 1968), p. 49.
12. On Mrs. Leigh Perrot's trial for shoplifting and other possible offenses committed by her, see Sidney Ives, *The Trial of Mrs. Leigh Perrot* (Boston, Mass., 1980), *passim*. In a note to the present writer, Mr. Ives quotes Alexander Dyce as saying that Mrs. Leigh Perrot "had an invincible propensity to theft" and the Austen family knew it. Still, she was never convicted of anything. Jane Austen, who did not like her aunt, was being malicious.
13. The information comes from some correspondence recently discovered at Castle Howard. See Elizabeth Jenkins, "Some Notes on Background," address given at the Annual General Meeting of the Jane Austen Society, *Report for the Year 1980*, p. 26.
14. Reginald F. Bigg Wither, *Materials for a History of the Wither Family* (Winchester, 1907).
15. Despite her avowed dislike of Jane Austen's novels, Charlotte Brontë seems to have remembered this section of *Mansfield Park* well enough when she came to write the scene in *Jane Eyre* (ch. 27) in the course of which the heroine reminds Rochester, "We were born to strive and endure."
16. To Cassandra Austen, 29 January 1813 (*Letters*, p. 298).
17. See Marilyn Butler, *Jane Austen and the War of Ideas* (Oxford, 1975), p. 243.
18. *Novels*, V, 223.
19. See Chapman's note on *Lovers' Vows* in *Novels*, III, 474.
20. Reported by Arlin Turner in *Nathaniel Hawthorne: A Biography* (New York and Oxford, 1980), p. 26.
21. To Francis Austen, 25 September 1813 (*Letters*, p. 338).
22. To Anna Austen Lefroy, 29 November 1814 (*Letters*, p. 415).
23. John Odmark, *An Understanding of Jane Austen's Novels: Character, Value, and Ironic Perspective* (Totowa, N. J., 1981), p. 102.
24. *Novels*, IV, 431.

3

On *The Ordeal of Richard Feverel*

> *Mamma, whose views on education are*
> *remarkably strict, has brought me up to be*
> *extremely short-sighted; it is part of her system.*
>
> – Gwendolen in *The Importance of Being Earnest*

Meredith's masterpiece, *The Ordeal of Richard Feverel* (1859), has sometimes been criticized for being inconsistent. How should one respond to a novel, it has been asked, which is two-thirds comedy (chapter 29 signals "The Last Act of a Comedy") and ends with a series of monumental tragedies?

Well, life too is a mixed *genre*; and many things which may seem amusing enough ultimately turn out, as Hardy says, to be not quite so amusing after all.

A reference to Hardy is not irrelevant here. For in writing a story which quite deliberately refuses to provide the mid-Victorian reader with the expected happy ending and a full round of poetic justice, Meredith – born thirteen years after Trollope, sixteen after Dickens, seventeen after Thackeray, and eighteen after Mrs. Gaskell – was in fact signalling a new direction for the novel. He is generally, and rightly, classified with the "later" Victorian novelists (Hardy, Gissing, Butler, Moore), who tended to find themselves at odds with contemporary standards and conventions, and whose novels present us with what Matthew Arnold termed a "criticism of life" (which Hardy thought of as the function of art) rather than with various examples of ways of accommodating ourselves to it. While Dickens, Trollope, and Mrs. Gaskell find plenty of things to complain about and to ridicule, in their novels the world is perceived as a place in which, finally, things are made to make sense, poetic justice flourishes, everyone gets his just reward. Do what is right, and you must come through: Thackeray and Wilkie Collins sometimes question this; the others, never. This is by no means the view of the later novelists; in their works we find no such confidence in the organization of the universe. The discoveries of the "New Sciences" and the difficulty of maintaining religious faith, the failure of economic prosperity (in the 1870s) and the collapse of the One Nation ideal – these, as well as creative sensibilities which, in good "modern" fashion, had been alienated, prevented the later generation of novelists from seeing their world as a benign place.

A pivotal figure here is George Eliot. The fact that *Adam Bede* appeared in the same year as *The Ordeal of Richard Feverel* has sometimes tempted literary historians to point to 1859 as a watershed moment for the novel. In this same year, doing business as usual, Dickens published *A Tale of Two Cities*, Mrs. Gaskell published *Round the Sofa and Other Tales*, Trollope published one of his most mediocre novels, *The Bertrams*, Wilkie Collins's *The Woman in White* was appearing serially, and Thackeray brought out what is arguably the worst book ever produced by a great novelist, *The Virginians*. (*The Origin of Species* also appeared in 1859.) But *Adam Bede* and *The Ordeal of Richard Feverel* pointed in a different direction. These are novels which emphasize psychological development and analysis of character over the demands – or perhaps in place of the demands – of plot, and many of the other conventional requirements of early Victorian story-telling. Perhaps 1859 was indeed the year in which the novel began to change. While such generalizations are both dangerous and often wildly overstated, this one may contain a few seeds of truth.

Like *Adam Bede*, *The Ordeal of Richard Feverel* focuses on the psyches of its characters; and, like *Adam Bede*, it has a highly controversial (for the time) seduction in it. The camera swings away at the crucial moment in both novels, however, in obeisance to contemporary taste; for novelists of this period were dependent for their livelihood on the puritanical requirements of Charles Edward Mudie and his colleagues in the circulating-library business. How the libraries reacted quite simply determined sales.

The seduction in *Adam Bede* is that of an inexperienced girl by a rich man – the standard type – and Arthur Donnithorne is given plenty of time to repent of his action before the novel comes to an end. And, while Hetty's baby is not allowed to live, she – unlike Tess, later – does survive, though in vastly changed circumstances. Dinah and Adam come together at the end, and the novel closes on a happy note. Born nine years before Meredith, George Eliot, though a transitional figure, is temperamentally closer to the early Victorian novelists than to her successors in the field. Her faith in the goodness of people, her "religion of humanity," allowed her to let her foolish people commit their folly early in the story, repent at their leisure, and survive. The idea that she is a tragic novelist surely invites re-examination.

In *The Ordeal of Richard Feverel*, the seduction is that of a virtuous boy by a woman of the world, and occurs near the end of the novel: different premises indeed. There is no happy ending. For these reasons, and for its irreverence, Meredith's novel got itself into serious trouble with the circulating libraries. While *Adam Bede*, doctrinally clean, was an immediate best-seller, *The Ordeal of Richard Feverel* initially became little more than a *succès de scandale*, not at all the same thing, and by no means as gratifying to an impecunious author as a healthy sale. But Meredith did not see life as a Dickens novel. For him acts had consequences, and the consequences of rash and foolish conduct were not easily sidestepped or atoned for.

It may be argued, then, that the appearance of *The Ordeal of Richard Feverel*, even more emphatically than that of *Adam Bede*, marks the beginning of the end of the "old" Victorian novel and the advent of something new. It was Meredith, not George Eliot, whom Gissing worshipped (*Feverel* was his favorite novel); nor was Gissing the only late Victorian novelist to lionize Meredith. It is difficult to appreciate now how towering a figure Meredith was for the novelists of the 1890s. Trollope was in eclipse, Dickens thought fit only for children. While Henry James read George Eliot and Gissing read Charlotte Brontë, Meredith and Hardy were the contemporary heroes, and the old-fashioned novel with a happy ending was an object of mirth. Writers simply didn't perceive their world that way any more. Meredith, who was born in 1828, had been seeing the universe as an ominous place, and writing about it that way, for a long time by the 1890s. He was a giant to the younger men in his trade, who noticed no similarity between the world they lived in and that depicted by George Eliot or Trollope or Dickens.

The setting of Meredith's great novel is shadowy, the chronology obscure. Still, one can place its action, roughly, from the late 1820s to the mid-1830s (like almost all Victorian novels, this one is set in the recent past). These dates are suggested by the fact that

Austin Wentworth, after four years abroad, is greeted upon his
return (ch. 41) by Adrian with news of the Reform Bill (1832) and
its consequences; by the dependence of most of the characters on
carriages and horses for long trips, and trains only infrequently –
in the 1840s they would have been jumping on one train after
another (like Dickens in many of his novels, Meredith wants the
atmosphere of an earlier time; horses instead of trains brought
with them the ambience of the late Regency and George IV); by
the description of Blaize as a "free-trade farmer," a characterization
that would have been relevant in the twenties and thirties but not
in the fifties, after the Corn Laws had been repealed; by the brief
debate in the novel over the comparative merits of Byron and
Wordsworth, which would not have been possible later (in the
1840s, say), when Wordsworth was a revered figure and Byron a
bad joke; by the mere presence in the story of a duel, something
in which no mid-Victorian gentleman, no matter how highly
strung, would have become involved, for Prince Albert had made
duelling not only illegal but, more importantly, both immoral and
unfashionable (the duel in which Trollope's Phineas Finn gets
himself embroiled is highly anomalous); and by the libidinous
evening party at Richmond, replete with unbuttoned ladies and
lascivious lords – again, a scene simply impossible to imagine a
few years after Victoria ascended the throne, in 1837 (the twenties
and thirties were the last decades, until the seventies and eighties,
when such things could be written about: the Nancy of *Oliver
Twist*, published 1837–9, could not be, and indeed was not,
repeated in any form in Dickens's later novels). For such amorous
adventures as Richard's, Meredith needed an earlier time, when a
hero with romantic illusions could jump on a horse.

But the debates over science that were taking place in the
middle of the nineteenth century are very much present in the
novel's main target, the spurious "scientific" System in which Sir
Austin Feverel brings up his son. Meredith believed in evolution –
the view of character-development in his novels is patently
evolutionary – and his protagonists are often changed by a kind
of organic growth. Undoubtedly he welcomed *The Origin of Species*
and the publications by Lyell and Darwin and others which had
preceded it. But one can believe in evolution and at the same time
abhor the application of scientific principles to human conduct,
and there can be no doubt that this is what Meredith is doing in
The Ordeal of Richard Feverel – whose villain is neither Lord

Mountfalcon nor Lady Mountfalcon nor anyone other than Sir Austin Feverel himself.

Only by involving himself with other people in society can a person learn what he is: it is this (very sound) principle which Sir Austin violently opposes. Now one of Meredith's most constant themes is what he calls the "comedy of egoism," which arises, he believes, out of man's failure to perceive his rightful place in the human hierarchy and his vision of *himself* at the center of the world. Meredith's important *Essay on Comedy and the Uses of the Comic Spirit* (1877), as well as the famous Prelude to his only other great novel, *The Egoist* (1879), make clear his commitment to the idea that the egoist must be ridiculed, not tolerated – and certainly not taken seriously or at his own valuation of himself. Meredith speaks of the virtues, indeed the necessity, of laughter, and of the need to recognize folly, advocating "Olympian" mockery rather than sympathy for the egoist. What Meredith calls the "Comic Spirit" provides moral progress by deflating egoism and establishing in its place a sense of proportion. It is the perspective of this "Comic Spirit" from which the story is told, and which we encounter in the narrative voice, from first to last, in *The Ordeal of Richard Feverel*; the result of this is an ironic, sometimes jeering tone which makes the novel complex, and perhaps hard-going for the reader unused to Meredithian mockery.

One form egoism frequently takes in Meredith's novels is the unreasonable desire of some to possess others entirely. Among the amazing gallery of egoists, hedonists, and solipsists in *The Ordeal of Richard Feverel* – extensively revised by Meredith in 1878, during the period when he was writing the *Essay on Comedy* and *The Egoist* – Sir Austin (like Dickens's Dombey) is prominent for his desire to possess completely the heart and soul of his son. "I require not only that my son should obey; I would have him guiltless of the impulse to gainsay my wishes," declares the baronet (ch. 16). The boy must not only be obedient; he must be innocent of Thoughtcrime. Indeed, there is something Orwellian about Sir Austin; he is the Victorians' most spectacular anticipation of Big Brother. In his wish "to be Providence to his Son" (ch. 4), he destroys him. Richard's "ordeal" is his moral education, which is the edifice of his father and which, due to his father's System, suffers fatal delays in construction. "His son's ordeal was to be his own," Meredith remarks of the baronet (ch. 28). Acts have consequences. What we do, how we act, inevitably affects others besides ourselves: it is one of Meredith's most deeply felt precepts. Unfortunately for the hapless Richard, all of Sir Austin's diseased chickens come home to roost in the breast of his romantic, idealistic, and tragically inexperienced son.

It is clearly wrong to have a "system" of any kind in dealing with others, especially those who are close to us. Meredith believed that the novel must affirm human freedom in the face of scientific determinism. Sir Austin places his faith in the scientific control of human nature; but human nature cannot be "controlled" – either scientifically or in any other way. Instinct, which finally "beats" the System, is alien to it, as is humor. It is indicative that the baronet has no sense of humor: "the faculty of laughter . . . was denied him" (ch. 22). "Honest passion," the novel reminds us, "has an instinct that can be safer than conscious wisdom" (ch. 29). It is instinct that Sir Austin fears above all, and rightly so. The System works, more or less, so long as Richard is young and malleable, without instincts of his own. Eventually he begins to think for himself. The combination of heroic idealism and personal naivety proves to be catastrophic.

Love – and what can be more instinctive than that? – marks the end of the System (the chapter titled "The Last Act of a Comedy" is that in which Richard is married); for science, as we have seen, takes no cognizance of instinct. The breach between Richard and his father begins when the boy is commanded to burn his poetry. Art, of course, is always anathema to tyrants, who fear what they cannot control; love, we remember, is the great enemy of the Party in *Nineteen Eighty-Four*. The gulf between Sir Austin and his son becomes impassable when Lucy enters the picture and Richard falls in love with her. The baronet refuses to accept her because she is not his own choice. There is an obvious irony here. The System has worked in so far as it has rendered Richard capable of choosing for his wife the one woman in the world with whom he has a chance of happiness. Indeed, when Richard meets and loves Lucy, "Then truly the System triumphed" (ch. 15), as Meredith observes. But the System, being a system, does not "know its rightful hour of exaltation" (ch. 19). A bad scientist as well as a bad father, Sir Austin cannot refrain from tinkering with a process which has, after all, turned out an admirable adolescent. In the paroxysm of jealousy and anger which overtakes him, the baronet never gives the marriage a chance to work; he has been balked in his chosen role as his son's one God. Nothing the boy does without his consent and encouragement can be acceptable. "It was the first of the angels who made the road to hell" (ch. 21), he remarks; but he seems to have forgotten that the original sin was Pride. That Sir Austin takes the Devil's side is clear enough. After Richard's marriage, in his determination to close his heart and mind against his son, the baronet "did not battle with the tempter. He took him into his bosom at once, as if he had been ripe for him, and received his suggestions, and bowed to his dictates" (ch. 33).

"Love of any human object is the soul's ordeal," Sir Austin observes (ch. 21); Meredith obviously agrees with him. But *how* we love is important. Sir Austin, and ultimately Richard too, can be seen as a person who loves the wrong way. To love possessively – so jealously as to turn vindictive and unreasonable – is the wrong way. But to love too selflessly, without any ego, is also dangerous, for it leaves us with no defenses, vulnerable to the smallest pinprick. Richard's blind romantic love, while morally preferable to his father's more selfish brand, is dangerous too. It is indicative that he is described as "an engine . . . at high pressure" (ch. 29); as having "the character of a bullet with a treble charge of powder behind it" (ch. 41); and, in an image which recurs, as "strung like an arrow drawn to the head" (ch. 15, for example). Those who recommend to his father what Lord Heddon calls "a little racketing" (ch. 18) for Richard are undoubtedly right. Had the boy been allowed some experience of the world before meeting the Mountfalcons and their set – had he, in short, stopped living in a dream of knight-errantry – the final tragedies might have been avoided. But Richard, until the end, exists in a world of his own, as his father does – different worlds, to be sure, but equally divorced from reality. One cannot make a career out of "saving" women any more than one can bring up a child scientifically. The old family doctor who declares that Richard "ought to see the world, and know what he is made of" (ch. 23) is ignored. So is Lord Heddon's prophetic warning: "Early excesses the frame will recover from; late ones break the constitution" (ch. 18). Even Mrs. Doria sees that Richard's "education acts like a disease on him. He cannot regard anything sensibly. He is for ever in some mad excess of his fancy, and what he will come to at last heaven only knows!" (ch. 35). The problem, of course, is the father. He understands as little of the world as the son; the egoist perceives nothing, being blinded by self-regard.

Indeed, we are told that "Sir Austin . . . knew less of his son than
the servant of his household" (ch. 12). When the baronet advises
Mr. Thompson (ch. 17) to let Ripton see the vices of London in
order to take away their mystery and allure, we know that he
won't allow Richard the same freedom. Feverels, of course, are
not Thompsons. It is all pride, Satanic pride.

Richard should have been sent to school, like Ralph Morton,
where he would have learned a few things worth knowing.
"Mystery is the great danger to youth" (ch. 25), as Adrian rightly
declares. But the father cannot let the son out of his sight; is it to
be expected that God should send his only son to Eton? The
father knows nothing; the son is brought up to know nothing.
"The danger of a little knowledge of things is disputable," the
novel reminds us (ch. 30), *"but beware the little knowledge of one's
self!"* (the emphasis is Meredith's). Sir Austin never has any self-
knowledge – not even, as Lady Blandish makes clear, at the end,
when he fails to see that he is responsible for all that has
happened. "As he wished the world to see him, he believed
himself" (ch. 40); yes, *believed himself.* It is here that the baronet's
egoism is thrown into greatest relief, in his putting himself and
his own wishes before the welfare of the son he claims to love.
"He lost the tenderness he should have had for his experiment –
the living, burning youth at his elbow" (ch. 22). For this, he
cannot be forgiven. Even when vaguely cognizant of some
possible guilt, Sir Austin manages to turn his conduct to his own
advantage: "His was an order of mind that would accept the most
burdensome charges and by some species of moral usury make a
profit out of them" (ch. 40).

What ultimately renders the novel so moving and so indelible is
the attractiveness of Richard Feverel himself, a character we so
readily and enthusiastically admire and commune with until, in
the final third of the novel, the results of his pernicious
"education" catch up with him and he behaves like an imbecile.
The tale is brilliantly and beautifully written from first to last,
however, and even in the final section Meredith is able to preserve
our feeling for Richard – most notably in the much-praised chapter
called "Nature Speaks" (ch. 43), in which, alone in the German
forest, Richard achieves some insight into himself and into the
meaning of his past actions. But it is the trimming of the bright
flame – the fact that "Richard will never be what he promised"
(ch. 46) – that we must come to terms with at the end. By then it

is too late; Richard is a failure. Meredith wishes us to see that acts *do* have consequences, that how we treat others *is* important, and that human interaction, since the ultimate results of it cannot be fully known or understood at the time, is a fragile thing, more deserving of our consideration than what we may conceive our own momentary needs and desires to be. And so there is no happy ending.

In the book's final chapters, though Sir Austin has met Lucy and surmised that only through "blind fortuity" could Richard have found such a perfect mate and that "instinct" has indeed "beaten science" (ch. 43), he still understands little more than that, as he says, "it is useless to base any system on a human being." Meredith comments on Sir Austin's error, "If instead of saying, Base no system on a human being, he had said, Never experimentalize with one, he would have been nearer the truth" (ch. 30).

Humans can be nurtured by love, but not by science. It is this lesson that Richard learns in the German forest: the value of unselfish love of another. But too much has happened that cannot be undone; Richard cannot escape fully the mad fancies and illusions fostered in him by his pernicious upbringing. Egoism and sentimentality, taken in large doses, are capable of turning comedy into tragedy after all. "The Fates must indeed be hard, the Ordeal severe, the Destiny dark, that could destroy so bright a Spring!" (ch. 12). Indeed they are. And so it is that in our last view of Richard Feverel we see the defeated hero lying silently in his bed, striving to imprint the image of his dead wife upon his mind.

4

Trollope's Conservatism

Trollope's conservatism was deep-seated, lifelong, and all-embracing. It was both a temperamental and a political conservatism, governing his perspectives on social conduct and embodying attitudes, often dogmatically and always clearly stated, on many of the issues of his day. I shall discuss the latter last: that is, his feelings about such questions as women and the new feminism, the emergence of the Jews in English society, and the position and condition of black men and women in the British Empire. The point, however, that I wish to make here is a more general one. Trollope is not simply, as he has often been taken to be,[1] the "normal" voice of the mid-Victorian middle class. He stands to the right of standard Victorian views on many issues – views that were, as we know, often conservative enough. Trollope's is not the voice of the middle-of-the-road "advanced conservative liberal,"[2] as he would have us believe, but rather that of the true conservative – and, in some cases, of the reactionary.

A number of critics have been misled by Trollope's own assessment of his political and social views; often such critics are men and women who believe that what the novelist says outside his fiction must be true, that a man apparently so honest in all his dealings with the world should have his word taken at face value. But it has been shown that Trollope does not always tell the truth, and that we are no more obliged to believe him when he speaks of himself than any other maker of fictions who may choose to pretend, at selected moments, that he is no longer writing what is not true.[3]

Yes, Trollope is sympathetic to "the English girl" (Henry James's phrase) and her inevitable dependence on marriage as an economic and social support: but this does not mean that Trollope, any more than Jane Austen, championed women's rights. Yes, he was involved in a number of progressive causes, often sided with the Liberals, and was associated with several moderately liberal journals: this does not speak to his political convictions, which we shall examine closely. The concept of Trollope as a moral casuist –

a believer in the doctrine of "live and let live," opposed to taking any rigid or even definable moral stance in his books – has been fashionable among some modern critics of the novelist. This view strikes me as lazy; it accepts Trollope's apparent moderation and tolerance, his notorious reluctance in his novels to find fault (for long) with anyone, as representing the way he actually looked at things. I believe something quite the contrary: that few men have held views – political, social, or otherwise – so tenaciously and consistently, and expressed them so positively.

I

In the political novels, a good place to begin unearthing what I have called Trollope's temperamental conservatism, the novelist shows us the connections between social and political, private and public life. One must be careful never to confuse party affiliation with temperamental inclination. Trollope was a Liberal because he was a conservative – the Conservatives seeming to him to be nothing at all. After all, the Whigs and then the Liberals were the party of the landed aristocracy and commanded, between them, majorities in the House of Lords throughout much of the nineteenth century. Trollope always revered the great Whig families and saw the Tory leaders, personified in Disraeli, as upstart con-men. The Liberal Party of Trollope's time was no more liberal than the Conservative Party; many of the most radical measures of the nineteenth century were enacted by Tory ministries. Trollope was really a Whig while Whigs were still Liberals and before they became Conservatives. Indeed, in his memoir of *Lord Palmerston* (1882) he declares that "Whig statesmen . . . were at heart Conservative."[4] There are always such people in the nominally progressive parties of English politics, as Arthur Pollard has written, and when such parties split, as they periodically do, the more conservative elements become Conservatives, whether as Unionists in the time of Joseph Chamberlain or as National Labour or Liberal in that of his son Neville.[5]

The tension between progressive and conservative elements is evident in Trollope's fictional realization of Plantagenet Palliser. This character stands between those, such as the Duke of St. Bungay, nearer to the Tories, and those, such as Turnbull, who represent the Radical pressures on traditional Liberalism. Trollope hated the Radicals and pillories them in book after book. One critic has argued that an important theme of *The Prime Minister* (1875–6) is the approaching demise of amateur political pundits amid the complexities of the modern state.[6] But Trollope is less interested in the modern state than in old-fashioned – not amateurish – political virtue. I have argued elsewhere[7] that Palliser is the justification and symbol of Trollope's social conservatism. A representative of the best traditions of the English aristocracy – "the very model of an English statesman," Trollope calls him in *The Prime Minister* (I, 24) – he personifies the novelist's faith in the free patrician life of England, the stratification of society, and the leadership of the aristocracy. Trollope wrote the Palliser novels to express this faith.

I shall be more specific about Trollope's views and why he held them. "No man has a right to regard his own moral life as isolated from the lives of others around him," the novelist declares in *Dr. Wortle's School*, a late masterpiece (1880); "A man cannot isolate the morals, the manners, the ways of his life from the morals of others. Men, if they live together, must live by certain laws" (pp. 84, 90). As Robert Tracy has argued, the novel shows that "Society and its laws must be placated . . . The man or woman who flouts the social order . . . is punished, but conformity earns forgiveness."[8] As he saw society, so Trollope saw politics – that is, as a continually shifting process of change and conciliation. He saw personal life in political terms, unable as he was to imagine it as something separate from the life of the community. In *Dr. Wortle's School* Trollope argues that a bad life cannot be led in a good community without infecting that community – and that a good life cannot be led in a bad community. Since social and political life are symbiotic in Trollope's view, the moral soundness of a nation will depend in large part upon the kind of people who constitute its political system – whether big men, like Palliser, Palmerston, or Lord John Russell, or smaller men, like Phineas Finn, Barrington Erle, or Laurence Fitzgibbon. There is little political *theory* in this point of view.

One notes Trollope's admiration for Palmerston, the memoir of whom was one of the last things he wrote (in 1881), and certainly his last work of non-fiction. Trollope praised Palmerston for his practical conservatism and his hatred of political theory. "He was more interested . . . in his own age than in the past or the future,"

Asa Briggs has written of Palmerston. "In his distaste for theory
. . . he reflected his age"[9] – a characterization applied as easily to
Trollope. Another of Trollope's great heroes – this one fictional,
but with many of Palmerston's traits – is the Dean of Brotherton
in another much-neglected late novel, *Is He Popenjoy?* (1877–8). In
a memorable moment in this novel the Dean says,

> 'It is a grand thing to rise in the world. The ambition to do so is
> the very salt of the earth. It is the parent of all enterprise, and
> the cause of all improvement. They who know no such ambition
> are savages and remain savage. As far as I can see, among us
> Englishmen such ambition is, healthily and happily, almost
> universal, and on that account we stand high among the
> citizens of the world. But, owing to false teaching, men are
> afraid to own aloud a truth which is known to their own
> hearts.'   (II, 286)

Like many of his contemporaries, Trollope believed instinctively
in the established institutions of his time: his lifelong veneration
of the House of Commons is just one example of this. In his
books he expresses some of the normal qualities of these
institutions and of those who people them (as a civil servant
employed in the Post Office for more than thirty years, he was
one of these people himself). It is characteristic that he puts into
the mouth of one of his heroes the following speech: "No man
has a right to be peculiar. Every man is bound to accept such
usage as is customary in the world" (*The Claverings* [1866–7], I,
282). This anticipates the lesson of *Dr. Wortle's School*. Trollope
was no radical and no revolutionary. "The people can take care of
themselves a great deal better than [politicians] can take care of
them," he wrote in *Phineas Finn* ([1867–9], I, 31). His distrust of
republican government, obvious throughout *North America* (1862)
and many of his other travel books, surfaces in his comparison of
the Speaker of the U.S. House of Representatives to "a croupier at
a gaming table who goes on dealing and explaining the results of
the game" as he deals (p. 176). What Trollope hated most about
the American experiment in democracy was its assumption that
"equality" among people is either possible or desirable. In several
of his novels "equality" is pronounced to be a dream.

Trollope's attachment to the Liberal Party of his day was less philosophical than social and temperamental. He knew personally many of the leading Liberal statesmen of the time and was invited to their homes. He disliked the unprincipled adventurers who seemed to have seized control of the Conservative Party. He was a man who liked to belong to things in any case – clubs, the Church, the hunts, the party – more for the sake of convenience than out of carefully developed conviction. Certainly he had a lifelong fear, no doubt a result of his disastrous childhood, of exclusion and isolation: and so his "heroes do not criticize the social order. . . . They accept it and are accepted by it."[10] Trollope describes his own untheoretical nature in what is perhaps his most autobiographical character, Sir Thomas Underwood in *Ralph the Heir* (1870–1; I have discussed this elsewhere in some detail[11]).

Trollope's conservatism is obvious everywhere in his thought. For example, he favored political rule by an oligarchy of aristocrats. "The few best men of a people are always those who should rule"; power is a "privilege . . . of some few who are specially chosen" to govern, he declares in *The New Zealander* (written 1855–6). He adds here that what he calls "the few best" are always "in some sort found. And so the government goes on and is conducted, in the one and only way in which the government of a people can be managed." Elsewhere in *The New Zealander* he says simply, "The aristocrat is . . . of all men the best able to rule."[12]

This is plain enough. It is an argument of each of the Palliser novels – in *Can You Forgive Her?* (1864–5), which asserts that a country is better off when its politicians have a personal stake in it; in *Phineas Redux* (1873), which declares that the rulers of England should be "looked for among the sons of Earls and Dukes . . . as [they] . . . may be educated for such work almost from their infancy" (II, 443); in the proclamation of the same novel that "some men . . . seem to have been born to be Cabinet Ministers, – dukes mostly, or earls, or the younger sons of such, – who have been trained to it from their very cradles and of whom we may imagine that they are subject to no special awe when they first enter into that august assembly, and feel little personal elevation" (I, 373–4); in *The Duke's Children* (1879–80), where Palliser argues eloquently that maintenance of the aristocracy is "second only in importance to the maintenance of the crown" (I, 213). Put simply, "the England which we know could not be the England that she is but for the maintenance of a high-minded, proud, and self-denying nobility" (*Phineas Redux*, II, 188). In *The New Zealander* Trollope speaks to the "danger" of aristocratic rule, so often a fact of nineteenth-century English life:

> We now hear much to the prejudice of the English aristocracy, and are told daily of our danger because the rule of the country is altogether in aristocratic hands. Would that it were! In what other hands can the rule of any country be safely placed? For what purposes have we an aristocracy here among us, if it be not that they may rule and guide us rightly?
>
> The main duty of all aristocrats, and we may say their only duty, is to govern; and the highest duty of any aristocrat is to govern the state.   (p. 18)

Here is an unmistakable anchor of Trollope's political philosophy.

Trollope's preference for aristocrats as political leaders takes us to the question of the great families. The Pallisers have always been Whigs; and the families Trollope most admired were the old Whig families, the conservative progenitors of Victorian Liberalism. A character in *Phineas Redux* articulates this cardinal point of Trollope's political faith:

> 'I do believe in the patriotism of certain families. I believe that the Mildmays, FitzHowards, and Pallisers have for some centuries brought up their children to regard the well-being of their country as their highest personal interest, and that such teaching has been generally efficacious. Of course, there have been failures. Every child won't learn its lesson however well it may be taught. But the school in which good training is most practised will, as a rule, turn out the best scholars. In this way I believe in families.'   (I, 216)

In another long passage in *Phineas Redux* the novelist pauses to discuss the superiority of Whig–Liberal governments to Tory governments specifically in terms of their aristocratic personnel:

> There is probably more of the flavour of political aristocracy to be found still remaining among our Liberal leading statesmen than among their opponents. A Conservative Cabinet is, doubtless, never deficient in dukes and lords, and the sons of such; but conservative dukes and lords are recruited here and

there, and as recruits, are new to the business, whereas among
the old Whigs a halo of statecraft has, for ages past, so strongly
pervaded and enveloped certain great families, that the power
in the world of politics thus produced still remains . . . With
them something of the feeling of high blood, of rank, of living
in a park with deer about it, remains. They still entertain a
pride in their Cabinets.   (I, 432–3)

This is a crucial statement. Trollope underscores his preference for
the Liberals – in this respect not at all like the Conservatives,
whose "great families" are only the most recent *nouveaux riches* of
the political arena; his admiration for the old families generally;
and his approval of their exclusiveness. The passage demonstrates
how Trollope's political Liberalism and temperamental conservatism are in perfect accord: he prefers the Liberals to the
Tories because the aristocracy of the former is purer and older.
This preference has nothing to do with "liberalism." Indeed, as
historian Donald Southgate has pointed out, mid-nineteenth-
century Whiggery, being aristocratic in terms of "personnel" and
oligarchic in terms of "influence," was "the most ostentatious and
self-conscious constituent of . . . 'the Establishment'" of the
time.[13]
    Nothing more plainly shows Trollope's dislike of the populist
vein of the Liberalism of his time than the series of attacks in the
Palliser novels on John Bright, who appears there in the person of
Turnbull, the Radical. In *Phineas Finn* Trollope lists the tenets of
Bright/Turnbull and calls our attention to the shallowness of the
way they are held:

> Progressive reform in the franchise, of which manhood suffrage
> should be the acknowledged and not far distant end, equal
> electoral districts, ballot, tenant right for England as well as
> Ireland, reduction of the standing army till there should be no
> standing army to reduce, utter disregard of all political
> movements in Europe, an almost idolatrous admiration for all
> political movements in America, free trade in everything except
> malt, and an absolute extinction of a State Church.
>
> (I, 198–9)

Trollope portrays the aristocratic Liberal leaders as statesmen,
products of an historical continuity which has eluded the Tories

and which they can only ape. But he has no use for Radical "popular" leaders, so-called men of the people such as Bright.

Trollope's preference for the privileged classes is made manifest in other ways and places. *Lady Anna* (1874) and *The American Senator* (1877) both emphasize the superiority of the upper classes and tell us how much pleasanter it is to be with the rich than with the poor. In *Can You Forgive Her?* the heroine's father declares, "Take them as a whole, the nobility of England are pleasant acquaintances to have . . . if I had a choice of acquaintance . . . I should prefer the peer" (I, 266). There is this from Trollope's *Thackeray* (1879): "A peer taken at random as a companion would be preferable to a clerk from a counting-house, – taken at random; the clerk might turn out . . . a scholar . . . but the chances are the other way."[14] In *Is He Popenjoy?* the same sentiments are articulated by the shrewd Mrs. Montacute Jones: "I like having lords in my drawing-room. They look handsome, and talk better, than other men. That's my experience. And you are pretty nearly sure with them that you won't find you have got somebody quite wrong" (II, 80).

In terms of what some Victorians thought, let us remember, Trollope's beliefs were less reactionary than simply normal. Theirs was indeed a conservative age. Lord Briggs has ably demonstrated Trollope's profound faith in Bagehot's concepts of the "old deference" and "dignity" of the English constitution as safeguards against the barbarisms of the rude democracy becoming ever more widespread during the nineteenth century.[15] "Deference" meant habitual respect for social superiors and contempt for urban radicalism. Gladstone himself acknowledged "the strong prejudices in favour of the aristocracy which pervade all ranks and classes of the community." The framers of the Second Reform Bill were no less aware in the 1860s that the prestige of the aristocracy must not be tampered with. The best government, that most likely to bring social peace and political tranquility, was thought by them to be government by a select few upper-class members of Parliament who were sufficiently educated and experienced – as well as removed from the material temptations of corruption – to undertake the work of leadership.

Bagehot's *The English Constitution* appeared serially in 1867 (the very year of the Second Reform Bill) in the *Fortnightly*, a journal with which Trollope was closely connected: we may be sure that he read Bagehot. Here he found defended the concept of government by a "select few" and emphasis on the contrast between the elite classes and the *demos*. Like Bagehot, Trollope had little sympathy for the poor, cared little about them, and knew even less about the social problems caused by extreme poverty. Wisely, he did not often write about the poor (equally wisely, there are no Marxist studies of Trollope). In his novels, if one may generalize, the working classes are often portrayed as greedy, unprincipled, or cretinous. The middle classes are seen as even less suited to hold or exercise political power: Trollope views them as especially susceptible to the temptations of material speculation, or economic gambling. Indeed, some of his harshest satire is directed against manipulative capitalists who are would-be statesmen; George Vavasor, Ferdinand Lopez, and Augustus Melmotte are but three examples. A virtue of aristocratic rule in the eyes of men such as Trollope and Bagehot was that it staved off the rule of mere wealth – the *merely* rich whose "religion of gold" (Bagehot's phrase) might enable them to vault to the top of the greasy pole. *The Way We Live Now* (1874–5) memorably articulates this fear. Speculation and stock-jobbing were seen by Trollope as inimical to honest political rule; the fact that the villains of his novels are often middle-class businessmen with political aspirations expresses this view. It should not surprise us, then, that in *Phineas Finn, The American Senator*, and elsewhere Trollope defends the "pocket boroughs" of rich aristocrats as being more likely than boroughs in which really democratic elections are held to send enlightened representatives to Parliament. He had nothing against the old system of aristocratic patronage and influence.

Trollope's conservative elitism, however, goes beyond love of aristocracy. "There are places in life which can hardly be well filled except by Gentlemen," he said. No "good can be done by declaring that there are no gates, no barriers, no differences" between the social classes. This is again similar to the outlook of Palmerston, who declared in 1850 that England was "a nation in which every class of society accepts with cheerfulness the lot which Providence has assigned to it."[16] "Could you establish absolute equality in England tomorrow," says the astute Sir William Patterson in *Lady Anna*, "the inequality of men's minds and character would re-establish an aristocracy within twenty years" (pp. 365–6). Differences in rank, the same novel declares, have been allowed and encouraged by "God Almighty . . . to carry out his purposes" (p. 244). In *The Claverings* Trollope goes so far as to declare that "some respect should be maintained from the low in station towards those who are high even when no respect has been deserved" (II, 225). As Arthur Pollard has said, Trollope admired good blood, the gentlemanly virtues, the "accumulated traditions of behaviour and belief," and had "a proper regard and regret for the passing of much that was valuable."[17]

In keeping with these attitudes, Trollope loudly opposed competitive examinations for places in the Civil Service: he felt they would not, as they should do, guarantee that appointments would be made whenever possible to "gentlemen," men of good family. He argues this unsubtly in *The Three Clerks* (1858), *The Last Chronicle of Barset* (1867), and *Marion Fay* (1881–2). Like Palmerston, he saw the stratification of society as inevitable. "I dislike universal suffrage; I dislike vote by ballot; I dislike above all things the tyranny of democracy," he proclaims in *North America* (p. 188). In one of his election addresses at Beverley in 1868 he went against the established policy of the Liberal Party that year specifically to denounce the concept of the secret ballot, which he called "unmanly."[18] He goes out of his way in many of his novels to ridicule Radicals and republicans: there are odious ones in *Ralph the Heir*, *He Knew He Was Right* (1868–9), *John Caldigate* (1879), and *Can You Forgive Her?* In *North America* Trollope defends the "Constitutional monarchy" as that type of government more likely than any other to give "a measure of individual freedom to all who live under it" (p. 55). He even proposes here that Queen Victoria send one of her sons across the sea to become King of Canada.

Like the true conservative, Trollope preferred the executive to the legislative branch of government – and in a bicameral system the upper to the lower house. It was the function of an upper chamber, he said, to protect the country against radical measures proposed by the lower; and he always looked with repugnance, as being extreme and dangerous, upon the periodical attempts by the Commons to abolish the Lords. The tendency of the Great Reform Act of 1832 to circumscribe somewhat the power of the peerage he sadly lamented. These feelings are stated openly in *The New Zealander* (pp. 107, 18), *Australia and New Zealand* ([1873], I, 487), and *The Fixed Period* ([1882], II, 87, 96). He couldn't get over the free mixture of classes in the classless train carriages and

hotels of America (especially in the West). Although he disliked
the Irish tenant-right system, he opposed any attempt to tamper
with free enterprise, as *Castle Richmond* (1860) makes clear enough
(for instance, p. 60).

Nor is Trollope's conservative elitism unconnected with his
lifelong passion for and interest in the classics, which was also
responsible for two of his published works: his edition of Caesar's
Commentaries (1870) and his two-volume *Life of Cicero* (1881). As
Robert Tracy has shown, Trollope saw Caesar as an instrument of
Providence in the destruction of the Roman Republic and the
initiation of the Empire – what the novelist termed a necessary
stage in "the gradual amelioration of the human race." Trollope
felt that British and other European civilizations derived in large
measure from Rome's imperial achievement, which made the
Empire "the common parent of modern nations." Caesar's career,
as Trollope remarked in a review of a history of Rome by his
friend Charles Merivale, helped bring this achievement about:

> The human mind cannot [accept] that the Creator would allow
> the career of an Alexander or a Caesar, a Frederick or a
> Napoleon, if the aggrandisement of man, or a nation, were to
> be the sole result of such violence and bloodshed; but when
> history shows us that the civilization of nations can be traced to
> the ambition of individuals, she teaches us her most useful
> lesson, explains to us why heaven permits the horrors of war,
> and vindicates the ways of God to man.[19]

Trollope never opposed "the ambition of individuals"; here he
comes close to giving us a moral justification of dictatorship.
Indeed, in one of his letters he remarked that Julius Caesar was
the greatest man who ever lived.

Interest in the classics is in itself indicative. A love of Greek and
Roman literature often suggests a conservative attitude of mind.
Familiarity with the classic literatures is usually considered a mark
of intellectual distinction; certainly this was true in the latter years
of the nineteenth century. Trollope's conservatism, like Gissing's
after him, is reflected in his lifelong interest in the ancient
cultures. I quote Samuel Vogt Gapp, who wrote on this theme
half a century ago:

> It is a familiar fact that the classic literature was an aristocratic

one. It took little account of slaves, of poor artisans, of the
hordes of freemen who filled the circus Maximus . . . It was a
literature written by men who reclined at ease in their villas. It
was often . . . the product of an imperial court . . . Proletarian
literature was simply inconceivable in ancient times. In the
education of modern times the classic literatures have found a
similar . . . destiny. They are not taught to artisans; a classic
education is synonymous with a professional training; it is the
privilege of the professional classes, of lawyers, doctors, divines,
or the wealthy classes, or of statesmen.[20]

Like the ancients, Trollope wrote nothing remotely resembling
proletarian literature. The number of genuinely poor people who
figure importantly in his books can be counted on the fingers of
one hand.

II

Trollope's anti-Semitism stemmed primarily from his hatred of
Disraeli, who was attacked in the Liberal press throughout the
1860s and 1870s as a foreigner and a Jew, and the Jewish
characters in his novels tend often to take on allegedly
Disraelian traits – charlatanism, untrustworthiness, audaciousness,
pushiness, a tendency toward "conjuring"; they often smell of
greasepaint and powder. In *The Bertrams* (1858) Disraeli is referred
to contemptuously, but not by name, as a "Jew senator" in whose
throat nothing will stick during the race to attain office. Disraeli
appears in the novels primarily as Daubeny, the Tory Prime
Minister who will use any trick, take any gamble, to maintain or
achieve office. There is also a good deal of Disraeli in Sir Timothy
Beeswax in *The Duke's Children* and in several other characters
who are not professional politicians – though all the Jewish
characters have some political instincts, as Trollope believed all
Jews to have.

We should do well to look at what Trollope says in his
Autobiography – written in 1875–6, when Disraeli was Prime
Minister and at the height of his influence – of Disraeli's novels:

An audacious conjuror has generally been his hero, – some
youth who, by wonderful cleverness, can obtain success by

every intrigue that comes to his hand. Through it all there is a feeling of stage properties, a smell of hair-oil, an aspect of buhl, a remembrance of tailors, and that pricking of the conscience which must be the general accompaniment of paste diamonds. (p. 223)

Trollope goes on here to talk about the "the wit of hairdressers" and "the enterprise of mountebanks" in connection with Disraeli's fiction. He consistently saw Disraeli as one of Disraeli's own novel-heroes; and if Disraeli's heroes are "audacious conjurors," Trollope's political villains are often Disraelian heroes. If Trollope could have considered Disraeli's politics more dispassionately, he might have seen how close, in many ways, the two men were in their political philosophies: it is a singular irony.

Four of Trollope's most conspicuous Jewish characters are Melmotte, Brehgert, Emilius, and Lopez. Melmotte is never actually proven to be a Jew, but it is generally considered that he is one (his wife is declared to be Jewish), and his shady origins are supposed to be somewhere in central Europe. One of his closest business associates, Mr. Cohenlupe, is a Jew. Melmotte's whole enterprise in *The Way We Live Now* may well stand for the sort of inroads into English society that Trollope saw the Jews making in the 1870s. Brehgert, the aggressive Jewish merchant, who is also part of Melmotte's financial empire, wishes to use his wealth as a means of connecting himself through marriage to the respectable upper-middle-class English squirearchy. The venomous reception he is given by the snobbish Longstaffes is treated ambivalently by Trollope – who, like Edith Wharton after him, worried about the dilution of the blue-blooded gentry through an unwelcome admixture of "foreign" blood.

Emilius is a "greasy Jew" pretending to be a Protestant who marries a rich widow and achieves for a while a certain fashion – an obvious swipe at Disraeli, who also married a rich widow and had been converted from Judaism to Anglicanism at an early age. Emilius is called "greasy" again and again; in *The Eustace Diamonds* (1871–3) there are numerous references to hair oil, as in the *Autobiography*. Emilius is glib but not deep, which is how Trollope saw Disraeli. But by far the most spectacular Disraelian figure in the novels is Lopez in *The Prime Minister*. Like Emilius and Melmotte, he is a European wanderer, presumably a Jew. But here we have something more specific: Lopez is said to be of

Portuguese extraction. It is impossible not to assume that in Lopez Trollope was still working off his hatred not only of the Jews, but of Disraeli personally – the Portuguese–Italian Jew who was Prime Minister of England as *The Prime Minister* was being written. Yet another of Trollope's treacherous, greasy, European–Jew adventurers who covets political place, Lopez, like Melmotte, dies "on stage," and violently. Such endings are unusual for Trollope; they are a measure of his growing impatience with such men. Before Disraeli came to power, Trollope's villains are given gentler treatment.

There are other anti-Semitic bits in Trollope. One is tempted to say that it was only a sign of the times, or to excuse Trollope by recalling how often he went back to Elizabethan drama to get his plots.[21] Still, one does not find the Brontës or Mrs. Gaskell or George Eliot or Meredith or Hardy or Gissing writing about "greasy Jews," whereas Trollope's novels are awash with them. About the kindest remark he can find to make about the Jews appears in his book on *The West Indies and the Spanish Main* (1859), where the novelist declares that he would "sooner dance with a Jew than pray with a Baptist" (p. 38).

III

"Can we forgive Miss Vavasor? Of course we can, and forget her, too," said Henry James,[22] and no one else has been particularly fond of the abrasive, platitudinous heroine of *Can You Forgive Her?*. Trollope is not shy about telling us what is wrong with Alice – "She thought too much," he says – nor about specifying her chief problem:

> What should a woman do with her life? . . . Alice was ever asking herself that question, and had by degrees filled herself with a vague idea that there was a something to be done . . . if only she knew what it was. She had filled herself . . . with an undefined ambition that made her restless without giving her any real food for her mind . . . How might she best make herself useful . . . in some [way] that might gratify her ambition . . . was the question which seemed to be of most importance to her. (I, 134–5, 401)

Thoughtful Alice, in her craving for independence and self-sufficiency, keeps changing her mind about whom she wants to marry – due, Trollope says, to absurd "ambitions": "All her troubles and sorrows . . . had come from an overfed craving for independence" (II, 38). The novelist explicitly condemns Alice for "that pride which had hitherto taught her to think that she could more wisely follow her own guidance than that of any other" (II, 368, 437). As P. D. Edwards has said, Alice is "a warning to other young women against over-reliance on their own judgement."[23] Such women, Trollope declares, inevitably wind up making fools of themselves (II, 500). The inflated estimation an "independent" woman has of her powers and abilities is responsible for a good deal of trouble in Trollope's novels. Let a woman recognize "the necessity of truth and honesty for the purposes of her life," he says in Can You Forgive Her? (I, 135), and she need not "ask herself many questions as to what she will do with it."

In creating one of literature's most perverse heroines who is not immoral, Trollope (as I have written elsewhere[24]) was expressing his distaste both for independent women and for the general evil of feminine self-indulgence. The other leading lady of Can You Forgive Her?, Lady Glencora Palliser, may seem at first glance to be even more self-sufficient and self-indulgent, but what is most significant in her story is that, despite much provocation, she continues to respect and cling to her husband. Thus at the end of the novel we have less to "forgive" her for.

When John Grey in Can You Forgive Her? resolves "to treat all that [Alice] might say as the hallucination of a sickened imagination" (I, 143), we are meant to see her ambitions for herself as the stuff and substance of romance, idle and unhealthy day-dreaming, a neurotic craving for excitement. Alice's "hallucination" is that she must "do something with her life" instead of becoming simply a wife. Can You Forgive Her? traces her journey from fiction to sense. As Juliet McMaster has pointed out, the anti-feminist theme in it is embellished by the presence of the two Misses Pallisers – suffragette types, stuffy, ineffectual, and in general unsympathetically drawn.[25]

In Can You Forgive Her? Trollope was concerned with the foolishness, as he saw it, of the new feminism, especially when it took the form of the too "thoughtful" woman – the "modern" woman stirred up by the new ideas of her time to find out what she should "do" with her life. Alice is Trollope's response to the

Woman Question. The *Westminster Review* observed this quickly
enough. In its notice of the novel the writer declared that Alice
"has, half-consciously, become deeply infected with the nineteenth-
century idea that there was something important to do with her
life."[26] It is worth noting that Trollope was reading *Emma* in 1864
as he was writing *Can You Forgive Her?* and spoke admiringly of
the way in which Jane Austen exposed the "folly," "vanity," and
"ignorance" of "the female character."[27]

Some recent critics have thought that Trollope often depicts
women as members of an oppressed second sex.[28] Certainly he
shows them, as Jane Austen did, being dependent upon men and
marriage for any sort of real freedom in their lives; but he also
shows them, in many cases, getting the better of recalcitrant
parents and finding the means to manipulate slower-witted lovers.
To depict women as economically and socially dependent upon
men was nothing new in the English novel. But Trollope never
goes beyond this, as some novelists did, to argue for women's
rights; and critics have sometimes interpreted the close sympathy
he gives many of his heroines as a political statement instead of
what in fact it is: fascination with female psychology and the
pathology of physical attraction. Again and again Trollope goes
out of his way to satirize the agitation for women's rights. An
interest in women need not, after all, be a political statement. The
anti-feminist sentiments of *Can You Forgive Her?* are by no means
anomalous in Trollope's work.

The theme commences as early as *The Kellys and the O'Kellys*
(1848). Lady Selina Cashel places herself above men and marriage –
resulting, it turns out, in her own unhappiness. A decade later, in
The Three Clerks, Trollope attacks the permissiveness with which
Mrs. Woodward brings up her three daughters: young ladies, he
states, should not be allowed to decide many things for themselves
(p. 27, for example). In *Phineas Finn*, written mostly in 1866, Violet
Effingham's energies are said to be devoted, fortunately, not to
"the sterile wastes of Women's Rights," but rather to being a wife
and mother. This makes her happy, while the frustration and
bitterness of Lady Laura Kennedy, who believes a woman can
live only half a life because she cannot sit in Parliament, destroy
both her own happiness and her husband's.[29] In *Sir Harry Hotspur
of Humblethwaite* (1870), Trollope recommends that women fall in
love, marry, and have babies. He specifically endorses the belief
of his heroine Emily Hotspur that "a woman should not marry

'

. . . unless she could so love a man as to acknowledge to herself that she was imperatively required to sacrifice all that belonged to her for his welfare and good" (p. 164).

This is certainly clear enough; and Trollope went on saying more or less the same things throughout the 1870s, as the women's-rights movement gathered steam. Both *Ralph the Heir* and *John Caldigate* specifically and spiritedly defend the institution of marriage; the hero of the last book argues that a woman's first and only duty is to cleave to her husband and child no matter what emergency may seem to weaken those ties.

Special mention must be made here of *The Vicar of Bullhampton* (1869–70), in which the Woman Question is reintroduced when the restless Mary Lowther debates with herself the issue of the day:

> When a girl asks herself that question, – what shall she do with her life? – it is so natural that she should answer it by saying that she will get married, and give her life to somebody else. It is a woman's one career – let women rebel against the edict as they may; and though there may be word-rebellion here and there, women learn the truth early in their lives. (pp. 259–60)

Let us "cease to hear of the necessity of a new career for women" (p. 260), Trollope declares here. He goes on to condemn the "mock modesty" of women *vis-à-vis* marriage, and concludes that a woman's desire to be married is natural and reasonable: furthermore, "the whole theory of creation requires it" (p. 260). As one critic has aptly said, Trollope's perspective upon woman reduces her realizable reality to marrying and having children "and being honest with an honest husband."[30]

It is also typical of Trollope's attitude (as, for example, in his lecture "On the Higher Education of Women," 1868[31]) that he advocated female education through programs of reading not in order to help women become productive citizens, but rather to help them find a way to exorcise boredom and loneliness. His unsubtle attack on organized feminism through the "Rights of Women Institute, Established for the Disabilities of Females" – abbreviated, ironically, to the "Female Disabilities" – is an unforgettable element of *Is He Popenjoy?* Here the women's-rights movement is said by one character to have its origin in "old maids who have gone crazy . . . because nobody has married them."

Some pages of this novel are occupied with the Baroness Banmann, a feminist who steals, perspires, and has a moustache. The Baroness belittles her rival in the feminist movement, Olivia Q. Fleabody, by calling her a female. Trollope's feelings about women's rights are articulated explicitly in *Is He Popenjoy?* when the worldly-wise Mrs. Montacute Jones warns the novel's heroine, Lady George, not to meddle with the "Disabilities": "I know my own . . . but I never think of interfering with Providence. Mr. Jones was made a man, and I was made a woman. So I put up with it, and I hope you will do the same" (II, 248). Lady George resolves to give up the "Disabilities" in future. Even Olivia Q. Fleabody has by the end of the novel – Trollope's wording is significant – "settled down into a good mother of a family" (II, 311), thus apparently coming to her senses.

Although such things must be speculative, it is tempting to see Trollope's animus against the feminists being stirred in part by the example of his mother. Fanny Trollope was a career woman (she wrote nearly eighty novels). At a tender age the young Trollope was abandoned by her when she went off to America with the rest of the family to gather material for a book. Trollope was left alone at school in humiliating circumstances. He never forgave her for this. Fanny Trollope was not fond of her novelist son (she favored his less ambitious brother Tom) and told Anthony repeatedly and emphatically that he had no talent as a writer of fiction. If one has an energetic, abrasive, unloving, and career-oriented woman for a mother, one is perhaps more likely than not to prefer passive women to domineering ones and to exaggerate homely virtues at the expense of public ones – especially if one's mother is in the same profession as oneself. Nor was Trollope always reticent about his mother's work. "No observer was ever less qualified to judge of the prospects or even of the happiness of a young people," he remarks in *North America* (p. 23) of Fanny Trollope's *Domestic Manners of the Americans* (1832), the book she abandoned him to write. It is a matter of record that Trollope married a quiet, pliant woman, and that in his novels he goes out of his way to satirize aggressive, publicity-minded ladies. Those who wish for any career other than wifehood and motherhood come, in the pages of his books, to a disappointing and sometimes disastrous end.

A decade before *Is He Popenjoy?*, in *He Knew He Was Right*, there appears "the republican Browning" – the feminist agitator

Wallachia Petrie. A poet and a bore, Miss Petrie believes she can get on well enough without the assistance of men; and she is able to persist in this delusion, according to Trollope, "because the chivalry of men had given her sex that protection against which her life was one continued protest" (p. 717). In *North America* Trollope had addressed this same question of male chivalry and female complacency. Women's "happy privileges," he declared there, are the result of male "chivalry. That spirit has taught men to endure in order that women may be at their ease" (p. 111). Years later Trollope said virtually the same thing in *Australia and New Zealand*: "Women all over the world are entitled to everything that chivalry can give them. They should sit while men stand. They should be served while men wait. They should be praised – even without desert. They should be courted – even without love" (II, 99). Is it possible to conceive of a less "feminist" statement?

Like most American women as viewed by Trollope, Wallachia Petrie fails to perceive the return which male chivalry demands. "The hope in regard to all such women," Trollope says in *He Knew He Was Right*, "is that they will be cured at last by a husband and half-a-dozen children" (p. 720). One "cures" a disease. In the same novel the sensible and kindly Charles Glascock, asked what he thinks of J. S. Mill's contention that women must eventually "be put upon an equality with men," replies with a question of his own: "Can he manage that men shall have half the babies?" (p. 521). Mill is also referred to twice in *Phineas Finn* (II, 45 and 243) – in each instance humorously by women who have no use for his feminist theories. It is difficult to see how readers of Trollope can justify the notion that the novelist supported Mill's efforts in the women's-rights movement or that *He Knew He Was Right* takes a "liberal view" of the new feminism.[32]

Mill's attempt to popularize the idea of the equality of the sexes profoundly affected social thought and even more customs as early as the 1860s; well before he died in 1873 the laws regarding women's property and personal rights had begun to be reviewed. The influential Society for Promoting the Employment of Women had come into existence in the 1850s; the Married Women's Property Act, though not passed into law until the year of Trollope's death, 1882, had been introduced in Parliament as early as 1856. Queen's College was founded in 1848, Bedford College in 1849, and Girton College later on, in 1872. But throughout the sixties and seventies Trollope's barren feminists and vulgar, meddling female careerists betray his contempt for the feminist movement. The social historian J. A. Banks is surely right to suggest that Trollope may be read less for information about the feminist movement than "for deep insights into the nature of the opposition which [it] had to face."[33] The novelist's lecture "On the Higher Education of Women," which I have mentioned and which, coincidentally or not, was delivered as *He Knew He Was Right* was appearing serially (1868), attacks the modern, too "thoughtful" woman, and anticipates the views of Mrs. Montacute Jones in *Is He Popenjoy?*

> As we cannot turn a man into a woman . . . so neither can we give to her the gift of persistent energy by which he does perform, and has been intended to perform, the work of the world. There is no doubt a very strong movement now on foot in favour of such assimilation, arising chiefly . . . from . . . jealousy and . . . ambition on the part of a certain class of ladies who grudge the other sex the superior privilege of manhood.[34]

Complaining in *North America* that American women talk too loudly and "know so much more than they ought to know," Trollope declares that in America "modesty has been put out of Court by women's rights." American women, he laments, are ignorant of "the virtue of obedience" and have a delusion "that destiny is to be worked out by the spirit and talent of the young women." He concludes with a bald assertion of his feelings in such matters: "I confess for me Eve would have had no charms had she not recognized Adam as her lord" (pp. 117, 200). Yet we find one critic asserting in the teeth of this that *North America* reveals Trollope's admiration for the emancipated girls of America and his support of the feminist theories of Mill.[35]

Trollope (like Gissing) felt that a woman could live a life both domestic and "full" – indeed, that she was most a force for moral order when presiding over the hearth and making its goodness radiate outward beyond the life of the home. If this point of view also reminds us of the creator of Mrs. Pardiggle and Mrs. Jellyby, Mrs. Clennam and Madame de Farge – and it should – it is in part because Dickens, less "radical" than many people still believe he was, made the same complaints, and made them before Trollope did. In 1851 he attacked the proselytizing fervor of the early feminists in an article called "Sucking Pigs," published in *Household Words*. The essay comes down heavily on the modern woman who feels the need to "agitate, agitate":

> She must take to the little table and the water bottle. She must be a public character. She must work away at the Mission. It is not enough to do right for right's sake. There can be no satisfaction . . . in satisfying her mind . . . that the thing she contemplates is right, and therefore ought to be done, and so in calmly and quietly doing it, conscious that therein she sets a righteous example which never in the nature of things can be lost or taken away.[36]

It is worth pointing out that both Dickens and Trollope were in fact less progressive than has been suggested by some recent academic criticism. Surely such men must have been like us and believed what we believe – yes? No. In Dickens and Trollope veneration of the past is only one product of a wholehearted temperamental conservatism. Both believed in God, in the virtues of money (in the novels of each, characters worthy of redemption are rewarded with it), and in class distinctions. Both, that is, believed in most of the deities and accepted most of the values that conventional, conservative Victorians believed in and accepted. Of course their sales were high. Both were skeptical about the virtues and effects of popular education and uneasy about the spread of a genuinely democratic spirit: in both there is a fear of the mob. Both were considerable capitalists; neither desired a political revolution. Like Trollope, Dickens hated American republicanism. Both held, as Gissing wrote of Dickens, "that *to be governed* was the people's good; only let the governors be rightly chosen . . . Dickens knew . . . how unfit are the vast majority of mankind to form sound views as to what is best for them . . . he knew that ignorance inevitably goes hand in hand with forms of baseness." All of this is equally true of Trollope. Gissing picks up the thread again in the recently discovered preface he wrote to the Rochester *David Copperfield* (for "Dickens" we may again read "Dickens and Trollope"):

> Dickens, with his intensely practical common-sense . . . never desired a social revolution. . . . He believed firmly in the subordination of ranks, and shows throughout his writings that

he regarded 'humility' as a natural and laudable attribute of
the lowly class. . . . Dickens . . . could not look with entire
approval on the poor grown articulate about their wrongs. . . .
He . . . thought that humble folk must know 'their station.' He
was a member of the middle class, and as far from preaching
'equality' in its social sense as any man that ever wrote.

Gissing characterizes "the conservatism which lay deep in
[Dickens's] mind" as "the root of so much in him that was good
and great."[37]

We may or may not agree; but on these issues, as on the issue
of the new feminism, Dickens and Trollope spoke with one voice.
Both men, beginning with little and achieving much, became in
the course of their lives middle-class snobs. In each there was a
subterranean fear of backsliding; in each lurked inordinate interest
in earning pots of money and living in big houses. Both were
correspondingly bored by the so-called deprivations of Victorian
women. Both portray women who want to become "independent"
as neurotic, unhappy, unfeminine – and, ultimately, embittered
failures. If a woman felt oppressed, the source of her feeling was
not some fault in society, but rather her own deviance.

"It is difficult," Lord Briggs remarks, "to consider Trollope 'a
feminist.' "[38] It is difficult to disagree with Lord Briggs.

IV

Both Dickens and Trollope defended what seemed to them the
brutal measures adopted by Governor Eyre in Jamaica in 1865–6
to repress what were represented in the British press as native
rebellions there – which takes us, conveniently, to the race
question.

We should not, in the 1860s and 1870s, expect of Trollope that
he sound an early clarion call for racial equality. Yet years after
Wilberforce's eloquence and the success of the abolitionists (in
Parliament, if not on the seas), what Trollope says about black
people is by any odds ungenerous. It is inconceivable to him, he
writes in *North America*, "that the Negro can be made equal to the
white man." After all, "the Negro is the white man's inferior
through laws of nature. . . . He is not mentally fit to cope with
white men" (p. 190). Though Empire was a concept close to the

heart of the hated Disraeli and anathema to Gladstone, whom Trollope admired, the novelist refers in *North America* to England's mission "to spread civilization across the ocean!" (p. 140) and to the acquisition of colonies as "carrying out the duty . . . of extending civilization, freedom, and well-being through the new uprising nations of the world . . . The national ambition [understands that] . . . there can be no glory to the people so great or so readily recognizable by mankind at large as that of spreading civilization from East to West, and from North to South" (p. 53). From the English government, Trollope declared two years later in *Can You Forgive Her?*, "flow the waters of the world's progress, – the fullest fountain of advancing civilization" (II, 54). On the question of Governor Eyre and the black natives of Jamaica, Dickens wrote: "That . . . sympathy with the black – or the native, or the devil – afar off, and that . . . indifference to our own countrymen at enormous odds in the midst of bloodshed and savagery, makes me stark wild"; and he ridiculed the idea that "New Zealanders and Hottentots . . . were identical with men in clean shirts at Camberwell."[39]

North America, however, is not the only one of Trollope's travel books in which the subject of English dominion over the blacks is treated so bluntly – as Lord Briggs's account of Trollope the traveler reveals.[40] Trollope's lifelong xenophobia (Palmerston is pointedly praised for his resistance to intimidation in the conduct of foreign affairs) coexisted with the novelist's passion for travel: what he says about the races in some of the travel books less well-known and pored-over than *North America* makes this clear enough. Throughout *The West Indies and the Spanish Main*, which Trollope thought the best of his various accounts of foreign travel, open distrust of both the negro and his "religion" are expressed. Jamaican black men, Trollope writes here, seldom understand "the purposes of industry, the object of truth, or the results of honesty." They would be "altogether retrograde if left to themselves. . . . [They] are a servile race, fitted by nature for the hardest physical work, and . . . for little else" (pp. 57, 62–3). He declares that the Jamaican blacks and their brothers in Bermuda entertain no idea of the purposes of work or the prospects of self-improvement. He goes on to attack the abolitionists, the Anti-Slavery Society, and those who object to the importation of "coolie labour" into the West Indies, noting that Trinidad is more prosperous than Jamaica because of the many immigrants imported from Madras and Calcutta, and that the economy of Jamaica has steadily declined after the abolition of slavery. He contends that, after all, "The negro's idea of emancipation was and is emancipation not from slavery but from work" (p. 92). He cites as proof of this that, following abolition, half the state of Jamaica lay fallow while the black natives squabbled over the form of government they wished to set up for themselves. No one in Jamaica, Trollope says, can possibly have "come across three of four [blacks] who are fit to enact laws for their own guidance and the guidance of others" (pp. 122–3).

In his book on the West Indies Trollope sometimes sounds like Kipling, assigning the roles of white and black men in these parts to the judgment of a beneficent Providence. He speaks here, as Briggs notes, about Britain's "noble mission" and about "the welfare of the coming world" as being in the hands of "the Anglo-Saxon race" (pp. 84–5). Briggs quotes, with approval, the opinion of Eric Williams, the late Prime Minister of Trinidad, that Trollope's book on the West Indies is "merely an expurgated version" of Carlyle's *Occasional Discourse Upon the Nigger Question* (1849) – for Williams "the most offensive document in the entire world literature on slavery."[41]

Trollope's chapter on slavery in *The West Indies and the Spanish Main* bears out Williams's charge. The novelist says here,

> A negro has not generally those gifts of God which enable one man to exercise rule and mastership over his fellow-men. I myself should object strongly to be represented, in the city of London, by any black man that I ever saw. 'The unfortunate nigger gone masterless,' whom Carlyle . . . commiserates, has not strong ideas of the duties even of self-government, much less the government of others. Universal suffrage in such hands can hardly lead to good results.   (p. 253)

One must remember that universal suffrage did not exist in Britain when this book was published in 1859, and that Trollope was not in favor of introducing it.

Trollope concludes *North America* by looking forward to the gradual extinction of the negroes in the United States and their replacement by "coolies from India and China as in Guiana and the West Indies." He reiterates here his belief in "the intellectual inferiority of the Negro" (pp. 88–9), and declares: "the preaching of abolition [of slavery] . . . is to me either the deadliest of sins or the vainest of follies" (pp. 85–6).

In *South Africa* (1868), Trollope speaks again of his Kiplingesque faith in the white man's mission to cultivate and improve the black native races through work, which he calls "the great civilizer of the world" (p. 317). He refers to the struggle already begun between blacks and whites for control of South Africa by affirming his opinion that "in one way or another a minority of white men will get the better of a majority of coloured men" (p. 22).

I do not wish to suggest that Trollope held these opinions in isolation: we have touched in passing on the views of Dickens, Carlyle, Gissing, and Kipling, who were not liberal on social questions. Comparisons are sometimes instructive. It is interesting to note that Trollope, on these matters, sometimes sounds more like an untutored child than a thoughtful adult. In the early 1860s Matthew Arnold, during a routine inspection of a school, found a third-year schoolgirl writing her history lesson for the day in these terms: "The aborigines (of New Zealand) are a degraded and ferocious cast of people but owing to the introduction of firearms and spirits they are gradually decreasing."[42] That Trollope's views on race may be roughly compared with those of a third-year schoolgirl may help to demonstrate that his was hardly the "normal" voice of liberal, middle-class Victorians.

V

In a recent article called "Trollope's Liberalism,"[43] the writer admits that *The Warden* (1855) shows Trollope out of sympathy with labor agitators, that Radicals in his novels are almost always portrayed in an unflattering light, and that not one of Trollope's books betrays as much sympathy with Radical causes as Disraeli's *Sybil* (1844). The explanation for what is admitted here to be a tepid "liberalism" is that Trollope had no intimate friends who were politicians – simply not true – and that the novelist wrote more about the country than the city, which inevitably dampens one's political fire. The article concludes with an interesting exercise in logic: "Believing that his countrymen" entertained "a certain sentimental reverence for outmoded forms" – that is, that most of them were reactionary – "the instinctively conservative Trollope . . . could *afford* to be an advanced Liberal."[44]

We need not belabor this. It is interesting to note that the author of an article called "Trollope's Liberalism" should conclude by calling the novelist "instinctively conservative."

We should do well to remember, with Robert Tracy, that although, "to the modern reader, Trollope's ideal social order may seem reactionary . . . we cannot condemn him because he does not share the democratic ideas of another time and place."[45]

NOTES

1. See, for example, Asa Briggs, "Trollope, Bagehot, and the English Constitution," in *Victorian People: A Reassessment of Persons and Themes 1851–1867* (London, 1954; Chicago, 1955), pp. 87–115.
2. Anthony Trollope, *An Autobiography* (2 vols, London, 1883); I am quoting from the Oxford World's Classics edition (1 vol., London, 1953; 1961), p. 253. Unless otherwise specified, all subsequent references to Trollope's works are to the World's Classics editions (page references in the text following citations).
3. See, for example, John Halperin, "Trollope's *Phineas Finn* and History," *English Studies*, 59 (Spring 1978). As examples of critics who have been misled by Trollope's claims of liberalism – or at the very least by his apparent political "casuistry" – I cite the following: Ruth apRoberts, *The Moral Trollope* (Athens, Ohio, 1971); A. O. J. Cockshut, *Anthony Trollope: A Critical Study* (London, 1955; 1968); Geoffrey Harvey, *The Art of Anthony Trollope* (London and New York, 1980); Walter M. Kendrick, *The Novel-Machine: The Theory and Fiction of Anthony Trollope* (Baltimore and London, 1980); James R. Kincaid, *The Novels of Anthony Trollope* (Oxford, 1977); Robert M. Polhemus, *The Changing World of Anthony Trollope* (Berkeley and Los Angeles, 1968); and R. C. Terry, *Anthony Trollope: The Artist in Hiding* (Totowa, N. J., 1977).
4. Anthony Trollope, *Lord Palmerston* (London, 1882), p. 80.
5. Review of John Halperin's *Trollope and Politics* (see n. 7), *Clio*, 8 (Spring 1979), 293.
6. See Polhemus, *Changing World*, passim.
7. See John Halperin, *Trollope and Politics* (London and New York, 1977).
8. Robert Tracy, *Trollope's Later Novels* (Berkeley and Los Angeles, 1978), pp. 262, 266.
9. See Briggs, "Trollope, Bagehot, and the English Constitution," *Victorian People*.
10. See Tracy, *Trollope's Later Novels*, p. 73.
11. See Halperin, *Trollope and Politics*, pp. 129–50.
12. Anthony Trollope, *The New Zealander*, ed. N. John Hall (Oxford, 1972), pp. 135, 144–5, and 13, respectively. Subsequent references are given in the text.

13. See Donald Southgate, *The Passing of the Whigs, 1832–1886* (London, 1962), p. 77.

14. Anthony Trollope, *Thackeray* (London, 1879), p. 84.

15. See Briggs, "Trollope, Bagehot, and the English Constitution," *Victorian People*, pp. 91–100, *passim*; my argument in the next several paragraphs is indebted to Briggs's.

16. See W. L. Burn, "Anthony Trollope's Politics," *The Nineteenth Century and After*, 143 (March 1948), 170–1.

17. Arthur Pollard, *Anthony Trollope* (London and Boston, Mass., 1978), p. 197.

18. See the *Beverley Recorder* for 14 November 1868.

19. See Trollope's "Merivale's History of the Romans," a review published in the *Dublin University Magazine*, 37 (May 1851), 611–12; and Robert Tracy, "*Lana Medicata Fuco*: Trollope's Classicism," in *Trollope Centenary Essays*, ed. John Halperin (London and New York, 1982), pp. 10–11.

20. See *George Gissing, Classicist* (Philadelphia, 1936), p. 94.

21. See Tracy, *Trollope's Later Novels*, *passim* (e.g., p. 55).

22. Review of *Can You Forgive Her?* in *Nation*, 1 (28 September 1865), 409–10; reprinted in *Notes and Reviews* (New York, 1921), but not reprinted (so far as I know) since. James was twenty-two when he wrote this review, one of his first to be published. I should like to thank Leon Edel for helping me to unearth it.

23. P. D. Edwards, *Anthony Trollope: His Art and Scope* (New York, 1977), p. 96.

24. See John Halperin, "Trollope and Feminism," *South Atlantic Quarterly*, 77 (Spring 1978), 179–88.

25. See Juliet McMaster, "'The Meaning of Words and the Nature of Things': Trollope's *Can You Forgive Her?*," *Studies in English Literature*, 14 (Autumn 1974), 603–18, esp. 609.

26. Unsigned, *Westminster Review*, 75 (July 1865), 284.

27. See David S. Chamberlain, "Unity and Irony in Trollope's *Can You Forgive Her?*," *Studies in English Literature*, 8 (Autumn 1968), 670–7, esp. 672–3 and n. 14.

28. See, for example, Polhemus, *Changing World*, p. 105; Kendrick, *Novel-Machine*; and Terry, *Anthony Trollope*.

29. My argument here in part follows that of an unpublished essay, a section of a Princeton dissertation, by Barry A. Bartrum. I am grateful to Mr. Bartrum for making a draft of his work available to me.

30. See George Levine, "Can You Forgive Him? Trollope's 'Can You Forgive Her?' and the Myth of Realism," *Victorian Studies*, 18 (September 1974), 15.

31. Reprinted in Anthony Trollope, *Four Lectures*, ed. Morris L. Parrish (London, 1938).

32. See, for example, Terry, *Anthony Trollope*; and Edwards, *Anthony Trollope*, p. 118.

33. See J. A. Banks, "The Way They Lived Then: Anthony Trollope and the Seventies," *Victorian Studies*, 12 (December 1968), 194.

34. Trollope, *Four Lectures*, ed. Parrish, p. 77.

35. See Terry, *Anthony Trollope*, pp. 154–6, *passim*.

36. Quoted by John Butt and Kathleen Tillotson in *Dickens at Work* (London, 1957), p. 96. "Sucking Pigs" appeared in *Household Words*, 85 (8 November 1851).
37. See Gissing's *Charles Dickens: A Critical Study* (Edinburgh, 1898); and his preface to the Rochester *David Copperfield*, ed. Richard J. Dunn, published for the first time in *The Dickensian* (Spring 1981), pp. 3–9.
38. Asa Briggs, "Trollope the Traveller," in *Trollope Centenary Essays*, ed. Halperin, p. 43.
39. Quoted by Norman and Jeanne MacKenzie in *Dickens: A Life* (New York and Oxford, 1979), p. 346.
40. Briggs, "Trollope the Traveller," in *Trollope Centenary Essays*, ed. Halperin, pp. 24–52, *passim*. Much of what I say in the following paragraphs about Trollope's racism is indebted to Briggs's discussion in *Trollope Centenary Essays* of the travel books.
41. See Eric Williams, *British Historians and the West Indies* (London, 1966), pp. 90, 80.
42. Quoted by Park Honan in *Matthew Arnold: A Life* (London and New York, 1981), p. 320. The paper in question, dated 20 July 1862, is in Balliol College; Arnold recorded the quoted excerpt in his diary in 1863.
43. See *Anthony Trollope*, ed. Tony Bareham (London and New York, 1980), pp. 161–81. This is a collection of new essays on Trollope (rather than reprints). The author of the article quoted here is A. O. J. Cockshut.
44. Cockshut, in Bareham, *Anthony Trollope*, p. 171.
45. See Tracy, *Trollope's Later Novels*, p. 81.

5

Trollope's *Phineas Finn* and History

When *Phineas Finn* finished its long run in *St. Paul's Magazine* and appeared in book form in 1869, Trollope was attacked by the *Daily Telegraph* (31 March 1869) for "ungentlemanly conduct" in drawing portraits of living politicians such as Disraeli, Gladstone, Derby, Russell, and Bright. It was widely assumed at least that the demagogue Turnbull was an unflattering likeness of Bright. In Trollope's reply to the newspaper he declared that it is neither "gentlemanlike" nor "right" to paint, malignantly, public men as they may appear in private, and that he had not done so in *Phineas Finn*. On the question of Turnbull and Bright he said this:

> In the character of Mr. Turnbull . . . I depicted Mr. Bright neither in his private nor public character; and I cannot imagine how any likeness justifying such a charge against me can be found. The character that I have drawn has no resemblance to [him] . . . in person, in manners, in character, in mode of life, or even in the mode of expressing political opinion. It was my object to depict a turbulent demagogue; – but it was also my object so to draw the character that no likeness should be found in our political circles for the character so drawn. I have been unlucky . . . but I protest that the ill-luck has not been the result of fault on my part. I intended neither portrait nor caricature, and most assuredly I have produced neither.[1]

Trollope was being considerably less than candid. While it is not true that Trollope ever "admitted that Turnbull was Bright," as Michael Sadleir erroneously reports,[2] the novelist does not in his letter to the *Telegraph* deny the paper's other identifications, which were that de Terrier was Derby, Daubeny was Disraeli, Mildmay was Russell, and Gresham was Gladstone. Indeed, in a letter written to Mary Holmes some years later (15 June 1876) in answer to questions she raised about some of the characters in *The Prime Minister*, Trollope writes in a strain significantly less militant:

> though in former novels certain well-known political characters, such as Disraeli and Gladstone, have been taken as models for such fictitious personages as Daubeny and Gresham, it has only been as to their particular tenets. There is nothing of personal characteristic here. When that has been attempted by me, – as in the Palliser people . . . there has been no distinct idea in my own mind of any living person. They are pure creations; and (as I think) the best I have ever made.[3]

In the same year he wrote in his *Autobiography*, "As to the incidents of [*Phineas Finn*], the circumstances by which these personages were to be affected, I knew nothing [in advance]. They were created for the most part as they were described. I never could arrange a set of events before me."[4]

Some scholars, naively asserting that a man so ferociously truthful as Trollope must always be believed, have accepted his denials. Chief among these has been A. O. J. Cockshut. Trollope was "a man who in his life was a byword for frankness," Cockshut believes; he cannot bring himself to think that in the letter to the *Telegraph* the novelist "was a liar." And Cockshut concludes, with marvelous bathos, "Now, if Turnbull really was drawn from Bright, then Trollope cannot have thought very highly of the latter." Less important than Cockshut's, but nonetheless indicative, is the work of Curtis Brown, who declares that all of Trollope's statesmen are "unidentifiable" and that any likenesses to real politicians are "far-fetched." Bradford A. Booth refers to "the absence of current political issues" in Trollope's political novels; and he cites Leopold Avery's comment about the novelist's "complete incapacity to be interested in, or understand, political issues." Even Sadleir insists that on the subject of politics Trollope was utterly untheoretical.[5]

Undoubtedly many of Trollope's political characters are either made up or composites of politicians known to him; others are simply illustrations of types. It is time to lay to rest once and for all, however, the notion that the Palliser novels deal with imaginary politicians and political events. Even without the substantial existing evidence connecting people and events in Trollope's political novels with contemporary politicians and political events, one is bound to question the assertion that Trollope must always be believed. Why? His letter to the *Daily Telegraph* is full of lies, as we shall see; and his other denials over the years may be equally distrusted. Trollope's chief occupation was making things up; what he made up he published. A letter, a newspaper article, a paragraph in the *Autobiography* – all intended for publication – represented to him pieces of work like any other, and he was little more specially zealous about "truth" in them than he would have been during his morning stint of fiction-writing.

He tells us in the *Autobiography*, for instance, that he wrote nothing while living and working in London in the 1830s and that the first time he ever "put pen to paper" was in September 1843. He would then have been twenty-eight. These statements are untrue; he kept both a diary and a commonplace book during these early years. And then of course there is the evidence of his own Charley Tudor in *The Three Clerks* – an obvious self-portrait – who scribbles away for magazine editors in his spare time while a young clerk in London. Of *The Macdermots of Ballycloran*, his first novel, Trollope says in the *Autobiography* (pp. 62–3) he expected nothing but failure, never heard of anyone reading it or saw any critical notices of it, but that nevertheless he was neither disappointed nor hurt. C. P. Snow points out that *The Macdermots* was praised by both the *Spectator* and the *Athenaeum*, that Trollope must have known this, and that no writer can release his progeny into the world without some hopes for them: "Unless Trollope was different . . . from any writer who has ever lived, or . . . from any young man who has made any kind of effort whatever, almost none of [what he says about *The Macdermots*] can conceivably be true: and where it can be checked some of it appears to be untrue." In his *Autobiography* (p. 306) Trollope says of *The Way We Live Now*, "I by no means look upon the book as one of my failures; nor was it taken as a failure by the public or the press." The latter part of this statement is not true, as Trollope knew very well; the book was reviled by press (except *The Times*, whose editor had suggested to Trollope some of the novel's paramount themes) and public alike. In 1875 "there was almost no one to say a good word for this magnificent book," as Booth rightly says. And then there is the *Little Dorrit* affair. When *The Way We Live Now* was published in 1874–5, Trollope was accused of deriving Melmotte from Dickens's Merdle. Trollope told

T. H. S. Escott – and Escott repeats this in this memoir as gospel truth – that he read *Little Dorrit* for the first time in 1878 while travelling to Germany. But in fact he had not only read it upon publication two decades earlier but had written an article on it. Such a deliberately misleading denial may seem surprising; but Trollope, remember, was also fond of saying that he had never met any clergymen before writing the Barset novels. He was, as Snow says, always a very "secretive" man. There is no particular reason to believe anything he says about his novels.[6]

In *Phineas Finn*, at least, it is clear that Trollope is drawing upon contemporary politicians and political situations. Critics of the 1860s understood this. Indeed, two major reviews of *Phineas Finn* commented upon the obvious similarities of Turnbull to Bright, for one. The *Spectator* said simply that Turnbull embodied the "worse parts" of Bright. The *Saturday Review* went farther and claimed there was no doubt whatever about Turnbull's identity: Trollope "is cruelly careful the veriest child shall not fail to recognize his pet aversion under the *alias* he has given him." Even Bright's clothes are accurately described: "The future historian may refer to [*Phineas Finn*] to discover what was the material of which Mr. Bright's waistcoats were made."[7] But the reviewer objected that Trollope's portrait contained a "curiously inaccurate estimate . . . of that gentleman's character," and that, since "the contemplation of Mr. Bright . . . acts upon Mr. Trollope as a red rag upon a bull," the portrait should not be taken seriously by anyone.[8]

Several incidents in *Phineas Redux* help confirm the conclusion that Turnbull is Bright; but *Phineas Finn* provides ample evidence. Turnbull, like Bright, is a Radical; like Bright he is a manufacturer; like Bright he is very rich, with a great many servants and thousands of acres of property; like Bright he is a fierce, loud, rough, overbearing man in public; and his cry, "free trade in everything except malt," would have been characteristic of Bright, a Quaker and a temperance reformer.[9] Beyond the careful description of Turnbull's public dress (*Phineas Finn*, I, 196), Trollope's picture of the man himself, coupled with the other evidence, could have left the reader of the 1860s in no doubt about his identity:

He was one of the most popular [politicians] in the country. Poor men believed in him, thinking that he was their most honest public friend . . . it could hardly be said that he was a great orator. He was gifted with a powerful voice, with strong . . . convictions, with perfect self-reliance, with almost unlimited powers of endurance, with hot ambition, with no keen scruples, and with a moral skin of great thickness.   (I, 197)

In the growing debate over the ballot question in *Phineas Finn*, Turnbull and Daubeny behave as Bright and Disraeli did in 1866 (as Trollope was writing the novel) during the agitation over household suffrage that was to lead directly to the Second Reform Bill. This occurred during Russell's second ministry (1865–6) and helped bring about its downfall. Bright favored household suffrage and led a great franchise agitation which aroused much feeling in 1866. Disraeli and the Conservatives cared little for Bright's bill, but when Russell's Liberal government opposed it as being too radical they joined with Bright on the chance of throwing out the ministry. In June 1866 a combination of Conservatives and forty Whigs voted together to defeat the Russell government's counter-proposals on extending the franchise, and the Prime Minister resigned. Derby took over for the third time, and the Tories were in. The agitation in the country, presided over by Bright, went on through the autumn of 1866 – "In vain the country houses were filled that Christmas with ladies and gentlemen abusing Bright"[10] – and in January 1867 Disraeli, always an opportunist on Reform and now convinced that Reform was coming one way or another, privately consulted Bright as to what measures of Reform could lay the question to rest.

The reader of *Phineas Finn* (which began to appear serially in October 1867) will see the similarity between this account and Trollope's description of the collusion between Turnbull and Daubeny – on such issues as the disenfranchisement of rotten boroughs and extension of the suffrage – for personal political ends (i.e., to confound and defeat the Liberals), despite the fact that they themselves agree on little. Here is part of Trollope's account of this:

With great dignity Mr. Daubeny had kept aloof from Mr. Turnbull and from Mr. Turnbull's tactics; but he was not the less alive to the fact that Mr. Turnbull, with his mob and his big petition, might be of considerable assistance to him in the present duel between himself and Mr. Mildmay. I think Mr.

Daubeny was in the habit of looking at these contests as duels between himself and the leader on the other side of the House, – in which assistance from any quarter might be accepted if offered.   (I, 283–4)

Bright constantly criticized Russell's measures on electoral reform as not going far enough and helped to get up a "big petition" in support of his cause. Disraeli aided and abetted Bright in the House of Commons for his own purposes: the machinations of Daubeny and Turnbull in *Phineas Finn* weaken Mildmay as Disraeli's and Bright's weakened Russell. The novel's political events reflect a tangible historical reality.

Trollope, who in his *Autobiography* (p. 253) called himself a "conservative liberal," liked political extremes of neither kind, and indeed often satirized the Radicals. In *The Fixed Period*, Trollope's little-known late fantasy, there is a gunboat called *H.M.S. John Bright* mounted with a huge gun, a "250-ton swiveller"[11] – a sort of ultimate weapon so powerful it can destroy a city with a single shot, and so devastating it need never, in theory, be used. However, the *John Bright* has to be called out at one point to help quell a Commonwealth rebellion at Gladstonopolis, Brittanula. The gun, Trollope comments, "has been prepared by the ingenuity of men, able to dominate matter though altogether powerless over mind" (II, 91).[12] This is perhaps the last of his published comments on Bright and his rhetoric – capable by its volume of stunning the senses but otherwise ineffectual and unimportant – but it is not his last reference to Bright. A letter dated 22 September 1882 (less than three months before Trollope's death), addressed to William Lucas Collins, refers to Gladstone and Bright thus: "I for one cannot forgive him the injustice which he has done in Ireland at the behest of Mr. Bright."[13] This supports the contention of the *Daily Telegraph* that *Phineas Finn* was written in part out of Trollope's hatred of Bright, a hatred which never abated. True, in one of his campaign speeches at Beverley, Trollope referred to Gladstone and Bright together as "great men . . . dear to your hearts . . . dear to mine," but the context shows that the novelist was appealing along partisan lines for his own candidacy; and the speech in question, one of Trollope's most Radical, was delivered before the Working Men's Liberal Association of Beverley, which would have had Radical sympathies.[14]

Daubeny becomes a major character in *Phineas Redux* and the later Palliser novels, where the identification with Disraeli is clear enough. In *Phineas Finn* it is also patent. We see Daubeny working with Turnbull to bring down Mildmay, as Disraeli worked with Bright to bring down Russell. "To crush the Whigs by combining with the Radicals was the first and last maxim of Mr. Disraeli's tactics," Lord Robert Cecil, younger son of the second Marquess of Salisbury (a Tory colleague of Disraeli's), wrote in 1860; "he made any Government while he was in opposition next to an impossibility." His tactics – "so various, so flexible, so shameless" – were always effective: "so long as his party backed him, no Government was strong enough to hold out against his attacks."[15] Lord Blake writes,

> Disraeli was perhaps the first statesman systematically to uphold the doctrine that it is the duty of the Opposition to oppose. Indeed, he might be said by this practice to have established the precedent on which all subsequent Opposition leaders have acted. Whatever proposal the Government put forward, whatever its merits, you could always find something wrong with it, some reason for attack. In the end, if you went on long enough, you would beat them in the House, or at the very least put yourself in position to beat them at the next general election . . . Disraeli's first instinct was to oppose, and, if he did not always do so, it was for reasons of expediency or because Derby overruled him. To Disraeli the object of politics was power and he never forgot it.[16]

We should have no trouble recognizing Disraeli in the Daubeny of *Phineas Finn* – a man who will use any means at his command to bring down his Liberal enemies. It is well-known that Disraeli and Bright were unconventional but nonetheless effective political allies in the Commons between 1848 and 1868;[17] and Daubeny's unholy alliance with Turnbull on the issue of Reform is Trollope's version of the real thing. Daubeny's attitude toward Reform, like Disraeli's, is essentially opportunistic; he will accept assistance from any quarter in his many duels with the Liberals, which he sees as personal contests to be won at any cost – as Disraeli did. As in the case of the Second Reform Bill of 1866–7, in *Phineas Finn*, despite the fact that the initiatives for Reform do not come from the Tory side of the House, the Conservatives are the chief

beneficiaries of such initiatives as do emanate from the divided
other side, and take maximum partisan advantage of the situation.
Having action of some sort forced upon them once the Liberals
had managed to defeat themselves by intra-party squabbling, the
Tory leaders of 1866–7 were determined to pass a bill – any bill –
in order to stay in office. "The reform bills of ministers" in this
period "were less triumphant vindications of principle than useful
political manœuvres," says Lord Briggs;[18] and we see in *Phineas
Finn* an accurate distillation of the historical reality. Derby and
Disraeli, that is, behaved at this juncture pretty much as de
Terrier and Daubeny behave in *Phineas Finn*, the political action of
which is set at the time of the Second Reform Bill. Later, in
Phineas Redux, Mr. Gresham says that before becoming Tory
leader Daubeny was aided in his audacious policies and private
ambitions by serving for years under "a leader who, though
thoroughly trusted, was very idle" (I, 53). Contemporary readers
must have seen the similarity to the relation between Disraeli and
Derby before the latter stepped down.

There is more evidence even than this. Daubeny's name is
shortened by friends and enemies alike to "Dubby," which of
course recalls Disraeli's nickname "Dizzy." When in *Phineas Finn*
Laurence Fitzgibbon tells Phineas that "Dubby would give his
toes and fingers to remain in" – and we learn immediately that
"Dubby was the ordinary name by which . . . Mr. Daubeny was
known: Mr. Daubeny, who at that time was the leader of the
Conservative party in the House of Commons" (I, 30–1) – every
Victorian reader would have known who was being referred to.
Daubeny is characterized as knowing "exactly the rules of
parliamentary combat" and as "a gladiator thoroughly well-trained
for the arena" (I, 72), which also describes Disraeli as a party
leader. Daubeny's hilarious and outrageous attempt at one point
to speak before an important division for hours late at night in the
hope that some of the ancient Liberals trundled in to vote against
him will either go to bed or die is something worthy only of a
Disraeli. We may also note that in *Phineas Finn* there is a party
hack named Barrington Erle whose chief activity is partisanship,
and that Ralph Earle was the name of the man who headed
Disraeli's notorious spy system in the Foreign Office in the late
1850s.[19] Finally, there is an interesting place in the holograph
manuscript of *Phineas Finn* at which, as can easily be seen today,
Trollope started to write "Disraeli" when he meant Daubeny:

"Dis" is crossed out and "Daubeny" put in its place. Trollope rarely corrected his manuscripts (now and then he called his heroine by different names in the course of a novel), but this "correction" he caught and made immediately.

Mr. Mildmay clearly is a version of Lord John Russell. He is, as we have seen, a victim of collusion between Daubeny and Turnbull on the ballot question as Russell was a victim of Disraeli and Bright in 1866, over a year before *Phineas Finn* began to appear in *St. Paul's*. Like Russell, Mildmay is related to all the great Whig families of the time. Mildmay is Prime Minister between Lord Brock and Mr. Gresham. There is something of Palmerston in Brock and of Gladstone in Gresham; Russell's second ministry (1865–6) came after Palmerston's death and before Gladstone's first ministry in the progression of Liberal cabinets in the sixties. Palmerston died in 1865. In Trollope's *Can You Forgive Her?*, which appeared in 1864–5, Brock is still the Liberal leader. In *Phineas Finn* he has been replaced by Mildmay, as Palmerston was replaced by Russell in the mid-sixties before Gladstone took over the Liberal leadership. Mildmay is an old man who is rumored to be near retirement. Russell, whose first ministry was back in 1846–52, had been around for a long time by the mid-sixties and was also close to retirement. In *Phineas Finn* it is said that Mildmay's "love of reform is an inherited passion for an old-world liberalism" (I, 330), which sounds very much like Russell's brand of old-fashioned (conservative) Liberalism. It is also worth noting that the reference in *Phineas Finn* to a quarrel and then a subsequent reconciliation between Brock and Mildmay recalls the bitter feud between Palmerston and Russell in the early fifties, healed after the Crimean War when Russell served in Palmerston's Cabinet. There are also a number of resemblances between Palliser and Russell,[20] and between Palliser and Palmerston;[21] Trollope often used bits and pieces of different men to make up his fictional politicians, as I have said. But some of the identifications seem clear enough.

There are obvious elements of Palmerston in Brock. Brock has quarreled with Mildmay and made it up, as Palmerston did with Russell. Brock is the Liberal leader in the early sixties in *Can You Forgive Her?*; Palmerston's last ministry stretched from 1859 to 1865, and he was succeeded by Russell, as Mildmay replaces Brock as Liberal leader between *Can You Forgive Her?* and *Phineas Finn*. (Trollope may have been working on his memoir of

Palmerston as early as 1866, though this is unlikely;[22] in any case
he began *Phineas Finn* just thirteen months after the death of
Palmerston, one of his great political heroes.) Brock's Cabinet
includes Gresham and Mildmay; Gladstone and Russell served in
Palmerston's. More to the point, Brock is said to have brought the
Crimean War successfully to a close and then, as Prime Minister,
has excellent luck in an Indian mutiny episode.[23] These
resemblances to Palmerston are unmistakable. In *Phineas Redux*
(II, 339) Monk says of Brock that he had "a thick skin, an equable
temper, and perfect self-confidence"; and in *The Prime Minister*
(I, 102–3) Mrs. Finn says of him, "He loved his country dearly,
and wished her to be, as he believed her to be, first among
nations. But he had no belief in perpetuating his greatness by any
grand improvements. Let things take their way naturally, – with a
slight direction hither or thither as things might require. That was
his method of ruling." Both of these characterizations could easily
fit Palmerston.[24] And it is also said of Brock in *The Prime Minister*
(I, 265) that he used "drawing-room influences" to help himself in
politics – something for which Palmerston was perhaps more
notorious than any other British statesman of the nineteenth
century.

Trollope, as we know, did not deny that Daubeny was Disraeli
or Gresham Gladstone. Gresham's hallmarks in the Palliser novels
are intellect, eloquence – "the greatest orator in Europe" (*Phineas
Finn*, I, 329) – arrogance, and temper, all of which point clearly to
Gladstone[25] (his being pictured briefly in *Can You Forgive Her?* as
Finespun does not negate this – we simply see him there in a
different role, as Chancellor of the Exchequer; Gladstone served
Palmerston and Russell in this capacity). Like Gresham as
described by Trollope in *Phineas Finn*, Gladstone wished to "fashion
[the future] anew out of the vigour of his own brain" (I, 330). It is
said at one point in *Phineas Finn* that, in all probability, it is on Mr.
Gresham's "shoulders . . . that the mantle of Mr. Mildmay would
fall" (I, 329) – which in fact is what happens in the second half of
Phineas Finn, just as Russell finally retired to make way for
Gladstone. Gresham favors disestablishment of the Irish Church,
as Gladstone did (this becomes a major issue in *Phineas Redux*). In
the late sixties, and particularly in 1868, Gladstone met fierce
opposition in both parties to his policy on Irish tenant-right. Now
Trollope tells us in the *Autobiography* (p. 275) that he finished

writing *Phineas Finn* in May 1867. But, as it ran serially until March 1869 in a journal of which he himself was editor, he would have had ample opportunity and time to make tenant-right the paramount issue for Phineas in the novel's concluding chapters. Gladstone persisted in his Irish policy despite great opposition within the Liberal ranks; this is what Gresham does, causing Phineas to resign at the end of *Phineas Finn*. The time element here, in other words, does not rule out the issue's relevance for the novel, though at first glance it might appear to be ruled out. Sadleir suggests that in Gresham Trollope blended Peel's character and Gladstone's views,[26] but I think there is more of Gladstone in Gresham than that. Only the *Spectator* among contemporary voices remained sceptical about the Gresham–Gladstone connection, basing its opinion on the tenuous ground that Gresham pays too little attention to "the past" to be Gladstone.

Lord de Terrier certainly seems to be Derby. Lord de Terrier is the Conservative leader in *Phineas Finn*; by the time of *Phineas Redux* he has given way to Daubeny. Derby resigned in 1868 and died in 1869, between the writing of the two novels. He was Prime Minister three times: February–December 1852, February 1858 to June 1859, and June 1866 to February 1868. *Phineas Finn* opens with de Terrier as Prime Minister, faced with Liberal majorities against him, dissolving the House and calling new elections. Derby's various short spurts of office-holding were due largely to continued Liberal majorities against him. Furthermore, Trollope tells us at the beginning of *Phineas Finn* (I, 5) that de Terrier "had now been in office for the almost unprecedentedly long period of fifteen months"; no other Conservative Prime Minister – indeed, no other Victorian politician – could have been twitted in this way. The tenure of Derby's last ministry, which went on for almost two years, would have been unknown to Trollope in 1866 when he wrote the opening chapter of *Phineas Finn* (of course he could have revised it for the 1869 edition, but Trollope rarely revised anything); as he was writing *Phineas Finn*, however, Derby was certainly Prime Minister. The fifteen months in office mentioned by Trollope corresponds exactly to the length of Derby's second ministry, during which Disraeli was Tory leader in the Commons, as Daubeny is during de Terrier's tenure as party chief. The uneasy relationship between Daubney and de Terrier resembles that of Disraeli and Derby in the early sixties.

Finally, de Terrier – "thoroughly trusted" yet "very idle," aloof and detached – presents an accurate picture of Derby during his years in office.

Escott and Speare both thought that Monk vaguely resembled Gladstone,[27] and the *Spectator* said he contained a few characteristics of Cobden. While the latter surmise has some plausibility, Monk is probably an original creation of Trollope's. His brand of selfless patriotism, however, also takes a direction which may remind us of a famous politician of an earlier era. One of Monk's greatest moments in *Phineas Finn* comes as he lectures Phineas on the necessity of devoting oneself to causes, even if they are lost or unpopular ones, if they seem truly worthwhile. If you argue persuasively enough for a measure, says Monk, you will at least force men to think about it; and

> 'Many who before regarded [it] . . . as chimerical, will now fancy that it is only dangerous, or perhaps not more than difficult. And so in time it will come to be looked on as among the things possible, then among the things probable; – and so at last it will be ranged in the list of those few measures which the country requires. . . . That is the way in which public opinion is made . . . it is a great thing to take any step that leads us onwards.'   (II, 421)

This is similar to Edmund Burke's well-known feeling that a good speech in the Commons which may not immediately change any votes is worth making in order to provoke members to think of the subject, thus preparing the ground for a more successful *sortie* on a future occasion.[28] Farther than this I do not wish to go.

Trollope's contemporaries thought that Lord Chiltern was an accurate portrait of Lord Hartington, later the eighth Duke of Devonshire; and Escott, Sadleir, and Pope Hennessy have since agreed to this pairing. The fact is, however, that Chiltern and Hartington have little in common, and in all likelihood the traditional idea is wrong. Chiltern's name, not to mention his life and habits, would make his being modelled on a political activist (the Duke served briefly as Prime Minister) very unlikely, not to say ludicrous; as Barry Bartrum points out, Chiltern more strikingly suggests the Marquess of Waterford or one of his horsy set.[29]

Surely the icing on the political cake is provided by the names

Trollope chooses. "Daubeny" and "Gresham" are obvious both in their first letters and in the number of their syllables. "Lord de Terrier" is not far from "Lord Derby"; and "Derby and Disraeli" is a combination close in sound, certainly, to "de Terrier and Daubeny." "Brock" is a sort of pun; it suggests a badger, a tenacious animal with sharp teeth – which recalls Trollope's conception of Palmerston (in his *Lord Palmerston*, Trollope refers to his protagonist as the "English bulldog incarnate"). Indeed, in *The Three Clerks* Trollope plays around with this pun a good deal. He uses the word "brock" for badger in the sentence, "Such a brock has not for years been seen in the country-side" (he is talking about badger-baiting here); and later he uses the word "badger" to signify the head of a political party, as in the phrase, "recommended . . . to the confidence of successive badgers" (pp. 394, 414). As a matter of fact, he takes the pun to its farthest extreme by actually naming the current Prime Minister "Badger": "Poor Badger, how much he has to bear!" (p. 430; Palmerston was out of office at the time, but he had just been in, and was about to come in again). To return to the others: "Mildmay" sounds like a gentle old man, such as Russell at the end of his career; "Turnbull" suggests the unpredictability and bellicose roughness of Bright; "Julius Monk" and "Edmund Burke" are names of equivalent length and sound, though that is more tenuous.[30]

Let us not forget Phineas Finn himself. Physically he is said by Escott to resemble Colonel King-Harman, a friend of Trollope's whom the novelist sometimes met at the Arts Club, and by Sadleir to suggest Joe Parkinson, an English journalist who married a millionaire's daughter and became a wealthy director of companies. Snow suggests as the original Sir William Gregory of Coole, a Harrow schoolfellow of Trollope's and a lifelong friend, who like Finn opposed his own party's Irish policy and supported tenant-right as an M.P.; Sir William, a Tory, finished his career as governor of Ceylon. Since he called Phineas Finn "a libel upon the Irish gentleman," it is unlikely that he would have thought much of Snow's suggestion. Another recent candidate, and a more plausible one, is Chichester Parkinson-Fortescue, later Lord Carlingford. Taken by some contemporaries as the model for Finn, Fortescue was a young, handsome, Irish M.P. who served both as Under Secretary of State for the Colonies and Chief Secretary for Ireland – offices held by Finn in, respectively, *Phineas*

Finn and *The Prime Minister* – and worked diligently for Irish land reform, as Finn wishes to do at the end of *Phineas Finn*. Fortescue did all of these things before Trollope began to write his political novels, so the chronology is all right; and an equally convincing part of the argument is that he ultimately became the fourth husband of Frances, Dowager Countess Waldegrave, in all likelihood Trollope's model for Madame Max Goesler (whose second husband, of course, turns out – in *Phineas Redux* – to be Phineas Finn).[31]

Sadleir, Pope Hennessy, and others, however, have pretty much come to agree, rightly or wrongly, that politically and circumstantially Finn is probably modelled on John Pope Hennessy (James's grandfather), a young Irish politician from Cork who came from "the same sort of dim, unpromising middle-class background as Phineas himself, and had much the same early, meteoric success in London society," becoming a protégé of Disraeli (Trollope, typically, makes him a Liberal, both to hinder possible identification and to leave the focus of his story on what to him was the more congenial part of the political spectrum), and ultimately marrying a daughter of Sir Hugh Low.[32]

Fortescue remains, I think, the most convincing model for Finn. But surely there is also a good deal of the novelist himself in his hero. For Phineas's political career, volatile as it is, must be in part sheer Trollopian wish-fulfillment. Booth and Escott both point to the account of Phineas's financial embarrassments, especially the twenty-first chapter ("Do Be Punctual"), as a light-hearted personal reminiscence of what Escott calls "Trollope's . . . out-at-elbows Post Office days"[33] (told in the third chapter of the *Autobiography*; Trollope's chief fictional version of himself as a young clerk is Charley Tudor in *The Three Clerks*, who is always in debt and being told to "be punctual"). And the seventieth chapter of *Phineas Finn* ("The Prime Minister's House"), which is an account of a huge party hosted by Mrs. Gresham, while clearly modelled on the sort of bash Lady Palmerston was famous for giving, is probably drawn first-hand from Trollope's own experience of political parties hosted by Lady Stanley of Alderley, in whose house he was a frequent guest from 1863 on. Her husband was Postmaster-General and therefore Trollope's Civil Service boss for some years, and it is known that Lord Stanley was fond of the novelist.[34] His house was a social center for Whig–Liberal politicians, especially after the death of Palmerston in 1865 (though her receptions never equalled Lady Palmerston's Saturday night gatherings at Cambridge House). In all probability Phineas's feeling of pride at being one of the few guests invited by Lady Glencora Palliser to dinner *before* one of her receptions (II, 23) reflects Trollope's similar sentiments on the arrival of such invitations from Lady Stanley.[35]

There is more. Finn, like Trollope himself, comes over from Ireland to find success in England, moves into the fashionable world, becomes disillusioned, yet keeps some of the passive detachment of an outsider.[36] Also relevant is the fact that Trollope was always saying – in his novels, in his *Autobiography*, in his letters and lectures – that a man should never be rewarded too early in life, before he has had a chance to know what he wants, work for it, and appreciate getting it. It took Trollope a long time to get where he wanted to be, both as a writer and in the Post Office. He had no literary success until the late 1850s, by which time he was in his early forties; indeed, he had to wait for it longer than any other Victorian novelist (Dickens, for example, was famous at twenty-three). The Post Office did not promote him to Surveyor until he was thirty-nine (in 1854); and the fact that he wrote of his promotion, late as it was, proudly to his mother "makes nonsense of previous protestations that . . . he hadn't worried much at being so often and pointedly passed over." "No work can be done, no pleasures received, no content obtained without an effort," he wrote a year later in *The New Zealander*.[37] So it is not surprising that people in Trollope's novels who get good things handed to them too early, before they have had a chance to earn and deserve them, almost always suffer. Trollope's early feelings of deprivation may help to explain his, as they help to explain Dickens's, acknowledged ability to describe so vividly some of life's most ordinary pleasures – that "complete appreciation of the usual" Henry James talks about in connection with Trollope.[38]

Early in *Phineas Finn*, Phineas paints for himself

a not untrue picture of the probable miseries of a man who begins life too high up on the ladder, – who succeeds in mounting before he has learned how to hold on when he is aloft. . . . If he did this thing [stand for Parliament] . . . he

might become utterly a castaway. . . . He had heard of penniless
men who had got into Parliament and to whom had come such
a fate.   (I, 9)

Mr. Low preaches the waiting lesson to Phineas throughout the
novel – telling him, for example, that anyone who is not financially
independent when he enters Parliament cannot be his own man
there and must come to either political or moral perdition. This is
indeed one of the major lessons Phineas is to learn. Getting to
Parliament too quickly and easily and tripped up by his own
premature success, Phineas personifies a point of view Trollope
involuntarily came to adopt as a result of his own unhappy and
frustrated early years.

Beyond his possible autobiographical connections, Phineas's
overall situation is believable enough, despite the scepticism of
some critics. Before the Fenian outrages which commenced in
1867, Irish members of Parliament did still attach themselves to
one of the major English parties, as Phineas does, instead of sit in
a bloc by themselves, as they were to do later. The positions he
takes once there border closely on Trollope's own commitment to
what might be called ecumenicism (*Autobiography*, p. 62). A product
of a mixed marriage (Catholic father, Protestant mother), Phineas is
brought up a Catholic and his sisters as Protestants – common
practice in nineteenth-century Ireland, as Janet Egleson Dunleavy
reminds us.

> As for being a Nationalist, Phineas is too much of a practical
> politician for that, even if his idealism did lead him to join a
> Cabinet Minister in support of Tenant Right. No Cabinet
> ministers in either fact or Trollopian fiction backed the incipient
> Irish party of the fifties and sixties, nor were the M.P.'s of this
> group sufficiently numerous (in *The Prime Minister*, Finn declares
> there to be 'about twenty') to have the significant impact
> realized later under Parnell. The verisimilitude of Phineas Finn's
> support of Monk's measure [regarding Irish tenant-right] in
> *Phineas Finn* and his later approval of disestablishment in *Phineas
> Redux* . . . [is] credible given his life history . . . and the
> opportunities he thus would have had for direct observation of
> the nineteenth-century Irish . . . scene. For such observations
> also would have provided awareness of the contradictions as
> well as the complexities of Irish social and political life, the
> ineffectual size of the Irish Party, and the odds against radical

change so long as neither Tories nor Liberals were dependent upon Irish votes to achieve or remain in power.[39]

As a former resident of Ireland and as a student of contemporary politics, Trollope was able to follow and understand the Irish questions which plagued English politics during his lifetime; as a result Phineas Finn, whatever his merits as the hero of a novel, is an authentic Irish politician of the 1860s. Whatever he may really have thought about Irish tenant-right,[40] Trollope sought always to give a true account of such matters in his novels. In a lecture "On English Prose Fiction as a Rational Amusement," delivered in 1869 (as *Phineas Finn* was winding to a close in the pages of *St. Paul's*), Trollope declared,

> A novelist is false who, in dealing with this or that phase of life, bolsters up a theory of his own with pictures that are in themselves untrue. There is at this moment a great question forward as to the tenure of land in Ireland. I may have my ideas upon it and may desire to promulgate them in a novel. But if for the sake of promoting my theory I draw a picture of Irish landlords which is not a true picture – which I have no ground for believing to be true – in which I make them out to be cruel, idle, and God-abandoned reprobates, because I have a theory of my own to support in my novel, then my book is a false book, and I am a liar.[41]

"There is at this moment a great question forward as to the tenure of land in Ireland. I may have my ideas upon it, and may desire to promulgate them in a novel." Yes, indeed.

In the 1860s Trollope helped found both *St. Paul's* and the *Fortnightly*, each of them a progressive voice devoted primarily to Liberal interests. Between 1865 and 1868, contemporaneous with the writing and appearance of *Phineas Finn*, he published in the *Pall Mall Gazette* – besides reviews of new books – articles on such politically sensitive topics as Lord Brougham, Lord Westbury, Lord John Russell, American conditions, Prevost Parodel, the St. Albans Raiders, church endowments, and clerks and usurers.[42] In 1868 he stood for Parliament. It is not surprising, then, that *Phineas Finn* deals with the real political problems of a real political system. The party structures and changes of leadership which both *Phineas* novels describe in some detail resemble those of the later 1860s, with the Conservative minority facing a disunited combination of Whigs, Liberals, and Radicals.[43] Written in 1866–7, when public opinion was causing the Second Reform Bill to be passed, *Phineas Finn* is narrated against this background, with a hero who succeeds initially as a Liberal who supports the party of Reform. The reviewers, even when they criticized the *Phineas* novels as novels, certainly recognized their own world portrayed in them. The *Saturday Review* commented that *Phineas Finn* shows "what was the bearing of the . . . Liberal leaders of the time in society"; and the *Dublin Review* observed that, despite its ostensible focus on the recent past, in telling the story of the disruption of a Liberal ministry over the Irish land question the novel was actually on its way to becoming prophetic.[44]

The *Dublin Review* also commented that Trollope understood the tenant-right question better than most Irishmen and almost all Englishmen and Scots. *Phineas Finn* demonstrates another kind of knowledge hardly surprising to anyone acquainted with the novelist's biography. I refer to Trollope's familiarity with the Civil Service of his time. Like his political heroes Palmerston and Russell, Trollope felt that competitive examinations for the service were likely to reduce rather than enhance the prospects for "government on principles of the strictest purity" – a pathetic ideal of the moment. Perhaps arising in part out of a conviction that, if "gentlemen" had been required to take examinations in his day he could never have been a public servant,[45] in his two novels of the Civil Service, *The Three Clerks* and *Marion Fay*, Trollope shows not the "best" but rather the most cunning and unscrupulous men winning jobs through examination. And, while he suggests that there are a lot of incompetents in the service, he has more sympathy for them than for the hard men who wish to hound them out of office in the interests of increased efficiency.

And yet a great many nasty things are said in *Phineas Finn* about civil servants and the system of political patronage which found jobs for them. Many of the negative comments are made by Phineas's voluble landlord Bunce, and some of the abuses are figured in characters such as Laurence Fitzgibbon and in such issues as the great parliamentary controversy over potted peas for the armed forces. Before 1870, certainly, Whitehall had been the happy hunting-ground of the political hack – the Taper and Tadpole of Disraeli's fiction, the Roby and Ratler of Trollope's. Ministers of all parties, Trevelyan tells us, "looked on . . . such patronage as the recognised means of keeping political supporters in good humour. The public services were filled with the nominees of peers and commoners who had votes in Parliament or weight in the constituencies." Gorged with incompetent and impecunious younger (and often illegitimate) sons of influential men, Whitehall's reputation for laziness and incompetence was proverbial; and Bunce's picture of it as a place where people sit drinking tea with their feet up on the desk is not far removed from the historian's allusion to the "heavy swells with long whiskers [who] lounged in late and left early."[46] The civil servant's usual office hours in these days were 10.00 a.m. to 4.30 p.m. Trollope himself used to come to work, when he came at all – he was allowed for years by his superiors at the Post Office to hunt two days a week – at around 11.30 a.m. Though he enjoyed his position he never liked administrative work, and did very little.[47] *The Three Clerks* and *Marion Fay* portray a great deal of lounging around, time-wasting, and absenteeism among civil servants.

Still, Civil Service "jobbing," as it was called, was regarded by most politicians as an indispensable tool of their trade; and, after Peel discontinued the distribution of honors and peerages on which Pitt had relied, "the Civil Service was the only field even of modified corruption left to Victorian statesmen."[48] Competitive examinations, recommended in 1853 by the Northcote–Trevelyan report on the Civil Service, did help to reduce jobbery after 1855, and in 1870 Gladstone managed to abolish patronage in almost all public offices and substitute competitive examinations in its place. In *Phineas Finn*, a novel of the sixties, jobbing is still very much part of the life of an aspiring politician, and indeed it is the last resource of young MPs such as Phineas Finn, who, without an independent income, must depend on government patronage for survival. How this affects the political system itself is a major concern of *Phineas Finn*.

Let those who still think the characters and events in the Palliser novels are wholly original creations look about themselves more carefully. *Phineas Finn*, for one, is a political novel whose people and issues reflect and revise various historical realities of the 1860s, and no amount of Trollopian denial and outrage, no amount of critical emphasis on Trollopian "daydreaming" and brilliantly "real" imaginary people, can erase this fact. I have no hesitation in saying that *Phineas Finn* could not have been written in any other time or place. Trollope, after all, was a man whose profession was fiction, which among other things is an acceptable form of lying. Why then should he not lie a little in a letter or two, or even in his *Autobiography* – when these, like his novels, were written for publication?

NOTES

1. The letter is dated 31 March 1869 and was published by the *Telegraph* on 1 April, p. 3. See *The Letters of Anthony Trollope*, ed. Bradford A. Booth (London, 1951), p. 241. (Note: this essay was written and published before N. John Hall's definitive two-volume edition of Trollope's letters appeared.)
2. See Michael Sadleir, *Trollope: A Commentary* (London, 1927; 1961), p. 418.
3. *Letters*, p. 355.
4. Anthony Trollope, *An Autobiography* (2 vols, London, 1883), Oxford World's Classics edition (1 vol., London, 1953; 1961), p. 274. Unless otherwise specified, all subsequent references to Trollope's works are to the World's Classics editions. Where possible, page references appear in the text following citations.
5. See A. O. J. Cockshut, *Anthony Trollope: A Critical Study* (London, 1955; 1968), pp. 241–9, especially pp. 241 and 245–6; Beatrice Curtis Brown, *Trollope* (Denver, 1950), p. 84; Bradford A. Booth, *Anthony Trollope: Aspects of His Life and Work* (Bloomington, Ind., 1958), p. 100; and Sadleir, *Trollope: A Commentary*, p. 418.
6. C. P. Snow, *Trollope* (London, 1975), pp. 66 and 83; Booth, *Trollope: Aspects*, pp. 119–20; T. H. S. Escott, *Anthony Trollope: His Public Services, Private Friends and Literary Originals* (London, 1913; 1967), p. 298; and Bradford A. Booth, "Trollope and *Little Dorrit*," *Nineteenth-Century Fiction*, 2 (March 1948), 237–40.
7. They were made of black silk, according to Trollope. For a detailed description of "Turnbull," see I, 196–8.
8. *Spectator*, 42 (20 March 1869), 356–7; and *Saturday Review*, 27 (27 March 1869), 431–2. Both are reprinted in *Anthony Trollope: The Critical Heritage*, ed. Donald Smalley (London, 1969).
9. Cockshut, *Trollope: A Critical Study*, pp. 244–5.
10. G. M. Trevelyan, *British History in the Nineteenth Century* (New York, 1922; 1966), p. 345. I am indebted here to Trevelyan's account (pp. 344–6) of the events leading up to the Second Reform Bill.
11. On one of the work sheets for *The Fixed Period*, Trollope wrote this note to himself: "What should be the weight of the gun?" Obviously he acquired some expert advice. Trollope Papers, II, 125 (Bodleian Library, Oxford).
12. I am indebted to the summary given by David Skilton in an article entitled "*The Fixed Period*: Anthony Trollope's Novel of 1980," *Studies in the Literary Imagination*, 6 (Fall 1973), 39–50.
13. I should like to thank N. John Hall for transcribing this letter for me.

14. The speech in question is reported in the *Beverley Recorder* for 14 November 1868.
15. Published anonymously in the *Quarterly Review* for April 1860 and quoted in Robert Blake, *Disraeli* (London, 1966), p. 426.
16. Blake, *Disraeli*, p. 355.
17. See, for example, Blake, *Disraeli*, p. 502.
18. Asa Briggs, "Trollope, Bagehot, and the English Constitution," in *Victorian People: A Reassessment of Persons and Themes 1851–1867* (London, 1954; Chicago, 1955), p. 90.
19. Blake, *Disraeli*, *passim*.
20. Blair G. Kenney, in "Trollope's Ideal Statesmen: Plantagenet Palliser and Lord John Russell," *Nineteenth-Century Fiction*, 20 (December 1965), 281–6, argues for this identification. Much of the summary of the Mildmay–Russell connection is based on information provided by his excellent essay.
21. See John Halperin, "Politics, Palmerston, and Trollope's Prime Minister," *Clio*, 3 (February 1974), 187–218.
22. Both Sadleir and Booth in their books date the memoir from this period, but without attribution or proof of any sort. There is nothing in Trollope's business papers to suggest that he was working on *Lord Palmerston* in 1866. There is, however, a memorandum in Trollope's hand (Bodleian Papers, II, 116) dated 24 August 1881, noting his agreement "to write a volume on Lord Palmerston – 200 pages – for £200 – for W. Isbister – to be delivered in March – 1882." The memoir did not appear until 1882; Booth and Sadleir are probably wrong. Booth, in fact, admitted in an article written later that there is no evidence that Trollope wrote *Lord Palmerston* in the sixties; he has come to assume, he says here, that it was "written to order in 1881." See Booth's "Author to Publisher: Trollope and Isbister," *Princeton University Library Chronicle*, 24 (Winter 1962), 58n.; and John Halperin, "The Composition of Trollope's *Lord Palmerston*," *Notes and Queries*, 222 (October 1977), 411.
23. Pointed out in F. E. Robbins, "Chronology and History in Trollope's Barset and Parliamentary Novels," *Nineteenth-Century Fiction*, 5 (March 1951), 310–12.
24. See J. R. Dinwiddy, "Who's Who in Trollope's Political Novels," *Nineteenth-Century Fiction*, 22 (June 1967), 31–47. Palmerston, incidentally, is mentioned twice by name in *Phineas Finn* (I, 195–6).
25. See R. W. Chapman, "Personal Names in Trollope's Political Novels," in *Essays Mainly on the Nineteenth Century Presented to Sir Humphrey Milford* (London, 1948), p. 75.
26. Sadleir, *Trollope: A Commentary*, p. 418.
27. Escott, *Trollope: His Public Services, Private Friends*, p. 258; and Morris E. Speare, *The Political Novel* (New York, 1924), p. 189.
28. Burke's feelings on the matter are available, among other places, in Boswell's account of a meeting of "The Club" on 3 April 1778, as reported in his *Life of Johnson* (1791). See also John Wain, *Samuel Johnson* (New York, 1975), p. 238; it is Wain's account that suggested to me the relevance of this aspect of Burke's thought.

29. See Escott, *Trollope: His Public Services, Private Friends*, p. 259; Sadleir, *Trollope: A Commentary*, p. 418; and James Pope Hennessy, *Anthony Trollope* (Boston, Mass., 1971), p. 280. Barry A. Bartrum has been kind enough to show me sections of his Princeton dissertation, which deals with such matters as these. Trollope, incidentally, always denied the identification of Chiltern with Hartington.

30. See Chapman, "Personal Names in Trollope's Political Novels," *passim.*, for more interesting speculation along these lines. Chapman, incidentally, identifies the Duke of St. Bungay as the third Lord Lansdowne (d. 1862).

31. See Snow, *Trollope*, p. 181n. (he later suggests, p. 182n., that John Pope Hennessy is a likelier model); Escott, *Trollope: His Public Services, Private Friends*, p. 266; and on Carlingford, Bartrum (n. 30, above). See also *T. P.'s and Cassell's Weekly* for 5 June 1926, in which T. P. O'Connor argues for the Pope Hennessy connection.

32. See Pope Hennessy, *Anthony Trollope*, from which the quotation is taken (p. 280), and Sadleir, *Trollope: A Commentary*, p. 418.

33. Booth, *Trollope: Aspects*, pp. 87–8; and Escott, *Trollope: His Public Services, Private Friends*, p. 37.

34. See Snow, *Trollope*, p. 135.

35. My information about Trollope's social connection with Lady Stanley is drawn largely from Barry A. Bartrum, "A Victorian Political Hostess: The Engagement Book of Lady Stanley of Alderley," *Princeton University Library Chronicle*, 36 (Winter 1975), 133–46.

36. Robert M. Polhemus, *The Changing World of Anthony Trollope* (Berkeley and Los Angeles, 1968), p. 151.

37. Snow, *Trollope*, p. 75; and Anthony Trollope, *The New Zealander*, ed. N. John Hall (Oxford, 1972), p. 170 (the essay "Society").

38. Henry James, "Anthony Trollope," originally published in *Century Magazine*, July 1883, repr. in *Partial Portraits* (New York, 1888), pp. 97–133, and widely thereafter.

39. Quoted from an essay by Janet Egleson Dunleavy entitled "Irish Politics and the Novels of Anthony Trollope." I am grateful to Professor Dunleavy for making a draft of her essay available to me.

40. Professor Dunleavy, in the essay cited in n. 39, suggests that Trollope, at least in retrospect, had some sympathy for the Tenant Right League; while historian Stephen Gwynn points out that, while Trollope in his Irish fiction attacks injustices within the land system, he never attacks the system itself, and that he seems to feel that if specific Irish landlords are bad they should simply be replaced by better ones – thus he would be likely to oppose any attempt by government to regulate free enterprise. See Gwynn's "Trollope in Ireland," *Contemporary Review*, 129 (January 1926), 72–9.

41. Anthony Trollope, *Four Lectures*, ed. Morris L. Parrish (London, 1938), p. 113. Here his view of tenant-right might seem to be closer to Gwynn's version than Dunleavy's, as indicated above. The rest of what Trollope says here seems to me to be a criticism of Dickens.

42. Booth, *Trollope: Aspects*, p. 80.

43. Dinwiddy, "Who's Who in Trollope's Political Novels," p. 33.
44. "Trollope's Irish Novels," *Dublin Review*, 65 (October 1869), 361–7; repr. in *Trollope: The Critical Heritage*, ed. Smalley.
45. Snow, *Trollope*, p. 43.
46. Trevelyan, *British History in the Nineteenth Century*, pp. 356–7.
47. Snow, *Trollope*, pp. 88–9 and 182n.
48. Trevelyan, *British History in the Nineteenth Century*, p. 357.

6

Trollope, James, and the International Theme

The last novel in Trollope's Palliser series, *The Duke's Children*, was written in 1876 but put away in a desk drawer by the novelist when its predecessor, *The Prime Minister* (1875–6), failed dismally with the reading public. James's *Daisy Miller* appeared in the *Cornhill Magazine* in June–July 1878 and his *An International Episode*, also in the *Cornhill Magazine*, in December 1878 and January 1879. One many be reasonably sure that Trollope, a voracious consumer of contemporary fiction and himself a former editor of *St. Paul's Magazine*, read them both. In June 1878 he sold *The Duke's Children* to *All the Year Round*. It did not begin its run, however, until October 1879, and James read it as he was finishing *The Portrait of a Lady*. Isabel Boncassen, the heroine of *The Duke's Children* and an American, does not appear upon the scene until a third of the way through the novel. Since Trollope had the manuscript of *The Duke's Children* by him during the three years preceding its publication, we cannot rule out the possibility that his portrait of an American in Europe was suggested in part by James's stories, even though Trollope himself had already dealt with the "international" subject (in much less depth, to be sure) in *He Knew He Was Right* (1868–9) and *The American Senator* (1877). Indeed, there is much in *The Duke's Children* that suggests both *Daisy Miller* and *An International Episode*; and, equally to the point, there is much in *The Portrait of a Lady* that suggests *The Duke's Children*.

On 15 April 1874, just two years before Trollope wrote *The Duke's Children*, Lord Randolph Churchill, third son of the seventh Duke of Marlborough, and Miss Jennie Jerome of New York City were married with much fanfare and publicity at the British Embassy in Paris. The Duchess of Manchester, of an earlier generation but no more removed from the social limelight, was also an American, and there were soon to be other international marriages of this sort, culminating some years later in that of Lord Randolph's nephew, the eighth duke, to Consuela Vanderbilt.

Undoubtedly the marriages of the Duke of Manchester and Lord Randolph Churchill were on Trollope's mind when, in *The Duke's Children*, Lord Silverbridge, elder son of the Duke of Omnium, contemplates his desire to marry an American: "there were certain changes going on in the management of the world which his father did not quite understand. . . . Some years ago it might have been improper that an American girl should be elevated to the rank of an English Duchess; but now all that was altered."[1]

The marriage of Caroline Spalding, an American, to the heir of Lord Peterborough in *He Knew He Was Right* recalls that of the Manchesters and anticipates that of the Silverbridges. When Charles Glascock, the future Lord Peterborough, virtually picks up Caroline Spalding during a trip to Florence, the themes of free association with whomever one pleases and of international differences on the subject gain substantial importance, as they were to do later in *Daisy Miller*. American women, Trollope tells us here, talk and move about with the freedom of men; and he comments,

> There is a feeling, however, among pretty women in Europe that such freedom is dangerous, and it is withheld. There is such danger, and more or less of such withholding is expedient; but the American woman does not recognize the danger; and, if she [should withdraw], it is because she is not desirous of the society which is proffered to her.[2]

When Caroline's sister tells her that "we are not in Boston" and that to have an intimacy with a male acquaintance only recently met "might be the most horrible thing in the world to do . . . in Florence," Caroline replies, "Why should that make a difference? Do you mean that one isn't to see one's friends? That must be nonsense" (p. 375). Caroline's uncle, the American minister in Florence, also has doubts about the proprieties involved:

> That their young ladies should walk in public places with unmarried gentlemen is nothing to American fathers and guardians. American young ladies are accustomed to choose their own companions. But the minister was tormented by his doubts as to the ways of Englishmen, and as to the phase in which English habits might most properly exhibit themselves in Italy.   (p. 517)

Surely the question of whether or not an American girl might properly walk in public in Italy with an unmarried male friend anticipates *Daisy Miller*, published a decade later. A constant supporting element in Trollope's version of the international theme (we find it in *The American Senator* and *The Duke's Children* too) is American antipathy to English titles, which, through association with English aristocrats, is transformed into admiration (Trollope was no enemy of an hereditary aristocracy). Caroline's uncle had made republican speeches at home attacking the idea of aristocracy, but when it seems that his niece may actually marry an aristocrat he changes his tune:

> Mr. Spalding was clearly of opinion that, let the value of republican simplicity be what it might, an alliance with the crumbling marbles of Europe would in his niece's circumstances be not inexpedient. . . . He had been specially loud against that aristocracy of England which, according to a figure of speech often used by him, was always feeding on the vitals of the people. But now all this was very much changed. . . . [At Caroline's wedding] he declared that the republican virtue of the New World had linked itself in a happy alliance with the aristocratic splendour of the Old.   (pp. 520, 817, and 824, *passim*)

I would add here, perhaps not irrelevantly, that in the same novel appears "the republican Browning" and women's-rights enthusiast Wallachia Petrie, a tedious and masculinely assertive woman who is called "Wally" by her friends, violently opposes the marriage of her friend Caroline, and has more than a suggestion of the lesbian about her. Whether or not she helped to inspire James's treatment of the subject in *The Bostonians* (1886) is a question that might well be asked (and answered elsewhere); in any case, Miss Petrie gives the lie to the assertion that James's novel is the first in English to address itself to this theme.

In *The American Senator*, Mr. Gotobed also begins his visit to England predisposed against aristocracy; he too, soon enough, changes his mind. Praising their "ease of manner," "grace," and physical appeal, Mr. Gotobed decides that "there is a pleasure in associating with those of the highest rank," that in being among aristocrats "he was surrounded by people who claimed and made good their claims to superiority," and that it is "more easy in this country [England] to sympathise with the rich than with the poor." Expressing at one point his astonishment over this and other matters to his English friend John Morton, Gotobed is told, "I suppose . . . the habits of one country are incomprehensible to another."[3]

At the end of the novel Trollope sums up his feelings about the international question in these terms:

> when an American comes to us, or a Briton goes to the States . . . the differences which present themselves are so striking that neither can live six months in the country of the other without a holding up of the hands and a torrent of explanations. . . . [Nevertheless] we Americans and Englishmen go on writing books about each other, sometimes with bitterness enough, but generally with good final results.[4]

James, no doubt, would have written his novels and stories on the international subject with or without such encouragement; the fact remains, for whatever it is worth, that *The American Senator* appeared just a year before *Daisy Miller* and *An International Episode*, and *He Knew He Was Right* a decade earlier.

In *Mr Scarborough's Family*, the great late novel which appeared in 1882–3 (four years after *Daisy Miller* and *An International Episode* and just a year after *The Portrait of a Lady*), Trollope, in his portrait of Florence Mountjoy, reverts to some of the themes treated in *He Knew He Was Right* (and of course in James's intervening stories). There is nothing "international" in Florence's engagement and subsequent marriage to Harry Annesley; both are English. But the paramount question at issue here is the degree of independence an unmarried woman may have in associating with an unmarried man whom she likes and intends to marry. "In America," Trollope reminds us here, young ladies "carry latch-keys, and walk about with young gentlemen as young gentlemen walk about with each other." Florence's mother complains that her daughter is more American than English in this respect: "she'll go out in the streets and walk with a young man when all her friends tell her not. Is that her idea of religion?"[5]

The "walking about" business is as central an issue in *He Knew He Was Right* and *Mr Scarborough's Family* as it is in *Daisy Miller*. After all, we think of James as the great comparer of America and Europe; but we perhaps have forgotten that Trollope produced a two-volume work on the international question. Entitled *North*

America and published in 1862, this study deals specifically with, among other things, the kinds of subjects I have mentioned here. Having just spent eight months in America and clearly paid much attention to American women, Trollope compares them to British women, and speaks often of the "different laws . . . which govern . . . different societies." He even devotes several paragraphs to the frequency with which he has seen, with dismay, American "young girls in the streets . . . alone" at night, coming home from tea parties and other amusements.[6]

Like Caroline Spalding and Isabel Boncassen, Bessie Alden, the heroine of *An International Episode*, is from Boston. Like Isabel, she is proposed to by a future English duke, and like Isabel Archer she turns down her aristocratic suitor, the first of James's international heroines to do so. She too respects the old-world aristocracy, even lecturing Lord Lambeth at one point on his duties as a nobleman. Lord Lambeth's family, like Lord Silverbridge's, objects to an American marriage: because of this, and also because, like Isabel Archer, Bessie has aspirations that go beyond an easy marriage, she rejects her duke – a reversal of the plot of *The Duke's Children*, though the situation is similar in other respects.

All of this is preface to and context for my main interest here, which is the similarity of Trollope's Isabel to the international heroines of James. Written in 1876 and published in 1879–80, *The Duke's Children*, let us remember, falls in the midst of a flurry of international stories by James, who was still experimenting with his subject.

Isabel Boncassen, like Mr. Spalding and Senator Gotobed, arrives in England prepared to dislike aristocrats. Soon thereafter, though she is not materialistic, Isabel is thrilled by the prospect of marrying a man she can love who also happens to be heir to a dukedom: very quickly indeed "a certain sweetness of the aroma of rank [began] to permeate her republican senses" (I, 315). More to the point, she bears a number of resemblances, beyond her name, to the heroine of *The Portrait of a Lady*. She is intelligent and quick-witted, though she is not intellectual or even overly bright. There is a touch of the snob in her. She is independent, spirited, open to experience, but she is no paragon, and she is never sentimentalized. She is prepared to laugh at English aristocrats but ends up admiring one of them. In all of these things she resembles her Jamesian namesake. She accepts her lord, and will presumably be happy. Isabel Archer lives in a universe less benign; to have accepted *her* lord (Warburton – also the name, incidentally, of the Duke's private secretary in the later Palliser novels) would have been too easy, a premature closing of the door of experience: or so it appears to her.

James seems to me to be responding in part to Trollope in *The Portrait of a Lady*; the unhappy ending of his novel declares that such matters are not always so easily or happily resolved. Could he be speaking directly to the author of *The Duke's Children*? I think it bears repeating that James was reading Trollope's novel in *All the Year Round* as he was completing *The Portrait of a Lady*; he finished it in July 1880, the month in which *The Duke's Children* ended its serial run. (*The Portrait of a Lady* then ran from October 1880 to November 1881 in the *Atlantic Monthly* in America.) Most interesting of all is the fact that the novelists' descriptions of their Isabels often sound strikingly similar. "She had a very high opinion of herself and was certainly entitled to have it by the undisguised admiration of all that came near her. . . . Her brain was firmer than that of most girls." This, astonishingly enough, is not James: it is Trollope (*The Duke's Children*, I, 315–16). A reading of the sixth chapter of *The Portrait of a Lady* will quickly show how similar James's conception of his Isabel is to Trollope's of his. James says of Isabel Archer,

> It had been her fortune to possess a finer mind than most of the persons among whom her lot was cast. . . . Whether or no she were superior, people were right in admiring her if they thought her so; for it seemed to her often that her mind moved more quickly than theirs. . . . Isabel was . . . liable to the sin of self-esteem. . . . It often seemed to her that she thought too much about herself.[7]

There is also more in *The Duke's Children* about American ladies "walking about" in public. Isabel Boncassen, when she takes a walk with Lord Silverbridge shortly after they have met for the first time, is immediately aware of the problem:

> 'In our country . . . [a] young lady may walk about with a young gentleman just as she might with another young lady; but I [think it is] different here . . . judging by English ways, I believe I am behaving very improperly in walking about with

you so long. Ought I not to tell you to go away? . . . I wish to
behave well to English eyes . . . when the discrepancies are
small, then they have to be attended to. So I shan't walk about
with you any more.'   (I, 268)

Trollope's Isabel, like James's Daisy, has a mind of her own in
such matters, however, and soon refuses to be bound by arbitrary
conventions: "the daughter hardly seemed to be under control
from the father. She went alone where she liked; talked to those
she liked; and did what she liked" (I, 294). Some of her friends
admire her sense of freedom, but Trollope himself is not so sure:
"There is . . . a good deal to be said against it. All young ladies
cannot be Miss Boncassens, with such an assurance of admirers
as to be free from all fears of loneliness" (I, 294). Isabel, like Daisy,
is warned about the conventions; Lady Clanfiddle, for example,
tells her that "Americans couldn't be expected to understand
English manners," but that they should not be ignored (I, 324).
Isabel suspects that "all conventional rules" of this sort "are an
abomination" (I, 378), but, more than Daisy, she heeds the
warning. Nevertheless, she will not be dictated to in love: in
America, "if two young people love each other they go and get
married" (II, 71), she tells Lord Silverbridge when he worries
about marriage settlements. Like Bessie Alden, she is both more
responsive to conventional expectations than Daisy and less
stubbornly imperceptive than Isabel Archer. And so, being
resident in a universe where marriages between Cinderellas and
princes may felicitously be made, she can live happily ever after
with her duke. The general situation is similar to many of those in
James's international stories, even if the resolutions are different.
  I am not concerned here with the possible real-life counterparts
of the two Isabels, though both characters seem derived from
actual platonic affections. If Isabel Archer is another version of
Minny Temple, Isabel Boncassen may be the youthful object of
Trollope's well-known esteem late in life, Kate Field, also from
Boston. Like Caroline Spalding and Isabel Archer, Kate went to
Italy as a very young woman. From all accounts she too was
"emotionally ardent and sensually cold." Kate apparently was
imperious in the same pleasant way Isabel Boncassen is imperious
with her admirers. The young man at a loss before a girl of spirit
fiercer than his own (Silverbridge) and an older man moved by an
emotion not entirely that of a decorous father-in-law (Palliser)

represent, perhaps, two aspects of Trollope's own response to Kate Field.[8] *The Duke's Children* was written at the same time (1876) as the *Autobiography*, which contains Trollope's famous outburst about "one of the chief pleasures which has graced my later years" and "a ray of light" encountered in the darkness of his old age.[9] He did not know many American women, after all; there has got to be something of Kate Field in Isabel Boncassen.

However, what matter most here are the literary connections. If James had, as I think he did have, Trollope's Alice Vavasor (the heroine of *Can You Forgive Her?*, 1864–5) in mind when dealing with the "thoughtful" woman theme in *The Portrait of a Lady*, he may well have had Isabel Boncassen in mind when dealing with the international theme. I suspect he also remembered Caroline Spalding. And it is likely that James's Daisy and his Bessie had some impact upon Trollope's heroine. My concern here is not so much with the question of "influence" as with the community of interests between the two novelists – with the fact that their themes are often the same themes.

There are, after all, other examples of this sort, not necessarily "international" in nature yet nonetheless interesting as part of the picture. One of these is the striking similarity between Trollope's odd little novel *Sir Harry Hotspur of Humblethwaite* (1870) and James's *Washington Square* (1880). In both novels a rich father prevents a marriage between his heiress–daughter and an unprincipled but clever and attractive cousin with whom she is in love. In each case the daughter thinks the would-be lover better than he is; and in each the father tactlessly proves to the daughter that the cousin is only after her money. Each daughter comes to see that the father has been right about the suitor, but loves neither the one better nor the other less for having her eyes opened; the interference in each case destroys forever the daughter's only chance for happiness. Neither daughter ever marries. The description of the one – "She suffered under a terrible feeling of ill-usage. Why was she, because she was a girl and an heiress, to be debarred from her own happiness? If she were willing to risk herself, why should others interfere?" – could easily fit both.[10]

In his essay on Trollope (1883), James says that "in these matters" (international matters) Trollope did well, though he comments that Isabel Boncassen is more an Englishman's American than an American's.[11] The *Spectator*'s reviewer had also suggested that Isabel Boncassen "is as English as the Duke himself, and not American at all."[12] Other adverse reactions to Trollope's Isabel have come more recently from the Stebbinses (Trollope, they say, did not understand Americans girls so well as James and Howells, and should have left the international theme alone), and Pope Hennessy (Isabel Boncassen "is convincing without being particularly interesting").[13] One of her most "interesting" properties, however, has been almost totally ignored: the possibility of her having inspired James to improve on her, to create a more domestic version of the real thing.

As Robert M. Polhemus has said, "A short while after he read Trollope's novel, James portrayed another American lady named Isabel who visits England and wins a proposal from a lord."[14] True enough; but there is more to say. Trollope and James in the late 1870s were writing about many of the same things; and it seems likely that they were responding in some of their fictions to each other, and that "influence," between them, goes in both directions. It appears at times as if a dialogue, an exchange of views, engaged them (it is known that they met one another several times[15]). What may be of most interest here is that James took from Trollope at least as much as Trollope took from him; whatever influence may have occurred is usually thought to have traveled in the other direction.

NOTES

1. Anthony Trollope, *The Duke's Children*, Oxford World's Classics edition, 2 vols (London, 1938), II, 204. Subsequent references appear in the text.
2. Anthony Trollope, *He Knew He Was Right*, Oxford World's Classics edition (London, 1948), pp. 373–4. Subsequent references appear in the text.
3. Anthony Trollope, *The American Senator*, 2nd English edn (London, 1878), pp. 146–7, 263, and 267, *passim*.
4. Trollope, *The American Senator*, p. 401.
5. Anthony Trollope, *Mr Scarborough's Family*, Oxford World's Classics edition (London, 1946), pp. 451 and 453.
6. Anthony Trollope, *North America*, abridged edn, ed. Robert Mason (Harmondsworth, Middx, 1968), pp. 102 and 42.
7. Henry James, *The Portrait of a Lady*, Riverside edition, ed. Leon Edel (Boston, Mass., 1963), pp. 52–5, *passim*.
8. See C. P. Snow, *Trollope* (London, 1975), pp. 126, 128.
9. Anthony Trollope, *An Autobiography* (2 vols, London, 1883), Oxford World's Classics edition (London, 1953; 1961), p. 262.

10. The quotation is from *Sir Harry Hotspur of Humblethwaite*, Oxford World's Classics edition (London, 1928), p. 263. Elsewhere, at greater length, I have written of the connections between *Washington Square* and *Sir Harry Hotspur*: see John Halperin, "Trollope, James, and 'The Retribution of Time,' " *Southern Humanities Review*, 19 (Fall 1985), 301–8.
11. James's memorial essay was originally published in *Century Magazine* in 1883 and later reprinted in *Partial Portraits* (New York, 1888). My reference here is to the latter, p. 121.
12. Unsigned notice, *Spectator*, 53 (12 June 1880), 754–5.
13. See L. P. and R. P. Stebbins, *The Trollopes: The Chronicle of a Writing Family* (New York, 1945), p. 296; and James Pope Hennessy, *Anthony Trollope* (Boston, Mass., 1971), p. 352.
14. See Robert M. Polhemus, *The Changing World of Anthony Trollope* (Berkeley and Los Angeles, 1968), p. 228.
15. At least twice; once aboard ship travelling from America to England in 1875, and again in 1877 at the home of Lord Houghton. My information is taken from Leon Edel, *Henry James: The Conquest of London 1870–1883* (London, 1962).

7

On *The Golden Bowl*

Since its publication in 1904, *The Golden Bowl* has been a focal point around which much of the literary criticism of the James revival has swirled. The novel is often cited by the Jamesians as the apotheosis of the art of the Master; Leon Edel calls it, simply, "the richest of all [James's] creations," the "summit" of "his career as a novelist." The anti-Jamesians have fastened onto it as an example of what is most spectacularly repugnant to them in James's work. James himself, who once referred to *The Ambassadors* as the "best, all round" of his novels, told his agent and his publisher as he was finishing *The Golden Bowl* that he was "producing the best book I have ever done." The novel, he wrote to Scribner's, was "the most composed and constructed and completed" of his "productions" – "the solidest, as yet, of all my fictions."

The Golden Bowl turned out to be James's last completed novel. It inevitably embodies many of the idiosyncrasies and displays the preciosity and brilliance of James's celebrated later style – that style both more praised and condemned for itself than any other element of the James canon. Hostile critics who prefer, to use their own terminology, "James the First" and "James the Second" to "James the Old Pretender," do so because they find James's later novels too ambiguous (Yvor Winters, Wayne Booth), stuffy, ponderous, disembodied evocations of abstract values (Wyndham Lewis), a retreat from life (Somerset Maugham), overelaborate, oversubtle, and synthetic (Glenway Wescott, F. R. Leavis), oppressive and unreal (Van Wyck Brooks, Granville Hicks), or simply dull (André Gide), superficial (H. G. Wells), or vacuous (J. M. Murry, Maxwell Geismar). Wells likened James's method in the later novels to that of a hippopotamus picking up a pea, and Edmund Wilson spoke for many anti-Jamesians when he said that the roundabout locutions and gratuitous verbiage of the later novels make them "unassimilably exasperating and ridiculous": unreadable, in a word. And yet the readers of James who find him brilliant, moving, always fascinating, tend to cite the three great novels of James's maturity – *The Wings of the Dove*, *The Ambassadors*, and *The Golden Bowl* – as ultimate proof of the Master's artistry. Thus we also find the later novels eulogized as profoundly beautiful and supremely intelligent masterpieces of realism (T. S. Eliot, Ezra Pound, Ortega y Gasset, J. W. Beach, Cyril Connolly, Morton Zabel, Lionel Trilling, F. W. Dupee) and, frequently, as dazzling symbolist poetry (Stephen Spender, F. O. Matthiessen, Richard Chase, Quentin Anderson, Leon Edel). For Eliot and Ortega, the Anglo-American novel came to an end with the death of James.

The complexity of James's later novels is largely the result of his theories of narrative point of view and of the epistemological structure of human perception. These theories evolved over a number of years into a polished yet orotund system of dramatic revelation of the dynamics of human vision. For James, what one sees determines in large measure what one thinks, and what is perceived helps reveal the mind perceiving it more than it defines the object of perception itself. The novelist's narrative system is designed to express the rhythms of imaginary psychology, the content of human thought. By the time James began to mull over what was to become *The Golden Bowl*, he had already accepted a plan that would enable him to combine the narrative and the dramatic elements of his story into a symbiotic union. After these early gropings with his subject – an "international" story with an "adulterine element" (disqualifying it for submission to *Harper's*) James calls it in a Notebook entry (14 February 1895) – the novelist toyed with the idea of refining even further the revolutionary narrative angle with which he had been experimenting over the past three decades.

From the solitary observer, a sentient center to whose mind the reader is largely limited, James moves in *The Golden Bowl* toward a division of the central consciousness into two minds, making the Prince his chief "reflector" in the novel's first half, with the Princess fulfilling the same function in the second. The novel is a series of meditations described for the reader by the Jamesian narrator and existing for the most part within the consciousnesses of the two imaginary reflectors. The subject of each reflector's meditations is almost always the other reflector. That is to say, Maggie Verver is presented to the reader through the Prince's "exhibitory vision" of her throughout the first half of the novel, and then the Prince is presented to the reader in the second half of the novel through his wife's vision of him – "the advantage thus being," James explains in the preface he wrote for the novel four years after its publication, "that these attributions of experience display the sentient subjects themselves at the same time and by the same stroke with the nearest possible approach to a desirable vividness." Thus the "scheme" of the novel, James says, is that, although we "see" very few persons in *The Golden Bowl* (no more than six, and of these only four in detail), "we shall really see as much of them as a coherent literary form permits." The narrative angle of the novel, then, is one designed to expose, as fully as possible, the minds of the protagonists. Since the human mind, as James conceives it, is often incoherent, indirect, analogical, and obscurely associative, what comes through to the reader is sometimes baffling.

Exacerbating this problem are several others which James confronts here perhaps more fearlessly and completely than in any of his other novels. For James, experience consists primarily of vision, of the ways people have of "seeing about" themselves. In "The Art of Fiction" (1884) he describes thus the "cluster of gifts" that may "be said to constitute experience": "The power to guess the unseen from the seen, to trace the implications of things, to judge the whole piece by the pattern." A man is what he sees; in James's novels, what is seen is the novel's content. Just as for James the most intelligent novelist is he upon whom nothing is lost, so his characters for the most part succeed or fail in accordance with their relative powers of perception. Maggie's ultimate ability to "guess," to "trace," to "judge," is the root of her success in *The Golden Bowl* (if success it is), and Charlotte's inability to do these things, or to do them as well, is the root of her failure (there is little doubt of her failure). James also speaks in "The Art of Fiction" of "the traditional difference between that which people know and that which they agree to admit that they know, that which they see and that which they speak of." Because we are not always able to recognize and understand these distinctions, James gives us in *The Golden Bowl* an intrepid interpreter, Fanny Assingham, and ensures that she will articulate her interpretations of the novel's action by providing her with a husband who refuses to involve himself in the kind of mental gymnastics required of anyone who would understand the moral intricacies of the Ververs' marriages.

But it is the *way* people think in this novel that is most

distinctive, and one must understand this in order to make sense of the organic intricacies of James's later style. In his preface to *The Golden Bowl*, James describes the narrative angle of his novel as "indirect and oblique" yet "the very straightest and closest possible . . . [It is] my account of somebody's impression." James's explanation could apply as well to all the novels from *The Portrait of a Lady* (1880–1) onwards. In almost every case the reader encounters an account of an impression, a vision of a vision, an image of an image. The vision the reader encounters is usually James's report of his observer's perceptions. This is what constitutes the narrative indirectness we often discover in James's novels. But James does not rest here. The narrative structure of his fiction also defines the nature of human perception itself. Vision, James seems to feel, exists symbiotically with mental nature, with psychological balance. In most of his characters the content of vision, as it is metamorphosed into thought, becomes analogical, indirect – and thus, ultimately, metaphorical. That is to say, James's people for the most part do not think of each other or of other things directly; their thoughts are less linear than circular or triangular. *A* does not think of *B* directly, but rather in terms of *C*. People who can identify things only by relating them to other things must inevitably think in terms of images, as Charles R. Anderson has argued in his essays on James; such people think of images of things rather than of things themselves. Indeed, this helps explain why in so many Jamesian passages of indirect discourse the phrase "it was as if" turns up. Simile becomes vision. James's characters experience their surroundings metaphorically, constantly incarnating experience into picture.

A prime example of this is the famous pagoda image which introduces the Princess as the center of consciousness in Book II of *The Golden Bowl*. Here the slowly encroaching evil in Maggie's domestic situation and the beginning of her reaction to it are projected in an elaborate metaphor which consists, basically, of a pictorial dramatization of consciousness. Maggie sees her situation in terms of a picture which is a spatial scene that can be brooded on. She sees her situation in terms of a picture of something else, confronts her image, and then goes around it. What the reader encounters in the pagoda passage is the narrator's account of Maggie's impression, his vision of her vision, an image of her image of her situation. In the same way, we are given in Book I an extended metaphor to describe Adam Verver's vision of his son-in-law in which Adam sees his relationship to the Prince in terms of a Palladian church. What the reader encounters is a vision Adam has of his idea of his son-in-law. James's characters often incarnate mental experience into picture. Perhaps such an indirect mode of thought is appropriate for people who sometimes shrink from direct physical encounters as well as personal and private revelations, people who on the one hand rarely exhibit sensual passion and on the other arrive at knowledge of themselves only after tortuous psychic struggle. In *The Golden Bowl*, Maggie eludes an understanding of her situation for a long time; the habit of circuitous cogitation is therefore an appropriate analogue of her nature.

Such cogitation forms the major part of the novel, and some readers have identified their distaste for *The Golden Bowl* with the scantiness of dialogue in the novel. But a novel which is about a character's mental growth is not likely to contain a great deal of dialogue. And in any case James believed in the sparing use of "scenes." For him, whatever is not scene in a novel – that is, dramatic confrontation between characters – must be picture, must be the leading-up-to of scene. As he says in the preface to *The Ambassadors*, fiction is comprised of scenes and preparation for scenes, and whatever is not scene is picture. James felt that a scene is most effective when it is awaited, anticipated, delayed. Thus there are several reasons why so much of *The Golden Bowl* is indirect discourse and why there are so few genuine "scenes" in the novel. The handful it does contain are thus made as dramatic as possible. For example, the confrontation between Maggie and Charlotte near the end, when Maggie brings the book out to her rival, is a scene made dramatic precisely through James's tactic of delaying this momentous meeting for as long as he can. Both the momentousness and the intense drama of the confrontation are implicit in Maggie's double-edged opening statement to Charlotte: "You've got the wrong volume, and I've brought you out the right."

Another controversial quality of *The Golden Bowl* is its ambiguous ending. Most of James's novels and stories do end in some sort of ambiguity, and James was very conscious of this. At the end of *The Portrait of a Lady*, for example, Henrietta Stackpole says to Casper Goodwood, after Isabel's return to Rome, "Just you wait!" The reader, like Goodwood himself, is invited to wonder whether Henrietta means that he should "wait" for Isabel to return to him, or simply that he is young and will eventually fall in love again. Clearly James means us to take up the latter interpretation, but some readers, perversely perhaps, have insisted upon the former. Though the final paragraphs of *The Portrait* are less ambiguous than those of *The Golden Bowl*, James felt compelled in his Notebook entry (n.d., probably 1880) for *The Portrait* to discuss its unfinished aspects, including his omission of any final scene between Isabel and Osmond upon her return from the journey he proscribed. What will the rest of her life be like? James declines to furnish this information. He says in his note,

> The obvious criticism of course will be that it is not finished – that I have not seen the heroine to the end of her situation – that I have left her *en l'air*. – This is both true and false. The *whole* of anything is never told; you can only take what groups together. What I have done has that unity – it groups together. It is complete in itself – and the rest may be taken up or not, later.

In *The Golden Bowl* James has left us – somewhat ambiguously, it is true – with what has grouped together. Maggie has grown from a daughter to a wife, the adulterous Charlotte and Maggie's father have been sent away, and Maggie is left with her husband, who now finds himself with a spouse and not just the innocent daughter of his mistress's husband. What will happen next is not told. While the story is not finished, the novel quite clearly is. After all, as James says, "the *whole* of anything is never told." Just two years after the publication of *The Golden Bowl*, in his preface to *Roderick Hudson*, James wrote, "Really, universally, relations stop nowhere, and the exquisite problem of the artist is eternally but to draw, by a geometry of his own, the circle within which they shall happily appear to do so."

James, who once described *The Golden Bowl* as, among other things, "a real feat of engineering," is concerned as an artist not with the complete story of human relations but rather with the amount of them that a novel may felicitously contain without bulging apart. In *The Golden Bowl*, a moral tale built out of geometrical symmetries and patterns, it is enough for him (as engineer), and it should be enough for us, to know that Maggie has preserved her husband for herself. Nevertheless, the novel's ending undeniably lends itself to an ominous interpretation: that Maggie's "victory" over Charlotte is Pyrrhic, that Maggie has lost in the process of winning. That is to say, she may have saved both marriages nominally, but the dark embrace described in the novel's final paragraph suggests that her marriage to the Prince may be incapable of redemption. Maggie, who "dreads" her husband's eyes at the end, has managed to keep the Prince for herself, but the stability of their future life together will be somewhat precarious. Perhaps one reason for this foreboding note at the end is that the stalemate Maggie achieves is a triumph of weakness, an unnatural containment of strong wills by a weaker one through evasion and strategy. When the novel is read in this way, Maggie becomes a villainess; she is seen as having ruined three lives in preserving her own. Thus R. P. Blackmur saw the novel's paramount theme as the destruction of life and the novel itself as a repudiation of human behavior. F. R. Leavis said that our sympathies in the novel can lie solely with Charlotte and the Prince, and R. W. B. Lewis emphasized the "cruelty of innocence" in the novel.

This is as good as any other reading of *The Golden Bowl*, which may be about the destruction of life as well as the recognition of life. Surely it is also about the gradual dissipation of innocence and illusion in the face of growing moral and psychological maturity and understanding. At the center of the novel is Maggie's movement from solipsism and naivety to wider perception. The movement is gradual, even at times ponderous, but there can be little question that, for James, Maggie's growth is inevitable. Maggie must first understand that both her marriage and her father's are threatened; it is then her task, eschewing passivity, to act to preserve them. For an essentially innocent, weak, and self-indulgent girl, such action seems at first impossible, unimaginable. The mere act of recognition itself is a long time in coming (all of Book I). What to do, after the situation has been understood, is even more difficult, for Maggie wishes to separate Charlotte and the Prince without alerting her father to the danger, without humiliating her own husband, and without publishing their difficulties to the world. Were Maggie more worldly and less fastidious, the problem would perhaps be more easily solved – and Maggie would be a character in somebody else's novel. But the brilliance of *The Golden Bowl* results specifically from the confrontation of innocence with evil, life's oldest dilemma. Here, as elsewhere in James's work, the question of what to do translates into the question of how to live. James's answer here and elsewhere seems to be that, while innocence is a moral state infinitely preferable to any other, life is meaningless without at least some of the understanding which painful experience brings. It may be that by the time one understands the nature of his existence it is too late to do much about it, since the fruits of experience can be plucked only when the tree has ceased to grow; but the unexamined life is a fool's paradise, divorced from human reality. This reality may not be worth our knowing, and innocence has the admirable property of being immune from the horrors of full comprehension: but illusion is sometimes even worse, especially when it forces us to perform in a moral vacuum detached from the realities of life and human behavior. This is also a central lesson of *The Portrait of a Lady*. Life is a poor thing, perhaps, but it must be at least partially understood and recognized for what it is before any accommodation is possible. Some of our illusions, such as the illusion of freedom, are good for us, even necessary; and yet life devoid of emotional maturity is irrelevant life. *The Ambassadors* tells us this too. It is right, then, that Maggie should attempt to understand her situation; and it is right, at least for her, that she should act to protect herself, her father, and her son. Not to do so would be to give up, to die. And while renunciation, for James, may be the noblest of human actions, it is not a substitute for life. Most of James's novels and stories argue something like this; he is the great delineator of the tragedies loss of innocence brings, and of the impossible alternative offered by sustained ignorance. Seen from this angle he is almost exclusively, as a writer, a tragedian.

We need not side with Maggie in her struggle with Charlotte and the Prince. The question of which team to root for in this novel is one that has exercised many critics, but in the final analysis it is probably a non-question. The duality of the narrative structure – first one perspective, then the other, each narrator concerned primarily with the other, the switch occurring in the middle of the novel – suggests, as Sallie Sears points out in *The Negative Imagination*, that a sustained *division* of sympathies is what James may have expected from readers of *The Golden Bowl*. As Ms. Sears says – and for much of what follows in this paragraph I am indebted to her provocative argument – "the luxury of single identification is denied the reader," the two views being more or less sustained throughout the novel, irrespective of where the center of consciousness actually happens to lie in any particular scene. We are simultaneously and for the most part consistently given two views of events as they happen: that of the reflector, and that of the subject of his or her reflections. This dual narrative perspective may also be seen as radiating outward toward a wider reference – toward, it may be, two different ways of looking at life. There is, for example, the moral versus the amoral view, the unworldly versus the worldly, the American versus the European. But none of these perspectives is ever seen as wholly triumphant, and none of them is ever wholly right. Thus in a moral sense no one in this novel has a monopoly on virtue. The chief characters may have different ways of looking at things, but by the end of the book all of their moral schemata have coalesced into a single collective state of ravaged exhaustion. Nominally, at least, Maggie and her father are the sacrificial dupes in the first half of the novel, Charlotte and the Prince those in the second half. But one might also say that Charlotte and the Prince are the victims of their own rapaciousness in Book I, while Maggie falls victim to the deceptions of her own selfishness in Book II. Whichever view we take, it is clear that Maggie is not simply heroic; with characteristic doubleness she is seen as both persecuted *and* persecutor, defendant *and* plaintiff. We may sympathize with Maggie more often than we sympathize with Charlotte or the Prince; but we must also recognize that Maggie's motivating impulse in Book II is to *annihilate* as much as it is to preserve and protect. In her fight to save her marriage, Maggie's values are, ironically, distorted and narrowed while her moral vision becomes focused and enlarged; and in her duplicity, her conscious hypocrisy, and her willing manipulation of others for selfish ends – as when, for example, she pretends to Charlotte to be heartbroken by the prospect of losing her father as a neighbor – she gives up any claim she may have had to moral superiority over her adversaries. It seems, as Ms. Sears concludes, that "the road to Heaven is paved with lies." Charlotte and the Prince appear to be agents of evil in Book I, but their crimes are palliated in Book II by the nature of the attack mounted against them. In all of this James seems less interested in the question of who is worse than whom than in the effects of adversity upon the human psyche. His position, if he has one, is probably closest to that enunciated by the Prince in a subdued yet ringing pronouncement made to his wife: "Everything's terrible, cara – in the heart of man."

Finally, there is the question of the golden bowl itself – a

symbol whose dark luminosity casts a lustrous glow over so many
of the novel's pages. The bowl is everywhere; it is both a cause of
and a determining factor in the phantasmagorically nightmarish
and emotively mingled tones of marvelousness, horror,
bewitchment, and fierce cruelty pervading the novel. To begin
with, the bowl is not really of gold – it is gilded crystal – and
furthermore it has a crack. The idea of the hidden defect gives us
from the start a sense of sinister foreboding, and many of our
worst suspicions are justified in this most erotic and symbolic of
all of James's novels. James's naturalism here, his tight-lipped
depiction of both the moral destructiveness of adulterous passion
and the selfishness that seeks to thwart it, is emphasized and
illuminated throughout by the ubiquity of the novel's chief
symbol. The bowl's camouflaged flaw is a constant reminder that
Maggie and her father both married under false, or at least only
partially understood, conditions. In fact it is the antique dealer
who gives Maggie the clue she needs to comprehend the actual
relationship between Charlotte and the Prince. The Prince married
for money on the rebound from Charlotte, and Charlotte married
for money on the rebound from the Prince. All they lacked was
money, and the Ververs supplied that. Presumably, neither the
Prince nor Charlotte married with the conscious intention to
deceive, to revive their affair, and yet they are as unable to resist
each other after their respective marriages as before. One feels that
both marriages were made in egregiously bad faith on the part of
the Prince and Charlotte, especially the latter. On the other hand,
Maggie and her father are also to blame, in their close attachment
and their solipsism, for driving their spouses back together.
Adam, after all, marries Charlotte not for love but only for
Maggie's sake: his chief motive is "the measure of relief" to be
effected for Maggie. And the Prince is arrogantly purchased by
the Ververs as if they were making a selection at Sotheby's.

Maggie's marriage, like the golden bowl itself, has been covertly
flawed from the start. The brilliance of James's metaphor,
however, is in the appropriateness with which it may be associated
specifically with either the Prince or the Princess, his two chief
reflectors and the novel's major protagonists. That is, the flawed
bowl is not only a symbol of Maggie's marriage; it also expresses
each partner in the marriage. The Prince is not what he seems; he
too is a flawed treasure. The flaw, however, is not obvious at first;
it comes to light in time. Like the golden bowl itself, the Prince, to

Maggie and her father, is an artifact, a European antique they have bought, the nicest piece in their collection. The international theme, the clash of cultures – present throughout this novel as throughout so much of James's fiction – gives us once again the novelist's vision of America as spiritually bankrupt, feeding off the decaying and often corrupt treasures of Europe. Here too Maggie and her father are to blame: it is only natural that the Prince, having given the Ververs an heir to their millions and then been put back by them upon his shelf, should seek the company of one for whom he is not merely an elegant ornament. There is also a symbolic association of the bowl with the Princess which may be sexual in part, but James undoubtedly did not intend only this. It is rather the deficiency of Maggie's moral vision that the symbolism of the bowl plays on. Her innocence, her illusions, and her final selfishness are her major flaws, flaws which first encourage, with the hope of undetection, the impropriety of Charlotte and the Prince, and then explode it with a cruelty which borders on the gratuitous. The golden bowl is central to Maggie's machinations in Book I. By purchasing it and displaying it to her husband, Maggie wishes him to see, without her having pointedly to tell him so, that her innocence is dissipated, that he is both found out and wanted back. Thus when the bowl is finally and climactically smashed (into three neat pieces, appropriately enough) by Fanny Assingham and its hollowness is exposed, we are meant to understand that more has been destroyed than an artifact. The destruction of the bowl is also the final destruction of illusion, of innocence, and therefore, ultimately, of deception itself: Maggie's, Charlotte's, and the Prince's. That hidden defect in the Ververs' marriages – the intimacy of the Prince and Charlotte – is both exposed and shattered along with the golden bowl, and Maggie is finally free to reconstruct, if she can, the lives of those whom she loves. The loss of innocence is always shattering.

There is no question, then, that the golden bowl is at the center of the novel and an inevitable candidate for destruction, for exorcism. Its symbolism is ubiquitous, as the novel's title acknowledges. James may have obtained his idea from an actual golden bowl, a gift from King George I to the Lamb family, builders of the house James owned in Sussex. This bowl, as Leon Edel tells us in the final volume of his life of James, was kept in the vault of a local bank, where the novelist apparently viewed it with interest. More likely the title's source is either Ecclesiastes or Blake. The relevant passage from Ecclesiastes (12:6–7) reads, "Or ever the silver cord be loosed, or the golden bowl be broken, or the pitcher be broken at the fountain, or the wheel broken at the cistern. Then shall the dust return to the earth as it was: and the spirit shall return unto God who gave it." Thel's lament, in Blake's *Book of Thel* (1789), seems a more logical candidate: "Can wisdom be kept in a silver rod? / Or love in a golden bowl?" Here life is evoked in patently sexual terms. Blake goes on in the poem to treat a subject even closer, in *The Golden Bowl*, to James's heart: the impossibility of legislating happiness through fiat or capturing it through an act of will. Living is hard work; there are no shortcuts to joy. The poet denounces those who, like Maggie and her father, have sought to catch sunlight and bring it into their house – thus darkening the rest of the world. And yet the impulse to capture and enthrall sunlight is perfectly natural; we all need it in order to live. Is it better to find the sunlight among the shadows than merely to curse the darkness? *The Golden Bowl* poses this question.

8

Leslie Stephen,
Thomas Hardy,
and *A Pair of Blue Eyes*

Much has been written about the famous scene in Hardy's *A Pair of Blue Eyes* (1872–3) in which Knight slips over the edge of a cliff and, while dangling over a deep chasm, reviews several thousand years of world history before being rescued by a rope of lady's underwear. Carl J. Weber says the scene was adapted by Hardy from an incident that occurred during a picnic he went on in August 1870 with his future first wife, Emma Lavinia Gifford, who lost an earring during the day in a rocky crevice and asked Hardy, despite the heavy rain, to look for it. According to Weber, Hardy sketched two pictures of the scene and afterwards wrote a poem, ''Where the Picnic Was,'' recalling the day's events. The fictionalized version in *A Pair of Blue Eyes* is ''the first indication in the novels of Hardy's ability to sustain interest in a tense situation by the sheer power of vivid description,'' Weber adds. Michael Millgate refers to Hardy's account of the cliffs along the coasts of Britain, of which this scene forms a part, as irrelevant picture-painting typical of a novel which is little more than ''a kind of rag-bag of information, ideas, descriptive vignettes, personal experiences, fragments of the author's brief literary past.'' J. O. Bailey says the scene is characteristic of a writer who enjoyed injecting into his novels spectacular events involving man and nature. Norman Page comments on the scene at some length; his assessment of it is particularly incisive:

> The vivid apprehension of a visual experience as an accompaniment to intense emotion or a moment of crisis, and the sense of the infinitesimal extent of human life in relation to the history of the earth as revealed by nineteenth-century science: these are . . . characteristic features of Hardy's literary technique and thought throughout the next half-century.

For Jean Brooks the "macabre" scene on the cliff is worthy to stand beside the treatment of Egdon Heath in *The Return of the Native* as a Hardyesque illustration of the "cosmic indifference" of the universe. In *A Pair of Blue Eyes*, Brooks adds, "Hardy scratches the surface of a tragedy to find a comedy in Knight's rescue from the cliff by Elfride's underwear."[1]

No one else says anything of substance about this scene; none of the critics except Weber takes any interest in Hardy's possible sources for the episode – and Weber is wrong. "Where the Picnic Was" came out of a very different picnic in 1912,[2] and in any case, as we shall see, the idea for Knight's ordeal had nothing to do with a picnic, whether in 1870 or in 1912.

Among Hardy scholars Robert Gittings, as might be expected, comes closest to the truth. Gittings is "pretty sure" that "some of the realistic detail" of the episode in *A Pair of Blue Eyes* in which Knight is described as hanging on the cliff-face was "based" on an essay by Leslie Stephen called "A Bad Five Minutes in the Alps." In this essay, Gittings notes, Stephen imagines himself in a similar situation on one of his mountaineering expeditions.[3] Gittings, however, offers no evidence for his hypothesis; he mentions the possibility of the connection – cautiously, tentatively, and briefly – and moves on. Nobody, in fact, has bothered to consider seriously the relation between Stephen's essay and Hardy's novel. It seems, then, that there may be a place in Hardy studies for a more thorough examination of the possible connections between *A Pair of Blue Eyes* and "A Bad Five Minutes in the Alps."

There can be little doubt, first of all, that the "Cliff without a Name" (as it is called) in *A Pair of Blue Eyes* is carefully drawn from Beeny Cliff and its coastline companions such as Pentargan Cliff, a little further south in Cornwall.[4] In this Hardy used his knowledge of the Cornish coast and got nothing at all from Stephen, whose essay is set in the Swiss Alps. Typically, Hardy makes us work to find out even this much about his cliff, describing it in the preface he wrote in 1895 for *A Pair of Blue Eyes* simply as an "enormous sea-board cliff." He adds here, "For some forgotten reason or other this cliff was described in the story as being without a name. Accuracy would require the statement to be that a remarkable cliff which resembles in many points the cliff of the description bears a name that no event has made famous."[5] Still he forbears to tell the name; such ingenuousness is characteristic of Hardy's more "personal" statements. In the

Life, as a matter of fact, he is especially vague when associating works of fiction and poetry with actual events and persons.[6] And in various works of fiction, as is well known, he was not above inserting into his stories without acknowledgment large chunks of material taken from other books, particularly when he was engaged, as in *The Trumpet-Major* (1880), in a piece of historical reconstruction for which methodical study was necessary. Indeed, Hardy was occasionally chided by reviewers for this unwholesome practice and became, ultimately, very sensitive about charges of plagiarism, especially after publication of *The Trumpet-Major*, some sections of which were cribbed directly from primary sources. So we need not be surprised if he says nothing about the debt he owed to Leslie Stephen in connection with *A Pair of Blue Eyes*.

Hardy's first meeting with Stephen, his senior by eight years, probably took place in December 1873 at Stephen's house in Kensington;[7] they had begun a correspondence in 1872, as we shall see. That first winter meeting is described by Hardy thus: "Hardy made the personal acquaintance of Leslie Stephen, the man whose philosophy was to influence his own for many years, indeed, more than that of any other contemporary."[8] This judgment is echoed by Hardy's biographer, who says the two men were "very close in personal and intellectual sympathy."[9] The *Life* goes on to describe the course of their growing intimacy throughout the mid-seventies, an intimacy punctuated by marathon late-night talks in Stephen's study about religion and metaphysics. These discussions contributed mightily to the loss of what little religious faith Hardy had retained as a young man (a gloss on the impact, to which he refers, of Stephen's philosophy upon him). Perhaps the most unforgettable moment of their friendship for Hardy occurred on 23 March 1875, when Stephen sent round a midnight summons to come to the house and witness the signing of his formal renunciation of Holy Orders.[10]

But their literary association predates their personal friendship. Stephen, who became editor of the *Cornhill Magazine* in 1871, had read and admired *Under the Greenwood Tree* when it appeared in 1872. In December 1872 he wrote to Hardy to request a serial novel for the *Cornhill*. This was by far the best offer the young novelist had had, and he readily agreed to terms. The novel turned out to be *Far from the Madding Crowd*, serialized (anonymously) in the *Cornhill* in 1873–4 and an instant popular success. Stephen collaborated closely with Hardy on the writing and revising of the serial for publication. *The Hand of Ethelberta*, Hardy's next novel, was published in the *Cornhill* in 1875–6. The literary collaboration ended abruptly in May 1876 when Stephen, worried about the various complicated love relationships he could see developing in early sections of the next novel, made one of the worst editorial decisions in the history of publishing and turned down *The Return of the Native*;[11] the two men nevertheless managed to remain friends until Stephen's death in 1904.

Most critical accounts of the Hardy–Stephen relationship come to an end with the *Cornhill*'s rejection of *The Return of the Native*. The *Life*, after all, does not mention Stephen's essay on the Swiss Alps, and except for Gittings, as we have seen, the subject is never broached. But there is a great deal more to the story.

In 1862 Stephen, then president of the Alpine Club – whose offices at 8 St. Martin's Place were in the same building as those of Arthur Blomfield, the architect for whom Hardy went to work in the same year – published *Peaks, Passes, and Glaciers*, describing his ascent of the Schreckhorn, a peak in the Swiss Alps over 13,000 feet high. Stephen was the first man to climb the Schreckhorn, and the book achieved some popularity. When Hardy, accompanied by his wife, toured Europe in 1897, his sight of this mountain peak[12] was inextricably associated with Stephen. Hardy later wrote of the experience,

> Then and there I suddenly had a vivid sense of him, as if his personality informed the mountain – gaunt and difficult, like himself. . . . As I lay awake that night, the more I thought of the mountain, the more permeated with him it seemed: I could not help remarking to my wife that I felt as if the Schreckhorn were Stephen in person; and I was moved to begin a sonnet to express the fancy.

The sonnet, written in June 1897, is called "The Schreckhorn" and first appeared as Hardy's contribution to F. W. Maitland's *Life and Letters of Leslie Stephen*, published in 1906.[13] The poem's subtitle is "*With thoughts of Leslie Stephen.*"

> Aloof, as if a thing of mood and whim;
> Now that its spare and desolate figure gleams
> Upon my nearing vision, less it seems
> A looming Alp-height than a guise of him

> Who scaled its horn and ventured life and limb,
> Drawn on by vague imaginings, maybe,
> Of semblance to his personality
> In its quaint glooms, keen lights, and rugged trim.
> At his last change, when Life's dull coils unwind,
> Will he, in old love, hitherward escape,
> And the eternal essence of his mind
> Enter this silent adamantine shape,
> And his low voicing haunt its slipping snows
> When dawn that calls the climber dyes them rose?[14]

Both the poem and the statement quoted from Maitland's *Life and Letters* make it clear that when Hardy thought of Stephen in later years he remembered him first as a climber of mountains rather than as a literary editor or an adviser on metaphysics. Gaunt, craggy, outwardly unprepossessing, the mountain, for Hardy, *was* Stephen; his friend *was* the Schreckhorn. "In its quaint glooms, keen lights, and rugged trim," Virginia Woolf wrote, quoting the sonnet, Hardy's portrait of her father "was incomparably the truest and most imaginative" she knew.[15]

Clearly Hardy had read Stephen's *Peaks, Passes, and Glaciers*, with its account of a dangerous ascent of a cliff-face, when it appeared – a decade, that is, before the publication of *A Pair of Blue Eyes*; and clearly it made a lifelong impression on him. But this is the beginning rather than the end of the story.

There is some question about when Hardy first began to work on the tale that was to become *A Pair of Blue Eyes*. Millgate, Weber, and Gittings all think that he had it planned before William Tinsley, in July 1872, asked him for a new serial.[16] This is speculation; no confirmation is possible. Hardy, who tells us in the *Life* that he began writing *A Pair of Blue Eyes* on the evening of 24 July 1872, that this was the first time he had any thought at all of the story, and that none of it was worked out in advance, may just as easily be believed. In any case, what we know for certain is this. Tinsley, who had published *Desperate Remedies* (1871) and was bringing out *Under the Greenwood Tree*, asked Hardy on 8 July 1872 for a new serial to begin in the September number (actually published in August) of *Tinsley's Magazine*. Hardy replied the next day that he had the beginnings of an "M.S." in hand – probably "The Poor Man and the Lady," later partially destroyed – but that it needed "a great deal of reconsideration." The novelist's account of the genesis of *A Pair of Blue Eyes* is consistent with what happened next. On 27 July 1872 he wrote to Tinsley to say that he was now working on the new story and that he agreed to the terms Tinsley had offered for the serial novel: twenty pages a month for twelve months, with eventual publication in three volumes, the remuneration to be £200. The tale would be called "A Willing Tongue Had He."[17] Shortly thereafter the title was changed to *A Pair of Blue Eyes*; eventually the number of serial installments was changed from twelve to eleven. The novel ran in *Tinsley's Magazine* from September 1872 to July 1873 and was published in three volumes at the end of May 1873. It is also clear from the correspondence between Hardy and Tinsley during the summer and autumn of 1872 that, when the novel began its serial run, Hardy had written out only a few chapters of it.[18] From this time until the following spring Hardy remained, the correspondence shows, between one and two months ahead of the printer. For example, the October number was said by Hardy in a letter to Tinsley dated 30 August 1872 to be "ready" to be posted the following week; and on 7 September he wrote to Tinsley to announce that copy for the October number had just been mailed. On 30 September another bundle of manuscript, presumably copy for the November number, was posted.[19]

Having now arrived at the month, the very important month, of November 1872, we must break away from this narrative. For in the November number of *Fraser's Magazine* appeared Leslie Stephen's "A Bad Five Minutes in the Alps."[20] *Fraser's* was edited by Stephen's friend J. A. Froude; Stephen had been contributing to it pieces mostly of an agnostic cast since 1867.

The cliff-hanging episode in *A Pair of Blue Eyes* occurs in chapters 21 and 22 of the novel. The sixth number, which appeared in February 1873, breaks off in the middle of this famous episode – that is, at the end of chapter 21 – leaving Knight, in good serial fashion, hanging in mid-air on the cliff-face. The seventh number, published in March, begins with the account in chapter 22 of Knight's rescue by Elfride. Presuming Hardy to be writing at the pace revealed by the first volume of *Collected Letters* (that is, between one and two months ahead of the printer), it is more than likely that the sixth number of *A Pair of Blue Eyes* was written in December 1872 and the seventh number in January 1873. Stephen's essay, appearing in November 1872, would have reached Hardy as he was finishing the fifth number (for January

1873 publication) and beginning to ponder the content of the sixth. It is a tight fit, but a very good one. Stephen's essay could not have appeared at a more convenient time, as a matter of fact, for anyone attempting to establish a connection between "A Bad Five Minutes in the Alps" and chapters 21 and 22 of *A Pair of Blue Eyes*.

We have seen how impressive and memorable Stephen's 1862 essay on the ascent of the Schreckhorn became for Hardy in later years; it is fair to assume that "A Bad Five Minutes in the Alps," widely read and commented upon at the time of its publication, was eagerly assimilated by the novelist as soon as it appeared, and that it too had an impact upon him. Most immediately, it had an impact upon the story he was writing. Starting to compose the sixth number of *A Pair of Blue Eyes* in December 1872, Hardy must have found Stephen's essay a heaven-sent clue for the sort of exciting climax the next number of his serial required.

The most revealing witnesses are, of course, the two texts; to place them side by side is to see exactly what and how much Hardy took from Stephen. Since no hard evidence of the relationship between the two texts has previously been offered, it may be worthwhile to show in detail here how closely Hardy's account of Knight's ordeal follows Stephen's description – also wholly fictional – of a similar ordeal.

Neither in "A Bad Five Minutes in the Alps" nor in *A Pair of Blue Eyes* is the cliff or peak called by any name. In both accounts it is raining heavily; everything for miles around is soaking wet. In each story the protagonist is wandering miles away from any commonly used footpath when the mishap occurs. Stephen in his essay and Knight in the novel both cross the cliff-face, lose their footing, slide over the side, grab a rocky outcrop at eye level, and shakily hold on to the jagged rocks with their hands while seeking, and in each case finding, some minimal support for their feet. In both versions a body of water is perceived by the unhappy man far beneath him; in both the word "cascade" is used to describe the movement of the water below. Each writer emphasizes the fierce primeval aspects of the cliff-face as they appear to the protagonist; each uses the word "grim" in the account. Stephen refers to "black rocks frowning above me and the pitiless chasm beneath"; in *A Pair of Blue Eyes* Knight is intimidated by the "blackish-grey" formation of rocks in front of him.[21] Each sufferer remarks pointedly upon the apparently alien aspect of the physical world. "Nature looked savage enough, marking my sufferings with contemptuous indifference," says Stephen. To Knight the cliff appears more ferocious than it rationally should; it seems, indeed, inimical to human beings, a mere caprice of nature with "a horrid personality" of its own.[22]

As he begins to lose his grip on the cliff-face, Stephen grabs a rhododendron root and hangs on; wondering how long he can keep hold, he considers letting go and giving up the ghost altogether: but of course he does not let go. Knight, also losing his grip on the cliff-face, grabs hold of some weeds growing out of the rocks; wondering how long he can hang on, he too considers letting go, but does not. Both try to climb back up the cliff-face but find the rocks too moistened by the rain to sustain any grip. Each man reminds himself of the importance of maintaining some presence of mind; each hits upon the idea of thinking about something else to make the time before a rescue becomes possible pass more quickly. At this point both begin to observe closely, as a sort of distraction, the rock formations directly in front of their eyes. In each case the rocks are perceived as types of geological specimens. The effect on Stephen is to make him think of his past life and to wonder about the meaning of experience. Prompted by a fossil he sees directly in front of him, Knight retraces several thousand years of past history; he too is led to wonder about the meaning of experience. "There is no place like a cleft landscape for bringing home such imaginings as these," *A Pair of Blue Eyes* tells us (p. 242).

Speculating on his chances for survival, Stephen finds himself suddenly galvanized by the acute (and unexpected) desire to keep on living. No faith can solace him, no stoicism can blunt his instinctual desire to live. Observing that "a believer in any creed would have been highly uncomfortable in my position," Stephen finds that "holding on" has become his single preoccupation. Speculating on his chances for survival, Knight also discovers a deep-rooted desire to live, nor can he bring either faith or the comfort of stoicism to his aid in this crisis. For him also, "holding on" becomes a monomania; loving Elfride, he hates the thought of losing her through his untimely death: "Love is faith, and faith, like a gathered flower, will rootedly live on."[23] Both men, then, are sustained in this emergency by a secular materialism (of the sort, perhaps, Stephen and Hardy were to discuss a year or two later during those nocturnal debates in Kensington) at times almost hysterical in its intensity. Stephen goes on to observe that, being a man out of the ordinary, his death would be more a loss than a gain to mankind; he wonders what work he might have done in future years. Knight too feels "his death would be a deliberate loss to earth of good material" (p. 245).

At this point in both narratives each man realizes he cannot hang on much longer. Each thinks more time has gone by than in fact is the case; in such moments "one lives fast," observes Stephen, whose opportunity for leisurely thought convinces him he has been on the cliff-face for thirty minutes when he has been there only for five. Knight, who thinks he has been hanging in space for ten minutes when he has been there only for three, also "lives fast": "These images passed before Knight's eye in less than half a minute, and he was again considering the actual present."[24] For each man, in other words, the present goes out of focus by being submerged in reverie. Stephen ultimately rescues himself by letting go of the cliff-face and simultaneously springing upward to a rocky projection; suspended by his arms for such a long time, he worries beforehand that they will not be strong enough to sustain the effort. Knight, also suspended by his arms and fearful of their weakness, is rescued in a somewhat similar way. He, too, must let go of the cliff-face and simultaneously spring upward; here, however, he has the help of a rope made out of Elfride's underwear which she has tossed over the edge for him to grasp. Each man has terribly cramped limbs immediately after the rescue.

Both stories, it is worth repeating, are entirely fictional, despite detailed descriptions of the ordeal.

Hardy's interest in Stephen's mountaineering experiences, the availability of them in print as he was writing *A Pair of Blue Eyes*, and especially the appearance of "A Bad Five Minutes in the Alps" as he was beginning work on chapters 21 and 22 of his novel, his lifelong association of Stephen's austere personality with a mountain peak, his intellectual sympathy with Stephen and his characterization of him as the man whose influence upon himself was stronger than that of any other contemporary, his tendency to lift what he liked without acknowledgment from other sources for his own purposes, and of course the similarity of the two texts, as described above, constitute enough evidence to make Gittings's cautious phrase ("pretty sure") about the possible connections between "A Bad Five Minutes in the Alps" and *A Pair of Blue Eyes* seem unnecessarily tentative. One can say more than that "some of the . . . detail" of Hardy's episode was "based" on Stephen's; substantiating evidence *is* available. There can be little doubt that Hardy got the whole of chapters 21 and 22 of the novel from Stephen's essay.

In "The Schreckhorn" Hardy speaks in the penultimate line of Stephen's "low voicing" haunting the mountain peak's "slipping snows." It was a voice he often listened to, not least when writing his own account of a slippery peak. Indeed, Stephen often seemed to Hardy like one of his own doomed heroes.[25]

NOTES

1. Carl J. Weber, *Hardy of Wessex* (New York, 1940; 1964), pp. 83 and 87; Michael Millgate, *Thomas Hardy: His Career as a Novelist* (London, 1971), p. 63; J. O. Bailey, *The Poetry of Thomas Hardy* (Chapel Hill, N.C., 1970), p. 281; Norman Page, *Thomas Hardy* (London, 1977), p. 97; Jean Brooks, *Thomas Hardy: The Poetic Structure* (Ithaca, N.Y., 1971), p. 150.
2. See Bailey, *The Poetry of Thomas Hardy*, pp. 307–8.
3. Robert Gittings, *Young Thomas Hardy* (London, 1975), p. 187.
4. See Gittings, *Young Thomas Hardy*, pp. 169 and 244n.; Weber, *Hardy of Wessex*, p. 86; and Denys Kay-Robinson, *Hardy's Wessex Reappraised* (Newton Abbot, Devon, 1972), pp. 249–50.
5. Thomas Hardy, *A Pair of Blue Eyes* (London and New York, 1962), p. vi. Subsequent references are to this (the Macmillan) edition.
6. Robert Gittings, *The Older Hardy* (London, 1978), p. 181. I refer, of course, to F. E. Hardy, *The Life of Thomas Hardy 1840–1928* (London, 1962), written, except for the last several chapters, by Hardy himself.
7. See Gittings, *Young Thomas Hardy*, p. 175.
8. See Hardy, *Life*, p. 100.
9. Gittings, *The Older Hardy*, p. 118.
10. See Hardy, *Life*, pp. 100 and 105.
11. See Gittings, *Young Thomas Hardy*, pp. 171–2; and Hardy, *Life*, p. 108.
12. Not the Jungfrau, as Gittings mistakenly says in *The Older Hardy*, p. 91.
13. Bailey, *The Poetry of Thomas Hardy*, p. 281; and F. W. Maitland, *The Life and Letters of Leslie Stephen* (New York and London, 1906), p. 277.
14. Quoted from *The Complete Poems of Thomas Hardy*, ed. James Gibson (London and New York, 1976), p. 322. The sonnet is poem 264 in this edition.
15. Gittings, *Young Thomas Hardy*, p. 187.
16. Millgate, *Hardy: His Career as a Novelist*, pp. 66–7; Weber, *Hardy of Wessex*, p. 84; and Gittings, *Young Thomas Hardy*, pp. 156 and 159.
17. R. L. Purdy, *Thomas Hardy: A Bibliographical Study* (London, 1954; 1968), pp. 11–12 and 332; Hardy, *Life*, p. 90; and *The Collected Letters*

of *Thomas Hardy*, I: *1840–1892*, ed. R. L. Purdy and Michael Millgate (Oxford, 1978), pp. 13–14 and 17.

18. See Hardy, *Collected Letters*, I, *passim*; Hardy, *Life*, p. 91 and *passim*; and Weber, *Hardy of Wessex*, p. 84.
19. See *Collected Letters*, I, 18; and Hardy, *Life*, p. 163.
20. *Fraser's Magazine*, 86 (November 1872), 545–61; repr. in Leslie Stephen, *Essays in Freethinking and Plainspeaking* (London, 1905), pp. 177–225. The essay, like most of Stephen's published in *Fraser's*, was unsigned, but no one could have been in any doubt as to its authorship; Stephen's feats of hiking and mountain-climbing were famous, and he was a frequent contributor of "outdoorsy" pieces to the magazines.
21. See Stephen, *Essays*, p. 206; and Hardy, *A Pair of Blue Eyes*, p. 232.
22. Stephen, *Essays*, p. 206; and Hardy, *A Pair of Blue Eyes*, p. 232.
23. Stephen, *Essays*, p. 221; and Hardy, *A Pair of Blue Eyes*, p. 245.
24. Stephen, *Essays*, p. 224; and Hardy, *A Pair of Blue Eyes*, p. 242.
25. Gittings, *The Older Hardy*, p. 118. I wish to acknowledge here my indebtedness to Donald Greene for his interest and encouragement.

9

How Gissing Read Dickens

The walls stood in a perpetual sweat; a mouldy reek came from the open door-ways; the beings that passed in and out seemed soaked with grimy moisture, puffed into distortions, hung about with rotting garments. . . . He went to work in a fog so dense that it was with difficulty he followed the familiar way. Lamps were mere lurid blotches in the foul air, perceptible only when close at hand. . . . Windows glimmered at noon with the sickly ray of gas or lamp; the roads were trodden into viscid foulness; all night the droppings of a pestilent rain were doleful . . . and only the change from a black to a yellow sky told that the sun was risen. . . . [Lambeth was] redolent with oleaginous matter; the clothing of the men was penetrated with the same nauseous odour.

This may sound like *Bleak House* or *A Christmas Carol*, but in fact I have strung together here passages from Gissing's *Thyrza* (1887) and *The Nether World* (1889). Gissing's accounts of the metropolis, especially the impenetrability of the atmosphere and its blearing effects on those it touches, often owe something to Dickens; indeed, in *Thyrza* there is in the midst of the slum a very Dickensian place indeed called "The Little Shop with the Large Heart."

In the prefaces he wrote for the Rochester edition of Dickens's works – the prefaces were composed between 1899 and 1901 – Gissing declares that the depiction of London was Dickens's *métier*. People still see London with Dickens's eyes, Gissing says in the preface to *Oliver Twist*: "To depict London was one of the ends for which Dickens was born."

Like Dickens, Gissing was a great walker, and the visual impact of the metropolis upon him was extensive. But, while the two often perceived the city similarly, the attitudes such perceptions wrought in them were often quite different. Consider the following passage – from *Thyrza*:

The life of men who toil without hope yet with hunger of an unshaped desire; of women in whom the sweetness of their sex is perishing under labour and misery; the . . . song of the girl who strives to enjoy her year or two of youthful vigour, knowing the darkness of the years to come; the careless defiance of the youth who feels his blood and revolts against the lot which would tame it; all that is purely human in these darkened multitudes speaks to you as you listen. It is the half-conscious striving of a nature which knows not what it would attain, which deforms a true thought by gross expression, which clutches at the beautiful and soils it with foul hands.

And this, from *The Nether World*: "On all the doorsteps sat little girls, themselves just out of infancy, nursing or neglecting bald, red-eyed, doughy-limbed abortions in every stage of babyhood, hapless spawn of diseased humanity, born to embitter and brutalise yet further the lot of those who unwillingly gave them life." These are not the innocent, dewy-eyed, lovable, playful progeny of Dickens's poor. The feeling expressed in these passages is quite clear: poverty *never* brings human nobility to the surface. Gissing did not equate poverty with virtue, as Dickens, in his most sentimental moods, was prone to do.

In his preface to *Oliver Twist* Gissing quotes the famous passage in which Dickens declares that the same qualities are impartially bred "in the finest lord and the dirtiest charity boy" – and says Dickens was wrong. Thackeray, he declares, is the greater "realist" – realism being defined as "a severe chronicle of actual lives." The realist, says Gissing in his preface to *Dombey and Son*, shows how things *would* turn out; Dickens showed how things may turn out for the best: "His view of art involved compliance with ideals of ordinary folk. . . . An instinctive sympathy with the moral . . . prejudices of the everyday man guided Dickens throughout his career. . . . [He was] a *representative Englishman of the middle class.*" The failure of *Nicholas Nickleby*, Gissing notes, lies in its sentimentality, which he traces in Dickens to "the great semi-educated class from which he sprang and to which, unconsciously, he so often addressed himself." He goes on to assert that Dickens's art is primarily concerned with the uncultured: "The uncouth and the underbred play so vast a part in human life that to neglect them is to falsify; but only the rarest genius can turn them to worthy use." Certainly Gissing viewed the uncouth and the underbred with much less sympathy. "Let the humbly born discharge the duties appointed to them by Providence," he says.

His preface to *Bleak House*, while praising the novel, attacks Dickens for the excessive attention paid to low life and the exaggerated delicacy of virtuous sentiment portrayed among the lower orders: "Though virtue may exist in the ignorant and the poor and the debased, most assuredly the delicacies of virtue will not be found in them." If anything is true of the English lower classes, Gissing declares, it is that, even "supposing them to say or do a good thing, they will say or do it in the worst possible way . . . we can only mark with regret how [in Dickens] the philanthropist often overcame the artist."

Like most studies of one writer by another, Gissing's prefaces primarily illuminate his own prejudices and perspectives. While Dickens sympathizes with the poor, "he never demands that they shall be raised above the status of poverty," Gissing declares – a statement which defines his own attitude towards the poor more nearly than Dickens's. *"Morally, he would change the world; socially he is a thorough conservative."* Gissing describes himself here; his view of Dickens is filtered through his own self-consciousness. Perhaps the most revealing of the prefaces in this regard is that to *The Old Curiosity Shop* – the work, says Gissing, of "an utterly conservative mind, ever looking backwards, lamenting every change, and dreading the new time that advanced." This is the archetypal reactionary view of Gissing in novel after novel, but I doubt that it accurately describes Dickens in all of his moods.

More revealing of his perspective on Dickens is the monograph Gissing wrote on his great predecessor, *Charles Dickens: A Critical Study* (1898); in the 1950s *The Times Literary Supplement* pronounced this still one of the best books ever written on Dickens, and I think this remains a just assessment today. Gissing's, incidentally, was also the first book on Dickens. It demonstrates Gissing's remarkable skill and insight as a critic. It pinpoints the sources alike of Dickens's genius and of his limitations; and, many years before Edmund Wilson's essay, it identified the "two Scrooges" pattern in Dickens's work. For better or worse, it was one of only three discussions of Dickens the late Dr. Leavis allowed his students to read (the others were those by Santayana and Wilson).

"Permit Dickens to show us the life he knew in its simple everyday course and he is unsurpassed by any master of fiction;

144 *Jane Austen's Lovers*

demand from him a contrived story, and he yields at once to the very rank and file of novelists," Gissing remarks. An explanation for the phenomenal hold Dickens had upon his contemporaries, Gissing declares, is the fact that he was "truly and profoundly national" in his point of view – and this "intense nationality" enabled him "to utter the thoughts of voiceless England." Gissing adds that Dickens's observations of apparently ordinary things was "wonderfully minute. . . . It is the property of his genius to perceive romance in the commonplace and squalid." Quite rightly, I think, Gissing attributes Dickens's "astonishing lack of skill when it came to inventing plausible circumstances" to his "love of the stage" and his usual failure "to see mentally as a whole the work on which he was engaged" as he wrote it. Another weakness Gissing shrewdly identifies in Dickens is lack of "historical knowledge . . . no true understanding of what is meant by history. . . . Few really great men can have had so narrow an intellectual scope," says Gissing, which also helps explain why "no distinctly intellectual person figures in his books."

I also agree with Gissing's intrepid assertion that, without qualification, Dickens's best novel is *Little Dorrit*. Gissing, remember, was writing at a time, twenty-seven years after Dickens's death, when Dickens's later novels were considered a falling off – when, that is, the achievement-and-decline view of his work was fashionable and he was considered fit only for children and Christmas. It is to Gissing's credit that he paid no attention to this Chestertonian absurdity.

Charles Dickens: A Critical Study also gives us a revealing glimpse into the complicated and ambivalent *personal* way in which Gissing reacted to Dickens. "It is the privilege of a great writer to put into his work the finest qualities of his heart and brain, to make permanent the best part of himself," Gissing says. "Be he a true artist, he gives us pictures which represent his own favourite way of looking at life; each is . . . the world as *he* prefers it." And so in the preface to *David Copperfield* Gissing says he can readily understand why that novel was always one of Dickens's most cherished: it was his most autobiographical tale.

Dickens's fascination for Gissing had a number of sources. Constantly overwhelmed by his own domestic disasters, Gissing was awed by Dickens's power, alien to him, "of pursuing his imaginative tasks amid distractions which most men would find fatal. . . . [His] fiction-writing went on as usual, with never a hint of difficulty owing to circumstances." On the other hand, he himself had done something which, he was certain, Dickens could never have done: "Dickens could never have struggled for long years against the lack of appreciation. In coldness towards his work he would have seen its literary condemnation, and have turned to a new endeavour." But it is in their similarities that Gissing is most interested. Both men loved to travel but hated "the supercilious Englishman abroad," as Gissing puts it; both loved the English countryside, and yearned for it most when penned up in the metropolis – both, indeed, were dissatisfied with their surroundings wherever they were; both venerated the past and detested many aspects of modern life – though Dickens, unlike Gissing, was interested more in the recent than in the remote past. Dickens's age and his own – not so very far apart, after all – appeared to Gissing to be periods

> in which the English character seemed bent on exhibiting all its grossest and meanest and most stupid characteristics. Sheer ugliness of every day life reached a limit not easily surpassed; thickheaded national prejudice, in consequence of great wars and British victories, had . . . developed . . . Power was passing to . . . [the] multitude, remarkable for a . . . ferocious egoism. With all this, a prevalence of such ignoble vices as religious hypocrisy and servile snobbishness.

All in all, Gissing sums up, "A time of . . . ugly religion, ugly law, ugly relations between rich and poor, ugly clothes, ugly furniture." When Dickens died at fifty-eight, Gissing was already in his thirteenth year; their hatred of the present age was a hatred of the same age. The London of the two novelists was essentially the same London, though observed four decades apart. Indeed, many scenes in a novel such as *The Nether World* could easily be transplanted to *Bleak House*, as we have seen. But it is typical of Gissing's hatred of the present to idealize the recent past as well as the long-ago past, finding his own time, "if more respectable," also "decidedly duller." Gissing's feeling that Dickens's "age" was better than his also leads him to see it as a period when "there was more of the picturesque, more of the beautiful, than we see today," and to speak of his own time as one in which there is

destruction of so much one would fain preserve. Think, for

instance, of Yarmouth as seen in *David Copperfield*, and the
Yarmouth of this year's railway advertisements. . . . Our people
. . . have advanced in the understanding of business, a word
which will justify most atrocities, and excuse all but every form
of shamelessness.

Hatred of the modern and veneration of the past are in each
novelist the products of a temperamental conservatism. In seeing
the so-called great radical of his time as a genuine conservative at
heart, Gissing is not indulging, as it might seem, merely in
psychological projection; he is being profoundly incisive,
articulating a point of view which was to escape Dickens's critics
for another half-century.

Dickens's conservatism lies, I think, in his unquestioning belief
in God, in money (characters worthy of redemption are rewarded
with it), and in class (his bourgeois characters speak a pure
English, no matter what sort of education they have had). He
believes, that is, in most of the deities, accepts most of the values,
that conventional, conservative Victorians believed in and
accepted. Gissing sees this. And in his study he strengthens the
case for Dickens's conservatism with a few additional observations.
As he points out, Dickens was skeptical about the virtues and
effects of "popular education" (as in the case of Charley Hexam in
Our Mutual Friend) and uneasy about "the spread of a genuinely
democratic spirit" (the fear of the mob is everywhere in Dickens –
most notably in *Barnaby Rudge* and *A Tale of Two Cities*). In these
matters the two novelists were as one. Dickens, himself "a
considerable capitalist," as Gissing points out, "never desired . . .
a political revolution"; Gissing reminds us how much he hated
American republicanism. He goes on,

> He was never a democrat; in his heart he always held that *to be
> governed* was the people's good; only let the governors be
> rightly chosen. . . . Dickens knew – no man better – how unfit
> are the vast majority of mankind to form sound views as to
> what is best for them . . . he knew that ignorance inevitably
> goes hand in hand with forms of baseness, and that though the
> voice of the people must be heard, it cannot always be allowed
> to rule.

In his preface to *David Copperfield* Gissing is equally explicit on this question: "Dickens, with his intensely practical commonsense . . . never desired a social revolution. . . . He believed firmly in the subordination of ranks, and shows throughout his writings that he regarded 'humility' as a natural and laudable attribute of the lowly class." In the same preface Gissing expresses approval of what he calls "the conservatism which lay deep in [Dickens's] mind"; indeed, the younger novelist characterizes this conservatism as "the root of so much in him that was good and great." On these matters the two novelists were again as one – another example of their temperamental affinity. "Every instinct of my being is anti-democratic," says Gissing's Henry Ryecroft, "and I dr.. d to think of what our England may become when *demos* rules. . . . Democracy is full of menace to all the finer hopes of civilisation."

Political action was not the answer; what, then, was one to do about the poor? Gissing's response was: nothing; the poor you will always have with you, no institutionalized scheme of relief can change that. Dickens's answer was almost identical – but with one addition: "He distrusted legislation; he had little faith in charitable associations. . . . His saviour of society was a man of heavy purse and large heart, who did the utmost possible good in his own particular sphere." In other words, Dickens put his faith in "private benevolence" rather than in public aid. Gissing's summing-up of Dickens's views on this question is a perfect synopsis of his own: "Dickens, for all his sympathy, could not look with entire approval on the poor grown articulate about their wrongs. . . . He . . . thought that humble folk must know 'their station.' He was a member of the middle class, and as far from preaching 'equality' in its social sense as any man that ever wrote." This is only a slight distortion of Dickens's views on such matters. Both men, beginning with little and achieving much, became in the course of their lives middle-class snobs. There was always, somewhere in the background, the memory in both men of early disasters unforgettable and unmentionable, a fear of backsliding. Well into middle age Dickens had nightmares about his deprived childhood: each house he lived in was more sumptuous than the last, and in his later years his love of money drove him to the kind of soul-destroying behavior he had so brilliantly satirized and condemned in one novel after another. Both men sympathized with the poor: how could they not? But in both the sympathy was more intellectual than practical. Dickens fought some abuses, but generally he tended more to sentimentalize the poor than to help them, though undeniably his work helped stimulate some reforms. An example of this sentimentality is Alice in *Dombey and Son*, who represents, Gissing says, "a total impossibility, the combination of base origin and squalid life, with striking mental power, strikingly developed."

Closely related to these questions in Gissing's mind as he wrote his study of Dickens were certain considerations about nineteenth-century puritanism – and what he calls "social tyranny." Gissing cites Dickens's distrust of institutionalized religion and religious fanaticism of all shades, his irritation with the English clergy, and goes on to discuss standards of social "respectability" created and maintained by English puritanism. "Since the Puritan revolution," Gissing says, "it has unhappily seemed necessary to our countrymen . . . to profess in a peculiar way certain peculiar forms of godliness, and this habit, gradually associated with social prejudices arising from high prosperity, results in the respectable man." Echoing a theme of his own novel *Denzil Quarrier* (1892), he adds, "Though the Englishman may dispense with a gig, and remain respectable, he must not be suspected of immorality. . . . We must hold it as an article of faith that respectability not only does not err, but knows not temptation." This sort of "social superiority," Gissing argues, which is "merely obstructive," earned Dickens's "boundless contempt."

When Gissing deals with questions of class in relation to Dickens, one hears again autobiographical echoes. Dickens was "by birth superior to the rank of proletary, inferior to that of capitalist," as Gissing was. Dickens's grudge throughout his life against his own unhappy childhood "was in essence a *class* feeling," Gissing declares. "To the end his personal triumph gratified him . . . as the vindication of a social claim." And, "he was one of fortune's favourites; what he had undergone turned to his ultimate advantage." How well Gissing himself knew most of these feelings! His literary success no less than Dickens's was "a social claim"; he too made literary use of "what he had undergone," though he was by no means "one of fortune's favourites." Dickens "wore himself to a premature end in striving to found his title of gentleman on something more substantial than glory," says Gissing, who was engaged in an identical kind of "striving," ultimately with similar results. "He treats . . . of the lower middle class, where he will be always at his best. . . . To the lower middle class, a social status so peculiarly English, so rich in virtues yet so provocative of satire, he by origin belonged."

Here again Gissing could be describing himself. His fascination with Dickens was largely personal. After all, the story of Dickens was that of a novelist from the lower middle class whose books made him rich and famous. This was a path Gissing, the son of a Yorkshire druggist, also wished to tread. And, to make the identification easier, Dickens had a "guilty secret": as a child he had seen his father go to prison for debt, he and the other members of his family had lived in jail with him for some time, and he himself had been forced to go out to work at a young age. This, Gissing rightly says, was always just beneath the surface of Dickens's novels: the recollection of humiliation, of being forced to work at a common job with common men and boys. "We know how sorely this memory rankled in the mind of the successful author; he kept the fact from his wife till long after marriage, and . . . could never bear to speak to his children of [it]." As a middle-aged man Dickens was still haunted by the prison and the blacking-factory. The jail haunted Gissing, and with even better reason: at the age of eighteen he had served a sentence of one month at hard labor for theft. So desirous himself of "respectability," the young Gissing had committed, of all horrors, a *working-class* crime, and paid for it. Nor did he ever speak of this to anyone in later years.

Among the reasons for the fascination of both novelists with low life, then, is that each, having been for a time "declassed," had only just escaped it himself. "In the only way possible he learnt the life of obscure London; himself a part of it, struggling in its sordid welter," Gissing writes of Dickens. Dickens's material, Gissing says, was "taken from the very dust-heap of . . . London life" – and so, at least in the early novels, was his own.

An important emblem of the "dust-heap" of metropolitan life in Dickens's novels, as in Gissing's, is the lodging-house. No doubt some day "it will cause laughter . . . to think that young men beginning life . . . should have fallen . . . into the hands of [a] Mrs. Crupp," says Gissing, referring to *David Copperfield*, but he isn't laughing, and neither was Dickens. For both, the London landlady represented the horrors of a deprived youth in London. Gissing wrote dozens of stories and several novels set in London lodging-houses. He knew Todgers's as well as Dickens.

Finally, and in some ways most crucially, Gissing's discussion

of Dickens's fictional woman is revealing. Both alternately
idealized and despised women. It is not to Gissing's credit that he
was enthralled by Dickens's most nauseatingly saccharin, lily-white
heroines. "One discerns absolutely nothing of 'exaggeration'" in
Dickens's women, Gissing says. "Not a word, not a gesture, goes
beyond the very truth." Everyone knows how completely Dickens
failed to bring to life most of his fictional women; Gissing, like the
rest of the Victorian audience, needed an angel of the hearth to
worship. Appropriately, then, his favorite woman in Dickens is
Ruth Pinch. "Ruth is no imbecile – your thoroughly kind-hearted
and home-loving woman never will be," says Gissing. Attacking
the "extravagant idealism" of some women and their desire for
"startling innovation," Gissing offers instead an example of what
he calls "safe reform" in the person of Ruth Pinch: "one humble
little woman, who saw her duty, and did it singing the while."
With his own peculiar and complicated feelings about women, he
was in many ways the perfect Dickens reader.

Both novelists were also good haters, and when it came to the
things they detested in women they were again on common
ground. Consider this remarkable passage:

> For incontestable proof of Dickens's fidelity in reproducing the
> life he knew, one should turn . . . to his gallery of foolish,
> ridiculous, or offensive women. These remarkable creatures
> belong . . . [mostly] to one rank of life . . . the lower middle
> class. In general . . . nothing is asked of them but a quiet and
> amiable discharge of household duties; they are treated by their
> male kindred with great . . . consideration. Yet their characteristic
> is acidity of temper and boundless license of querulous or
> insulting talk. The real business of their lives is to make all
> about them as uncomfortable as they can . . . they are
> unintelligent and untaught; very often they are flagrantly
> imbecile . . . their voices shrill upon the terrified ear. It is
> difficult to believe that death can stifle them; one imagines them
> upon the threshold of some other world, sounding confusion
> among unhappy spirits who hoped to have found peace. . . .
> Many a woman . . . has brought the arts of ill-temper to high
> perfection. Indeed . . . if Dickens were now writing . . . he
> would have to add to his representative woman the well-
> dressed shrew who proceeds on the slightest provocation from
> fury of language to violence of act. . . . Nowadays these ladies

would . . . systematically neglect their children . . . and soothe their nerves, in moments carefully chosen, by flinging at the remonstrant husband any domestic object to which they attached no special value . . . these women [produce] more misery than can be calculated.

The lower-middle-class woman, choosing to cultivate "acidity of temper," "querulous or insulting talk," "ill-temper," "fury of language," "violence of act," who is capable of "flinging at the remonstrant husband any domestic object" and producing "more misery than can be calculated," is in fact Edith Gissing, *née* Underwood, the novelist's second wife, from whom, when he wrote this passage, he was hiding in Siena. Gissing took the Dickens shrew and recast her as the wife he had just left: Edith had threatened to fling a plate at his own "terrified ear." Dickens's shrews do not resemble Edith so perfectly in his own pages as they do in Gissing's. Such women, Gissing declares, bring their households "to the verge of despair by . . . persistent sourness and sulkiness":

No reason whatever can be assigned for it; when she takes offence, it pleases her to do so. She has in perfection all the illogicality of thought, all the maddening tricks of senseless language, which, doubtless for many thousands of years, have served her like for weapons. It is an odd thing that evolution has allowed the persistence of this art, for we may be quite sure that many a primitive woman paid for it with a broken skull. . . . Such women are incapable of change; they will but grow worse, till the pangs of death shake them.

So much for Edith, whom he may well have wished to pay back with "a broken skull," did the law allow it, for all her abuse of him. Consider this passage on Mrs. Joe Gargery in *Great Expectations*:

Mrs. Gargery shall be brought to quietness; but how? By a half-murderous blow on the back of her head, from which she will never recover. Dickens understood . . . that there is no other efficacious way with these ornaments of their sex. A felling and stunning and all but killing blow, followed by paralysis and slow death. A sharp remedy, but no whit sharper than the evil it cures.

It is probably a good thing that Gissing left home when he did.

"It was (and is) precisely because so many men admire the foolish in girlhood that at least an equal number deplore the intolerable in wives," Gissing says. This was his own sad story. Few passages in *Charles Dickens: A Critical Study* so plainly show the extent to which he was writing about himself and his own feelings in this work of literary criticism. Indeed, from first to last Gissing's reading of Dickens takes on a characteristic cast: that of self-scrutiny. In almost everything he wrote, Gissing wrote of himself. He was his own most fascinating, inexhaustible subject. This is as true in *Charles Dickens: A Critical Study* as in any of Gissing's twenty-three novels and 111 stories. The fact that the two men were alike in so many ways accounts for Gissing's remarkably intuitive understanding of Dickens and the undiminished value and insight of his book. In addition to the monograph and the eleven prefaces Gissing wrote for the short-lived Rochester edition of Dickens's works, he also published several articles on Dickens and did an abridgment of Forster's *Life of Dickens* for Chapman and Hall. There was long-lived interest here. The two men had much in common – most important, their lifelong scrutiny of the lower middle class and the class immediately beneath it. As Gissing's friend Morley Roberts says, "These were the only classes that [Gissing] knew well." Like Dickens's, Gissing's was a reactionary nature – though more consistently so than Dickens's. And, like Dickens's, Gissing's attacks on the Establishment had their origin not in liberalism or sympathy for the suffering of others but rather in his own past miseries and trials.

Both men, in the last analysis, saw themselves as exiles, living in an alien time. But whereas Dickens was concerned chiefly to tell a story that would engage his readers and maintain his popularity, Gissing felt obliged in his novels to report the truth he saw, no matter what the consequences. Nothing more clearly pinpoints this most revealing difference between the two novelists than an entry Gissing made in his Commonplace Book in 1889 on the antithetical ways he and Dickens dealt with the poor in their novels. "I am constantly astonished to think of the small use Dickens made of his vast opportunities . . . in the matter of observation among the lower classes," Gissing noted. "The explanation . . . is, that he did not conceive of a work of fiction as anything but a *romance*. The details which would to me be the most precious, he left aside as unsuitable because unattractive to the multitude of novel-readers." In other words, Dickens had in him a streak of his own Mr. Podsnap, obscuring as he did many of the real ills of the world in order to leave his audience good-humored and, though concerned, undisturbed. But Gissing was no romancer; the "details . . . most precious" to him were those which most illuminated the ordinary daily existence of the poor. "I have not the true English note – the foolish optimism which is indispensable to popularity," Gissing wrote to Gabrielle Fleury in 1899. One may be reminded of the differences between Tennyson, so ready to give the public what it wanted, and Browning, who went his own way. Of a section of *Idylls of the King* Browning commented, "We look at the object of art in poetry so differently! Here is an Idyll about a knight being untrue to his friend and yielding to the temptation of that friend's mistress after having engaged to assist him in his suit. I should judge the conflict in the knight's soul the proper subject to describe: Tennyson thinks he should describe the castle, and the effect of the moon on its towers, and anything *but* the soul."

If Dickens, as Gissing said, perceived romance in the commonplace and squalid, Gissing himself never did. He understood well enough what Somerset Maugham wrote in *Of Human Bondage*: "You will hear people say that poverty is the best spur to the artist. They have never felt the iron of it in their flesh."

10

Eminent Victorians and History

SWINDON. *I can't believe it! What will history say?*
BURGOYNE. *History, sir, will tell lies, as usual.*

– Shaw, *The Devil's Disciple*

I

In an essay called "English Prose between 1918 and 1939" (1944), E. M. Forster takes some trouble to describe Lytton Strachey's method as an historian. He worked from *within*, says Forster, thus rendering his characters psychologically alive. By managing to get inside his subjects he was able to bring whole societies to life, and in so doing he revolutionized the art of biography. According to Forster, Strachey was implacable in his pursuit of truth.

But which truth, and whose? Forster acknowledges that Strachey was uninterested in politics, no doubt a serious flaw in an historian; and he admits that Strachey must have got some of his biographical subjects wrong – most likely, General Gordon.

As usual, Forster himself is wrong; for if Strachey ever got anyone right, it was General Gordon. Certainly there is little else that he got right in *Eminent Victorians*. As Leon Edel has remarked of Strachey, "One may expect that the reverse of what he says is usually the truth"; his most characteristic vein is that of "malice and subterfuge." Strachey's motive in *Eminent Victorians* was to mock, to startle, to debunk – and to make himself famous. All of these things the book managed to do. But it did not manage to become history. Strachey got only a second in the historical tripos at Cambridge. He had wanted to be a history don but was considered by his examiners not good enough. He got even with them by making a farce of historiography. The readers of *Eminent Victorians* (1918), emerging wearily from a war brought about largely, so they thought, by the bungling and blundering of their fathers and grandfathers, were perfectly content, as Edel says, "to overlook [Strachey's] mannerisms, his inaccuracies, his wantonly imagined details. . . . It was too easy to laugh at the past. And it was too easy to take shortcuts with documents." The result was "skillful *collage* and *pastiche*" – but not, certainly, history.

It has been suspected for many years that Strachey was not a dependable historian. The questions still worth asking and answering are these: what exactly did he do to the historical record, and why did he do it?

Strachey's boredom with the facts of political history was a reflection of one of Bloomsbury's most obvious traits. (One night at dinner Vanessa Bell turned to the gentleman seated next to her, a friend of J. M. Keynes, and asked him if he were interested in politics. The gentleman's name was Asquith, and he was Prime Minister of Great Britain.) Surely Virginia Woolf is right when she says in her essay "The Art of Biography" that Strachey succeeded when he treated biography as a craft and failed when he treated it as an art. Biography, says Mrs. Woolf,

> imposes conditions, and those conditions are that it must be based upon fact. And by fact in biography we mean facts that can be verified by other people beside the artist. If he invents facts as an artist invents them – facts that no one else can verify – and tries to combine them with facts of the other sort, they destroy each other.

The biographer, she says – reaching a conclusion very different from Strachey's – is *not* an artist; at least, he shouldn't be.

Strachey's method as biographer, to use Mrs. Woolf's terms, is that of an artist rather than that of a craftsman. Bloomsbury's ideas about "significant form" govern his approach to history. His books are less objective than "autonomous": works of "art" with their own internal coherence and logic but with only some relation to what lies outside them – in this case, historical truth. Just as Roger Fry believed that paintings need express only themselves – that they need not, above all, be representational – so Strachey's biographies are less representational, less reproductions of exterior reality, than artistic creations, like novels, true only to themselves, to what the artist sees. Strachey's own philosophy of historiography, set forth in an essay in the *Spectator* in 1909, allows the historian to be – indeed, declares that he must be – an artist. Art, Strachey says here, is the great interpreter: through the artist's personal revelation only may bare facts be transformed into readable history. History, he says, is less a science than a branch of literature; good history-writing is as personal as poetry, and requires literary method.

All Strachey's talk about art is nonsense. He wrote about history as art, but he wrote history itself as polemics. His very personal approach to his subjects assured the destruction of "pure" historiography. He did not believe in placing historical facts before the reader and letting him form his own conclusions. His method rather was to select his presentable facts in order to force the reader to reach the same conclusions he himself had reached before he began to write. He usually had in his head the plan of a book, including what he was going to say, long before he commenced reading and research on his topic. He took more interest in his characters than in their milieux, and unfairly, I think, applied to them and to older customs and beliefs the modern standards of a less reverent age. In his books the events of past history often seem little more than a series of farcical imbecilities, trivial eccentricities, bigotries and crimes resulting from a human nature consistently imperfect. In Strachey's tendency to focus too much on personality and too little on the outside forces shaping personality, we can once again see the influences of Bloomsbury's theories of form. For, if Bloomsbury was anything, it was anti-historical. Strachey's biographies are chiefly interesting as an expression of his age's perception of others – the English Renaissance, in *Elizabeth and Essex* (1928), and the nineteenth century, in *Queen Victoria* (1921) and *Eminent Victorians*.

Both Leonard and Virginia Woolf perceived the extent to which their generation was writing *against* preceding generations. Of his circle of friends at Cambridge (Strachey was one), Leonard Woolf wrote, "We were part of a negative movement of destruction against the past." In "How It Strikes a Contemporary" Mrs. Woolf said,

> We are sharply cut off from our predecessors. A shift in the scale – the war, the sudden slip of masses held in position for ages – has shaken the fabric from top to bottom, alienated us from the past and made us perhaps too vividly conscious of the present. Every day we find ourselves doing, saying, or thinking things that would have been impossible to our fathers. . . . No

age can have been more rich than ours in writers determined to give expression to the differences which separate them from the past and not to the resemblances which connect them with it.

II

"Je n'impose rien; je ne propose rien: j'expose," says Strachey in the preface to *Eminent Victorians*. Like almost everything else in the book, this is pure fabrication. Strachey gets some of his facts right, principally in the account of General Gordon, but most of the rest of the time he distorts or simply changes what he knows to be the truth. Certainly he understands Cardinal Manning's cruelty, cunning, rigidity, megalomania, and hard-heartedness. Equally well does he understand Florence Nightingale's passion for medical reform, her hatred of bureaucracy and bungling, her genius for organization. In both of these studies he perceives the ways in which simple human affection and warmth have been obliterated by the cold ambition of aspiring natures. But he wants us to laugh at Victorian earnestness and devotion to duty, and in order to get us to do this he revises and flattens many of the facts of the lives of both. The account of Dr. Arnold is fabrication from first to last. The story of Gordon is brilliantly incisive, though even here Strachey was unable to resist some distortion of history.

Eminent Victorians is an attack upon Victorianism – more than anything else upon fanatical evangelicalism, which Strachey and some of his contemporaries felt had made the Great War possible. It is for this reason that *Eminent Victorians* begins with a study of a famous Victorian cleric – even though the equally famous schoolmaster, Dr. Arnold, was born thirteen years earlier than the Cardinal and died half a century earlier.

After a series of loaded rhetorical questions, the portrait of Manning commences its improbable, incredulous, preposterous path. Very like Butler in *The Way of All Flesh* – surely, much more the Bible of Bloomsbury than G. E. Moore's *Principia Ethica* – Strachey is so eager to condemn that he sometimes forgets to do the most important thing in satire: to bring his subject–target to life through plausible description. No one could have been as diabolical as Manning is said to be here; no one, not even Machiavelli's Prince, could always be so prescient, so politically astute.

Of course the details of Strachey's story are tailored to fit the protagonist. According to Strachey, Manning consciously blotted all memory of his wife from his mind after her death, destroying in the process every memento of their married life. The fact is that on his deathbed Manning pathetically produced from under his pillow his dead wife's pocketbook and a bundle of her letters and committed them to the care of a friend. But it is Strachey's account of Manning's conversion that has caused most the controversy, especially Manning's famous meeting with Pius IX. In fact, there was nothing mysterious about the reasons for the meeting; Manning had been asked by Sir Charles Trevelyan to deliver personally to the Pope a British government pamphlet recounting British activities undertaken to relieve the starving population of Ireland (this must have been one of history's briefest pamphlets, since the British, under Trevelyan's heartless direction, were engaged at this time in systematically starving the Irish to death). But in Strachey's hands Manning and the Pope are transformed into cunning co-conspirators, whispering to each other secret ambitions.

Strachey assumes that Manning's decision to convert was based purely on political considerations, including his assessment of the clerical job-market. Nowhere does he allow for the possibility of a reason beyond secular ambition. There is no account of any spiritual struggle, doubting, worry about heaven and hell. Having no interest in religion himself, Strachey could not believe that such a thing as a spiritual dilemma might be brought about by theological uncertainty. And yet the nineteenth century in England was very much an age of doubt. Lyell's *Geology*, the discovery of new fossil remains, the writings of Darwin, the growth of the new sciences, the so-called "higher criticism" – these things battered the citadel of Victorian faith and forced many a man and woman to worry, to doubt, to wonder. Religious conversion was in the air; and the Anglican establishment was in trouble, especially in the latter half of the century. In 1850 roughly half of the undergraduates at Oxford and Cambridge were studying for Holy Orders; by the 1880s the churches of England were half empty. Nowhere does Strachey suggest that Manning's struggle with his Anglican faith was a historical and cultural phenomenon of the nineteenth century, as well as a personal one; he writes of it as of a rhetorical or dramatic exercise. For Manning, in fact, the rites and the protectiveness of the Roman Catholic Church were appealing and soothing, the liberalized Anglicanism of his time hard to swallow. His was indeed a conservative nature. But for Strachey all religions were forms of fanatical superstition – which, happily for his own purposes, lent themselves to satirical presentation. Himself an atheist, he could not credit that his grandfather's generation might find itself buffeted by genuine spiritual uncertainty, nor that a man might be concerned about believing the wrong set of dogma and thus going to hell instead of heaven.

Much of what Strachey says about Manning is credible. He was a very hard man, he was ambitious, he was often unprincipled. Someone observed that Manning's famous magnificent forehead was a result of the fact that he had no face – an exaggeration, but he does resemble the insatiable swooping eagle of Strachey's description. Strachey's portrait of Newman here is absurd, written entirely for dramatic effect to carry forward the account of the uneven battle between the eagle and the dove. Newman was about as much like a dove as Palmerston was. Later Strachey was forced to admit that his portrait of Newman was sentimentalized. It is more than that, however; it is, like the portrait of Dr. Arnold, a fabrication from first to last. Newman was famous among other things for his violent temper; one of his biographers says that he had a tongue that could clip a hedge. Newman was impatient, unforgiving, and a good hater. But, as Michael Holroyd has pointed out, Strachey needed a passive, sweet man as a foil to Manning's hardness, and so Newman was screwed into the role. The account *Eminent Victorians* gives of Newman's return to Littlemore, for example, is wholly an invention of Strachey's.

Strachey was interested in Manning less as a real man than as a representative, as Holroyd has written, of "certain abhorrent aspects of Victorianism, particularly the fanaticism and adherence to a rigid code of behaviour." A more accurate account of Manning's life would have emphasized the struggle in the man between his desire for earthly advancement on the one hand and his yearning for spiritual peace on the other. But, instead of any sense of inner torment, we are given a caricature of a man who, for Strachey, represented everything unlikable about the previous generation.

III

To Strachey, Florence Nightingale was less objectionable than Manning, but again in his account of her he used those aspects of her character he found repellent to illustrate characteristics of the age he abhorred. He attacks her for repressing her erotic feelings and for her indifference to human relationships while he praises the energy with which she fought, all of her life, bureaucracy and convention. Strachey's picture is that of a sort of Amazon whose humanitarianism was based on a system rather than real feeling, whose sexual instinct became sublimated in good works. As so often in Strachey's biographies, there is a little truth in this picture, but again a good many facts are wrong – because of deliberate distortion or careless historiography. One result of his distortions has been to turn a genuine nineteenth-century epic into a twentieth-century mock-epic. For Florence Nightingale *was* a great woman; in Strachey's hands she appears less great than merely eccentric.

It is not true, as Strachey says, that in childhood Florence Nightingale practiced nursing methods on her dolls. The famous dog with the wounded paw is another fabrication. And so on throughout the memoir. Strachey's Florence is demonic, a megalomaniac whose psychosis took the form of a desire to heal all of mankind. He emphasizes the violence of her compassion, her pitiless philanthrophy. His description of her work at Scutari, vivid as it is, is written largely to support the theme of a being possessed. As Holroyd has said, Strachey simply distorts the facts. He calls the hospital orderlies who assisted Florence Nightingale in the Crimea a "miserable band of convalescent soldiers"; in fact, they were mostly able-bodied non-commissioned officers. He says she appointed herself purveyor of clothing to all the hospitals; she did not. He says the report she published after the Crimean War became "the leading authority on the medical administration of armies"; in fact it was privately published, little read, and entirely out of print by the time Strachey wrote *Eminent Victorians*. He says she continued to write voluminous memoranda even while she was flat on her back with exhaustion after the war; in fact, she wrote practically nothing.

Strachey's manic treatment of Florence Nightingale, so arranged as to throw into relief the deficiencies of her personality, transforms her in *Eminent Victorians* into what Holroyd has called "a schizophrenic monster, a female Dr. Jekyll and Mr. Hyde, at one moment a saintly crusader in the cause of hygiene, at the next a satanic personality, resorting to sardonic grins, pantomime gestures and sudden fits of wild fury." As in Manning's story, what changed Strachey's account from history into polemics was his hatred of the age she represented; in her as a real person he had next to no interest. He makes her into a symbol of the Victorian matriarchy that, he felt, emasculated men and bred neuroses – an embodiment of the woman who sublimates her sexual feelings in her pursuit of power over men. His suggestion that by her continued demands for reform and action she murdered both Sidney Herbert and Arthur Clough is absurd. His account of Herbert's death is another fabrication; he doesn't even get his governments right – in 1862, when Herbert died, the Prime Minister was Palmerston, not Gladstone. The story of the post-Scutari years is largely made up.

Notoriously fanatical on the subject of sunshine and fresh air, Florence Nightingale, according to Strachey, lay for fifty years in a dark, stuffy room; downstairs, supposedly, hundreds of dignitaries milled around begging for a chance to meet her. In fact, her biographers agree, her rooms, which had large windows without curtains and were painted white, faced south and were always light and airy. Visitors came to the house by appointment and were never kept waiting.

"You can feel reading the book," Duff Cooper says, that Strachey "is pleased that Miss Nightingale grew fat and that her brain softened."

IV

"Nowhere," Dr. Arnold once said, "is Satan's work more evidently manifest than in turning holy things to ridicule." Strachey's "caricature essay" – the phrase is Edel's – on Thomas Arnold isn't even remotely accurate. It is not only inaccurate: it is irresponsible and malicious. Strachey's dislike of Arnold undoubtedly stemmed in part from his own unpleasant school experiences at Abbotsholme, in part from his dislike of the pious biography of Arnold by Dean Stanley and of the more popularized account of Rugby given by Thomas Hughes in *Tom Brown's Schooldays*, a best-seller of the 1850s. Strachey's response was to exclude all documentary evidence from his discussion of Arnold and to construct a caricature rather than a portrait.

Holroyd thinks that Strachey was right to label Arnold a mediocre educational thinker and reformer; that, far from improving the curriculum of the public schools, Arnold discounted intellectual achievement in favor of good form; that he therefore changed nothing at all. In short, says Holroyd, Arnold "asked for it." Michael Holroyd rarely writes nonsense, but here, for perhaps the only time in his superb biography of Strachey, he is doing just that. Half of the things Strachey says about Arnold are inventions; his historical judgment of the man is nil. He admitted that he made up the fact that Arnold's legs were too short for his body. If they weren't "they ought to have been," he told a friend. His statement that Arnold hated democracy and wanted to rule Rugby like Jehovah over the Chosen People is rubbish. "If the King of Prussia were as sincere a lover of liberty as I am," Arnold wrote in 1829, the year after he took over Rugby, "he would give his people a constitution – for my desire is to teach my boys to govern themselves – a far better thing than to govern them well myself." Bruce Haley has said,

> His most influential reforms included turning the sixth form into a disciplinary body by making prepositors of . . . its members; eliminating fagging by restricting the privilege . . . using other sorts of persuasion than flogging; and quickly expelling troublemakers from the school. It was this series of . . . changes and the philosophy underlying them that gave Rugby its special character.

Lord Briggs has reached a similar verdict:

> He refused to rule as a tyrant or a jailer, preferring to delegate authority to the . . . oldest, strongest, and cleverest boys in the sixth form. Such delegation insured a regular government among the boys themselves and avoided the evils of anarchy, in other words, of the lawless tyranny of physical strength. From 1829 onwards he and the senior boys met from time to time, almost as equals, to consider ways of improving the school.

It was Arnold's purpose in all of this to *avoid* wherever possible rule by the physically strong and aggressive in his school.

Frederick W. Farrar's *Eric, or Little by Little* (1858), another best-selling schooldays story (twenty-four editions by 1889), does not mention Arnold by name, but has this to say on the monitorial system:

> Ill indeed are those informed who raise a cry, and join in the ignorant abuse of that noble safeguard of English schools. Any who have had personal and intimate experience of how schools work *with* it and *without* it, know what a Palladium it is of happiness and morality; how it prevents bullying, upholds manliness, is the bulwark of discipline, and makes boys more earnest and thoughtful, often at the most critical periods in their lives, by enlisting all their sympathies and interests on the side of the honourable and just.

So much for Jehovah and the Chosen People. Equally ridiculous is Strachey's charge that the boys at Rugby often left the place without ever having spoken to the Headmaster; in fact Arnold kept a flag flying outside his study to indicate when he was free to speak to pupils, which was most of the time.

Above all Strachey is dead wrong to say that Arnold adhered to the old system of education, leaving it even more firmly entrenched in the public schools than when he accepted the headmastership of Rugby. These things are not just distortions; since Strachey had at hand the material that would have refuted such charges, they are deliberate lies. As we know, Strachey was writing at a time when it was fashionable to take the Victorians apart. The disillusionment of post-war Britain found one of its voices in mocking what then seemed the useless pretensions, the moral earnestness, the high seriousness, of the previous two generations. Arnold was an easy target. After the Great War the Victorians appeared to many, because of their priggish blundering and their passion for Empire, to be largely responsible for the holocaust then just over. In more recent years, we have looked back upon the nineteenth century with more nostalgia and more affection – wishing, perhaps, that some of that idealism, that faith, that ideal of duty could become part of our lives, as they were so much a part of the lives of many Victorians. Surely this is one explanation of the tremendous explosion of interest in the nineteenth century, and especially in the Victorian novelists, that began near the end of the Second World War.

Thomas Arnold especially infuriated Strachey, and may especially appeal to us, precisely because he represents so much that we associate with Victorianism. I quote Basil Willey on this theme:

> Leading men, of whom Arnold was a type, were then conscious of a destiny and a duty, whose fulfillment, whether conceived as an obligation to God or to one's fellow-creatures, would make life significant and satisfying. This unquestioning sense that life has momentous meaning, and the 'unhasting, unresting diligence' in the effort to realize it, gives to the great men of the last century a quality which inevitably overawes the present generation – a generation which has so largely lost its sense of direction and of any distinct moral summons, and yet is anxious to recover both.

Willey assumes unhesitatingly that Thomas Arnold was one of the great men of the nineteenth century, and surely he is right. The fact is, despite Strachey's feeble disclaimer, that Arnold almost single-handedly changed the face of education all through the public schools of Britain. An important element of his greatness, as Willey says, was his ability to translate his ideas into action, actually to get things changed for the better; and of how many men, living or dead, can that be said?

Arnold believed that the common goal of men should be *good* rather than *truth*; the former was possible to attain, the latter impossible. His students loved and respected him, and when he died, at the age of forty-seven, men recognized that a great presence had disappeared from among them.

What was it, exactly, that Arnold did at Rugby to revolutionize the nine British public schools? His reforms were not so much educational as spiritual: he was interested less in how much his boys knew than in what kind of people they turned out to be. He thought it was the special opportunity of the public school to encourage moral development – inward examination and self-improvement. Despite Strachey's sneering, we all know that we measure others less by the comprehensiveness of their book-learning than by their moral qualities as human beings.

The state of the British public schools in the 1820s was extremely unpleasant. The boys slept about six to a bed, discipline was non-existent, learning virtually nil. Rugby boys, said a master in the

1820s, were "the excrescence of pond life." Anarchy prevailed. The schools were run by the biggest bullies among the boys, for whom cruel and unusual punishment of others was of course one of the pleasures of life. Besides bullying, stealing, poaching, drinking, and sodomy flourished. There was the occasional murder. By the 1850s, the public schools, having been reformed from within, were beginning to overcome many of their worst abuses, due largely to Arnold and the influence of the disciples he sent out into the world to become headmasters of other public schools, such as Harrow and Repton.

Arnold believed in the character-forming role of the public schools, and it was for this reason that he introduced a curriculum which put a more strenuous demand on the minds and bodies of his students: harder work, more athletics, intense moral instruction. It *mattered* to Arnold whether Rugby turned out good or bad young men, something for which Strachey seems unable to forgive him. Arnold made "earnestness" the guiding principle in Victorian public-school education, and it was "earnestness" above all that Strachey, seeing it as the chief emblem of the age he hated, wished to attack. Arnold's emphasis on character development was a response to the failure during this period in the public schools to care about such things. He was not anti-intellectual, nor did he stress character development at the expense of learning, as Strachey suggests. Arnold has been accused of anti-intellectualism because he did indeed believe that character development and good behavior should be the highest priorities of a public school; but he believed that these things could be acquired only through intellectual development, and he said so. Coming into a school in which the students were housed and fed in a manner inferior to that of the average early Victorian jail or workhouse, Arnold tried to give his students an ideal of responsible public service. His teaching that social duty was as important as good form was not only ambitious but also courageous – especially the latter, for the public schools of the early nineteenth century catered largely to the social rather than the intellectual requirements of the upper middle classes. Nevertheless, he accomplished most of his goals. In fact, there is little doubt that Thomas Arnold, more than anyone else in nineteenth-century Britain, was responsible for making reform in the public schools both possible and fashionable. His work inspired other schools to follow the example of Rugby. In 1861 the

Public Schools Inquiry Commission, in its report to Parliament, paid special tribute to "the personal influence and exertions of Dr. Arnold."

Let us not forget that the early and middle years of the nineteenth century in Britain were years of idealism and optimism. Arnold deserves to be judged by the standards of his own time, not those of Lytton Strachey. "In an age when Christian values were the central values of society and all deep individual problems were related to Christian morals," Lord Briggs reminds us, "Arnold's sense of spiritual insight was of fundamental importance." Arnold did nothing, as Briggs points out, to place games on an equality with work at Rugby, and this part of Strachey's attack is also spurious.

> He would have disapproved of the late-nineteenth century fetish of games on the grounds that it vulgarized intellectual labour, that it substituted self-indulgence for self-denial, and that it placed those boys in positions of command and influence who were frequently most unfit to exercise authority. Arnold . . . spurned the example of Sparta, and saw in cultivated athleticism "brutality of soul," not embryonic team spirit.

Arnold went out of his way to warn his boys against the notion that physical fitness was the only equipment they needed for life. Despite his association in the minds of many with that branch of nineteenth-century evangelicalism known as Muscular Christianity, "he never seems to have adopted a serious attitude toward games," remarks Bruce Haley, who has studied the subject carefully. Arnold was interested in athletics only for their educative value. When he spoke about "manliness," as he often did, he meant maturity of mind, not body; this was the ultimate goal of his system of education. Even *Tom Brown's Schooldays* nowhere suggests that Arnold actively promoted games or saw any real value in them. Strachey's attempt to make him out the patron saint of athleticism and anti-intellectualism is nonsensical.

One of Arnold's most famous "reforms," as Briggs points out, was to insist that all of his students speak the truth all of the time. He took a boy's word as his bond, and as a result the feeling became widespread at Rugby during Arnold's time that it was a shame to tell the Headmaster a lie, because he always believed it. Such an attitude on the part of boys in a public school was unheard of in the 1830s, but thanks to Arnold's influence it was widespread by the 1860s. The novelists, Trollope especially, were fond of trying to define a gentleman, and one of the most popular definitions of the time was that a gentleman never told a lie. Arnold's influence was everywhere.

His changes at Rugby became famous and soon spread. If a boy graduated from Rugby, it was generally thought he must be a reliable, solid sort; the universities sought Rugby graduates, and the other public schools began to feel that they should make some changes too. It had been predicted in one of Arnold's testimonials that if he were appointed head of Rugby he would change the face of education all over England. This prophecy was fulfilled – largely, says Lord Briggs, through Arnold's "simplicity of purpose and the force of his personality." He improved the tone and the atmosphere of the schools by sheer force of will, purging them of their obvious abuses while retaining many of their essential characteristics. In the hands of a less capable man, such attempts at reform would have come to nothing. His son Matthew Arnold, for many years an inspector of schools, laid plans for a national system of education which was steered through Parliament by his brother-in-law W. E. Forster in 1870. The Forster Act, which established British education on modern lines, would have been impossible without the inspiration of Thomas Arnold. Strachey's criticism of him resembles the attack of an ant on an elephant.

Bonamy Price had this to say of Arnold:

> Every pupil was made to feel that there was work for him to do – that his happiness as well as his duty lay in doing that work well. Hence an indescribable zest was communicated to a young man's feeling about life . . . and a deep and ardent attachment sprang up towards him who had taught him thus to value life and his own self, and his work and mission in this world.

But perhaps Arnold's most eloquent epitaph was that composed by his son on the fifteenth anniversary of his father's death. Having just finished reading *Tom Brown's Schooldays*, which ends with the funeral of Dr. Arnold in the chapel at Rugby, Matthew Arnold in "Rugby Chapel" (written 1857; first published 1867) invokes the memory of his father in these terms:

And through thee I believe
In the noble and great who are gone;
Pure souls honour'd and blest
By former ages, who else –
Such, so soulless, so poor,
Is the race of men whom I see –
Seem'd but a dream of the heart,
Seem'd but a cry of desire.
Yes! I believe that there lived
Others like thee in the past,
Not like the men of the crowd
Who all round me to-day
Bluster or cringe, and make life
Hideous, and arid, and vile;
But souls temper'd with fire,
Fervent, heroic, and good,
Helpers and friends of mankind.

V

On 10 February 1885, William Ewart Gladstone, Prime Minister of Great Britain, along with his wife, was seen attending a play in a West End theater. That same night the death of General Gordon and the massacre of the garrison at Khartoum were announced. It was largely for this failure and this insensitivity that not long afterward the British public substituted a Tory government under Lord Salisbury for the Liberal one of Mr. Gladstone. Long known as the G.O.M. (Grand Old Man), Gladstone was called instead the M.O.G. (Murderer of Gordon); the disaster at Khartoum kept him out of office for years.

It has been said, with some justice, that while Gladstone could persuade most people of most things, above all he could persuade himself of almost anything. There can be no doubt that Gladstone deserved much of the blame for what happened at Khartoum. He accepted the suggestion of Gordon's appointment without taking the trouble to find out what sort of man or soldier he was, and this despite the fact that shortly before Gordon left for the Sudan, as Strachey points out, Gordon had published in the *Pall Mall Gazette* (8 January 1884) an inflammatory interview on the situation in Africa.

Gladstone had always hated the idea of imperialism. This was largely because Empire was a concept dear to the heart of the Conservative Party, especially its late chief Disraeli, and to Queen Victoria, who loved to hear herself referred to as the Empress of India. The Queen hated Gladstone, and he never liked her. Nor did Gladstone's high-minded theories of political liberty accord well with the principle of British dominion over subject peoples. During these, his later years, Gladstone was interested in little except Ireland; he thought that God had put him on earth to settle the Irish question. Needless to say, Gladstone was wrong. Indeed, no British statesman has ever succeeded in anything undertaken in connection with Ireland. Rigid, dogmatic, inflexible, Gladstone was a religious fanatic, with no sense of humor and little common sense. Unbelievably, he had no interest in foreign policy, which he left mostly in the hands of others. It was always a matter of objection for Queen Victoria that Gladstone would never talk to her of foreign affairs, about which she was surprisingly well-informed. The subject bored him, she complained to anyone who would listen – including, over many years, the Archbishop of Canterbury who was the father of E. F. Benson; the Queen's conversations with the Archbishop are vividly sketched in Benson's *As We Were* (1930). At any rate, this lack of attention to details abroad brought Gladstone's government crashing down; and so he was prevented, as he came to believe, from saving Ireland.

Within Gladstone's government there were men who wished to see Britain's imperialist ventures broadened, despite the instinctive hatred of Empire harbored by their chief. These people were instrumental in the appointment of General Gordon, as Strachey suggests. Sir Evelyn Baring (later Lord Cromer), who had known Gordon in China and understood perfectly what sort of man he was, opposed the appointment to the end. Wolseley and Granville had no understanding of Gordon's character. By ignoring the matter himself, Gladstone made possible – indeed, made inevitable – the famous disaster at Khartoum. To send such a man as Gordon only to ascertain the facts of the situation at Khartoum and to manage, if necessary, the retreat of the garrison there, was asking for trouble – as Sir Evelyn Baring knew very well. The government picked for this job a fanatic who had never been able to follow orders. It was like asking a mouse to retreat from a piece of cheese. On this Strachey is incisive indeed:

The whole history of [Gordon's] life, the whole bent of his character, seemed to disqualify him for the task for which he had been chosen. He was before all things a fighter, an enthusiast, a bold adventurer; and he was now to be entrusted with the conduct of an inglorious retreat. He was alien to the subtleties of civilised statesmanship, he was unamenable to official control, he was incapable of the skilful management of delicate situations; and he was now to be placed in a position of great complexity, requiring at once a cool judgement, a clear perception of fact, and a fixed determination to carry out a line of policy laid down from above.

If Gladstone hadn't the vaguest idea of Gordon's character, Gordon, though he never really understood the Prime Minister either, understood enough of him and of the way governments work to assume that the expeditionary force sent to save him would arrive too late. Strachey's brilliantly written version of Hartington's role in this disaster of timing is largely accurate. The famous account of Hartington's slowness is among the best passages of prose Strachey ever composed:

Lord Hartington was slow. He was slow in movement, slow in apprehension, slow in thought and the communication of thought, slow to decide, and slow to act. . . . The fate of General Gordon, so intricately interwoven with such a mass of complicated circumstance . . . was finally determined by the fact that Lord Hartington was slow. If he had been even a very little quicker – if he had been quicker by two days . . . but it could not be. The ponderous machinery took so long to set itself in motion; the great wheels and levers, once started, revolved with such a laborious, such a painful deliberation, that at last their work was accomplished – surely, firmly, completely, in the best English manner, and too late.

"The history of failure in war can be summed up in two words: Too late," Douglas MacArthur once observed. It is typical of Gladstone that several years after Khartoum, looking back on Hartington's performance at the War Office during the Sudanese crisis, he remarked to Lord Granville, "I don't think he ever came to any sharp issue."

As usual, Strachey exaggerates some things, and his prejudice against any kind of religious conviction is as virulent as ever, but in the main he captures accurately the spirit of the events that led up to the tragedy at Khartoum. Indeed, "The End of General Gordon" is probably his finest piece of writing – better even than the chapters on Melbourne and Disraeli in *Queen Victoria*, certainly better than anything in *Elizabeth and Essex*. To send a Christian fanatic to Africa to effect the retreat of Christians from the onslaught of Moslem fanatics must be one of the greatest pieces of political stupidity on record. Even Lord Morley, Gladstone's admiring biographer, admits that "to dispatch a soldier of this temperament on a piece of business . . . needing vigilant sanity and self-control was little better than to call in a wizard with his magic." Gordon was the last man in the world to hold himself bound by official or any other instructions.

When the catastrophe had struck, Gladstone, in his characteristically stubborn way, refused to accept the blame. In response to an angry (and uncoded) telegram from the Queen, he wrote: "neither aggressive policy, nor military disaster, nor any gross error in the application of means to ends, has marked this series of difficult proceedings, which, indeed, have greatly redounded to the honour of Your Majesty's forces of all ranks and arms." Years later, when criticism of the government's handling of the affair had turned Gordon in memory into a heroic martyr victimized by bureaucratic incompetence, Gladstone in a letter said this of Gordon: "It was unfortunate that he should claim the hero's privilege by turning upside down and inside out every idea and intention with which he had left England, and for which he had obtained our approval. . . . My own opinion is that it is harder to justify our doing so much to rescue him, than our not doing more." In 1898 Kitchener's victorious Khartoum expedition dramatically avenged the death of "Chinese" Gordon, but Gladstone's posthumous reputation has always had to shoulder the blame for the original debacle. Indeed, a decade after Gladstone's death, Sir Evelyn Baring wrote in this account of the Khartoum affair that "it is improbable that the verdict of Gladstone's death, Sir Evelyn Baring wrote in his account of the of the Soudan will ever be reversed."

One of Strachey's rare virtues in *Eminent Victorians* is that he manages to capture and portray the stubbornness and the fanaticism of both Gordon and Gladstone. Both were rigid and violent in their prejudices, and, once they found themselves on

opposite sides of an issue which involved the potential loss of
human life, it was inevitable that blood would flow. Strachey for
once did not have to invent; the neuroses and megalomania were
there in his subjects. He did not need to change historical facts in
order to indict the government of the most staunchly religious
British statesman of the nineteenth century; that government
indicted itself. "The End of General Gordon" is the best of the
portraits in *Eminent Victorians* not only because of the brilliance of
its narrative but also because of the few distortions of fact.
Perhaps Strachey blames Gordon a bit less than he should – for
Gordon, as Holroyd says, was in truth a half-crazed romantic, a
manic-depressive fatalist, high on brandy and the Bible throughout
much of his life. To portray him as a nineteenth-century Don
Quixote, both comic and heroic, a man more sinned against than
sinning, is to ignore the fact that much of the trouble in the Sudan
came about as a result of Gordon's own absurdities. But of course
Strachey would take the side of a rebel against Victorian authority.

The two most controversial aspects of Strachey's version of the
Khartoum disaster have been his revelation of Gordon's
unpredictable drinking habits and his portrait of Baring. Strachey
is unnecessarily hard on Baring, whose published version of the
Sudan campaign is very close in slant to Strachey's own in
Eminent Victorians. Surely Baring is right when he says the
expedition to save Gordon was sanctioned too late because "Mr.
Gladstone would not accept simple evidence of a plain fact." As
for Gordon's drinking – for once the weight of published evidence
is on Strachey's side. Certainly what Strachey says fits what we
know of Gordon's other habits. He was a man who drank to
excess occasionally – a nervous drinker, abstemious most of the
time but prone to get very drunk when he drank at all. As
Holroyd says, Strachey "believed that Gordon's addiction to
religiosity and to alcohol sprang from the same epileptic source.
In this way he could bring out Gordon's intoxicated, muddled,
transcendentalist thinking which, allied to his thirst for fame, led
inevitably to his self-destruction."

Strachey was equally successful with Gladstone, who has
puzzled posterity as much as he puzzled his own contemporaries.
Did he – a model, upright man – believe everything he said, or
was he a detestable arch-hypocrite? I think Strachey and Holroyd
have the right answer: that Gladstone was really a sort of moral
opportunist – not a hypocrite or a humbug but rather a man often

self-deceived, who in the Khartoum crisis was honestly befuddled by the varying demands of conscience and policy, enemies and friends in and out of his government, and whose hatred of Empire prevented him from acting decisively in its defense.

VI

Holroyd's claim that "Strachey's influence as a biographer has matched that of Plutarch and Boswell" is exaggerated; but controversy has kept *Eminent Victorians* alive for over six decades now and will probably continue to keep it alive. In his preface to the book, Strachey advocates detachment as a necessary attitude of mind for the would-be historian; we have seen that his biographies, if they lack anything, lack detachment. Still, in his philosophy of historiography, in his pronouncements upon biographical form, Strachey has had some influence, and his books undoubtedly will continue to be read if for no other reason than that they are entertaining to read.

"We are going I think to have a new age in English literature," Gerald Brenan wrote to Strachey in 1921. "*E.V.* will then be on the border-line between new and old." The passage of time has made Strachey's age seem as remote to us as the age of Manning and Arnold seemed to him.

11
Bloomsbury and Virginia Woolf: Another View

"It had seemed to me ever since I was very young," Adrian Stephen wrote in *The Dreadnought Hoax* in 1936, "that anyone who took up an attitude of authority over anyone else was necessarily also someone who offered a leg to pull."[1]

In 1910 Adrian and his sister Virginia and Duncan Grant and some of their friends dressed up as the Emperor of Abyssinia and his suite and perpetrated a hoax upon the Royal Navy. They wished to inspect the Navy's most modern vessel, they said; and the Naval officers on hand, completely fooled, took them on an elaborate tour of some top-secret facilities aboard *HMS Dreadnought*. When the "Dreadnought Hoax," as it came to be called, was discovered, there were furious denunciations of the group in the press and even within the family, since some Stephen relations were Naval officers. One of them wrote to Adrian, "His Majesty's ships are not suitable objects for practical jokes." Adrian replied, "If everyone shared my feelings toward the great armed forces of the world, the world [might] be a happier place to live in . . . armies and suchlike bodies [present] legs that [are] almost irresistible." Earlier a similarly sartorial practical joke had been perpetrated by the same group upon the mayor of Cambridge, but since he was a grocer rather than a Naval officer the Stephen family seemed unperturbed by this, which was not so patently a thumbing-of-the-nose at the Establishment. The Dreadnought Hoax was harder to forget, however, and it was one of the first of a series of instances in which the so-called Bloomsbury Group received a bad press.

Later in the same year, 1910, Roger Fry gave London its first real taste of Post-Impressionism at the Grafton Gallery. The exhibition, with its emphasis on the works of Cézanne and Matisse, symbolized another Bloomsbury characteristic: its francophilism. This too infuriated Londoners. For a while Fry was the most hated man in the British art world. Clive Bell as a critic and Vanessa Bell and Duncan Grant as painters were also involved in the controversy by their public support of Fry. Nor did it help matters that Vanessa and Virginia Stephen went to the Post-Impressionist Ball as barefoot, saronged, nearly naked Tahitian girls. It was whispered, says Quentin Bell, that at Gordon Square, Vanessa and Mr. Maynard Keynes copulated on a dining-room table in the midst of a crowd.[2]

A few years later came the First World War, which Bloomsbury loudly and undiplomatically opposed. It was, to them, horrible, unnecessary, and ridiculous – "a war about nothing, a war that could do no good to anyone," as Quentin Bell puts it in *Bloomsbury*.[3] It is perhaps worth comparing this attitude toward the Great War with that of Bloomsbury's arch-enemy D. H. Lawrence: "I am mad with rage. . . . I would like to kill a million Germans – two million."[4] Most of the Bloomsbury people declared themselves pacifists or conscientious objectors. At this point public hostility toward them reached a sort of crescendo, and many, says Michael Holroyd, "who had hitherto dismissed the group as a bunch of harmless prigs, now pointed with alarm to the explosive danger, in the very centre of London, of an obviously militant pro-German force."[5] There is a famous anecdote of these years that goes as follows. An angry old lady asks an elegant young man-about-Bloomsbury if he isn't ashamed to be seen out of uniform when other young men are off fighting for the survival of civilization. "Madame," the young man replies, "*I* am the civilization they are fighting for."

Bloomsbury very early was perceived as a vortex of disaffection and license, as well as a purveyor of incomprehensible aesthetics. "An over-serious, self-important Bohemia, Bloomsbury was said to be composed of highly pretentious, ill-mannered dilettanti, who derived a masochistic excitement from casting themselves in the role of supersensitive martyrs to the coarse insensitivity of the barbarian world of twentieth-century London."[6] They were supposed to be arrogant, squeamish pedagogues, contemptuous of the less well-educated – symbolized for them by Lawrence, who had a provincial accent and was poor. They were described as insular, awkward in the company of people they did not know, and notorious for their private-signal system of grimaces, sarcasm, and infantile practical jokes. By outsiders these things were perceived, often, as merely the symptoms of a rigid and reactionary (rather than revolutionary) social perspective. Pretending to be ascetic world-shunners, they were instead, it was thought by some, ruthlessly ambitious. In his *Modern English Painters*, Sir John Rothenstein says this:

> I doubt . . . whether more than a few people are . . . aware how closely-knit an association 'Bloomsbury' was, how untiring its members were in advertising one another's work and personalities. . . . They would have been surprised if they had known of the lengths to which some of these people . . . with their gentle Cambridge voices, their informal manners, their casual unassuming clothes, their civilised personal relations with one another . . . were prepared to go in order to ruin, utterly, not only the 'reactionary' figures whom they publicly denounced, but young painters and writers who showed themselves too independent to come to terms with the canons observed by 'Bloomsbury' . . . There was nothing in the way of slander and intrigue to which certain of the 'Bloomsburys' were not willing to descend. I rarely knew hatreds pursued with so much malevolence and over so many years.[7]

After the war Bloomsbury continued to be perceived as exclusive, practicing a supercilious, studiously cultivated priggishness, too clever and too busy to perform ordinary services on behalf of the community, impervious to contemporary events or even charitable causes, yet too "arty" and unreliable to find places in the universities, where they might perhaps have been of some use.[8]

To the extent that Bloomsbury could be said to have sexual attitudes, these too were perceived as unusual and threatening. There is no doubt that, if Bloomsbury had any coherent theories of sex, these were among other things simultaneously homosexual and feminist. Keynes, Strachey, Duncan Grant, Virginia Woolf, and Forster were all homosexual, or at the very least bisexual. Bloomsbury's militant feminism challenged the ethics of a society which saw man as the natural source of power and authority, and so it also found itself challenging the entire system of morality upon which the system was based. In *A Room of One's Own* (1929) Virginia Woolf attacks Galsworthy and Kipling among others for celebrating almost exclusively male virtues and emotions – most of which, she says, are incomprehensible to women. Sex, says Mrs. Woolf, gets in the way of the artist; he must surmount it and become, as an artist, sexless – or, rather, male and female simultaneously. That is, he must have the sensitivity of a woman and the intellect of a man but the prejudices of neither, and thus be, in the least pejorative sense, androgynous. Virginia Woolf especially resented the fact that she was not sent to university while her brothers were – although, as she remarked once to Clive Bell, "It certainly doesn't seem to have improved all of you much."[9]

Bloomsbury's perceived exclusiveness and snobbery continued for years to antagonize others. "There was no flow of the milk of human kindness in that group of Lytton Strachey and [the] Bloomsburies, not even a trickle," Frieda Lawrence said. "They were too busy being witty and clever."[10] The poet E. W. Fordham wrote some lines on Bloomsbury's celebrated liberation: "Here verse and thought and love are free;/Great God, give me captivity." Another poem on Bloomsbury, by Roy Campbell and entitled "Home Thoughts on Bloomsbury," goes like this:

> Of all the clever people round me here
> I most delight in me –
> Mine is the only voice I hear,
> And mine the only face I see.

According to Campbell, the Bloomsbury equivalent of shaking hands was a pinch on the bottom accompanied by a mouse-like squeak. The Bloomsbury "voice," according to another arch-enemy, Wyndham Lewis, reminded one of "the sounds associated with the spasms of a rough Channel voyage"; it must be said that Lewis never forgave the group for meeting with serene indifference all the scandalous reports he circulated about it. Osbert Sitwell on the "Bloomsbury voice": they were unemphatic except when emphasis was not expected – "then there would be a sudden sticky stress, high where you would have presumed low, and the whole spoken sentence would run, as it were, at different speeds and on different gears, and contain a great deal of expert but apparently meaningless syncopation." David Cecil on Bloomsbury: "It [was] more important to be clever than good, and more important to be beautiful than to be either."

Between the two world wars opinions of Bloomsbury began to change. Its members were perceived less as dangerous and obnoxious rebels than as dreamers who had been living in a fool's paradise, stupidly cut off from the realities of the contemporary world. It is interesting to note that members of the original Bloomsbury Group who remained alive in the late 1930s were in the forefront of the anti-fascism forces and among the first to denounce England's neutrality. Nor could any group that included J. M. Keynes and Leonard Woolf rightfully be accused in the 1930s of imperviousness to social or political issues.[11]

In 1949 an anonymous essay on Bloomsbury appeared in *The Times Literary Supplement* for 17 June, from which I quote the following passage:

> For those too young to have known it, the Bloomsbury world is like the memory of a legendary great-aunt; a clever, witty, rather scandalous great-aunt, who was a brilliant pianist, scholar, and needlewoman, who could read six languages and make sauces, who collected epigrams and china and daringly turned her back on charity and good works. The influence of Bloomsbury can still be found in the adulation of France; in the mixture of delicious food and civilised values, and in 'saying what you mean.' Religion was covered by a belief in the importance of human relationships, and the belief seems reasonable enough, though one gets the impression that the milk of human kindness was kept in the larder and that the tea was usually served with lemon.

This is a slightly less acerbic view of Bloomsbury than that of the previous generation. As time passed, perspectives on Bloomsbury became less sharp and less virulent; today it is generally regarded as a group of writers and artists who were not particularly pleasant people but who contributed a good many books and paintings to the world's storehouse of art treasures and who can be excused most of their eccentricities on these grounds. Indeed, as time has passed there has been less and less agreement as to what Bloomsbury actually was and what it represented, as to who was in it and when, as to when it began and ended, even whether it ever existed or not. Perhaps all we may ever know for sure is that, in Bloomsbury, "all the couples were triangles and lived in squares."[12]

My own feeling is that, since Bloomsbury, like any other artistic movement, consisted of people, all of whom were different from one another, it is impossible to say exactly what it was at any particular time. "Any group," T. S. Eliot remarked in an essay on

Bloomsbury, "will appear more uniform, and probably more intolerant and exclusive from the outside than it really is." He adds that Bloomsbury could never really have been as orthodox and homogeneous in its views as others thought.[13] "The spectacle of gifted people enjoying themselves is never one to give pleasure to the onlooker," observed an anonymous writer on Bloomsbury in *The Times Literary Supplement* (4 July 1958). All one can really say about it, adds this writer, is that it "avoided bores as far as possible, disliked pretences, and felt a marked partiality for . . . friends." Nowadays Bloomsbury seems less revolutionary than reformist; and, in as much as its work represents the culmination and ultimate refinement of the aesthetic movement, it seems as much identified with the nineteenth century as with the twentieth. Indeed, in his brilliant biography of Virginia Woolf's father, Noel Annan takes Bloomsbury farther back even than this. Of the intellectual basis of its thought Lord Annan says,

> The doctrine of original sin was replaced by the eighteenth century belief in man's fundamental reasonableness, sanity, and decency. They violently rejected Evangelical notions of sex, tossed overboard any form of supernatural belief as so much hocus-pocus, and set their sails in the purer breezes of neo-Platonic contemplation. And yet one can still see the old Evangelical ferment at work, a strong suspicion of the worldly-wise, an unalterable emphasis on personal salvation and a penchant for meditation and communion among intimate friends.[14]

Various members of the Group have of course written reminiscences of it; most of these accounts differ widely, except insofar as they acknowledge the eclecticism and variety of the Group's interests. Vanessa Bell says,

> We did not hesitate to talk of anything. This was literally true. You could say what you liked about art, sex, or religion; you could also talk freely and very likely dully about the ordinary doings of daily life. There was very little self-consciousness I think in these early gatherings . . . but life was exciting, terrible and amusing and one had to explore it thankful one could do so freely.[15]

Vanessa's husband Clive Bell, in *Old Friends*, says this of the Bloomsbury Group:

> Beyond mutual liking [the members] had very little in common, and in mutual liking there is nothing peculiar. Yes, they did like each other; also they shared a taste for discussion in pursuit of truth and a contempt for conventional ways of thinking and feeling – a contempt for conventional morals, if you will. Does it not strike you that as much could be said of many collections of young and youngish people in many ages and many lands?[16]

Leonard Woolf has probably said both more and less about the Bloomsbury Group than any of the others – more in terms of square-footage, less in terms of information. Of his own Cambridge years Woolf remarks,

> Our youth, the years of my generation at Cambridge, coincided with the end and the beginning of a century which was also the end of one era and the beginning of another. . . . We already felt that we were living in an era of incipient revolt and that we ourselves were mortally involved in this revolt against a social system and code of conduct and morality which, for convenience sake, may be referred to as bourgeois Victorianism. We did not initiate this revolt.[17]

On the London years of Bloomsbury, Woolf said in 1964,

> What came to be called Bloomsbury by the outside world never existed in the form given to it by the outside world. For 'Bloomsbury' was and is currently used as a term – usually of abuse – applied to a largely imaginary group of persons with largely imaginary objects and characteristics. . . . Its basis was friendship, which in some cases developed into love and marriage. . . . But we had no common theory, system of principles which we wanted to convert the world to; were not proselytisers, missionaries, crusaders, or even propagandists.[18]

I am inclined to accept this as the truth. The available evidence indicates that far from having an orthodox or consistent position on most matters, Bloomsbury was often racked by internal disagreements, and to expect of it a coherent body of developed views is as absurd as to expect people always to agree with one another. Virginia Woolf attacked Strachey's methods as a biographer in her essay "The Art of Biography"; she said he was not "first-rate." In private she declared that she found his books unreadable (she was also jealous of their huge popular success). Strachey said that Forster's novels were incomprehensible (true), pronounced Clive Bell's *Art* "utter balls," and thought Bell and Roger Fry were wrong to admire Matisse and Picasso. Strachey disliked Post-Impressionism and Cubism; he also disliked Roger Fry, whom he once called "a most shifty and wormy character," and was delighted by the publication of I. A. Richards's *Principles of Literary Criticism* (1925), which went out of its way to attack Fry. Vanessa Bell thought that Fry "managed to reduce [painting] to . . . a dead, drab affair." Forster had reservations about Virginia Woolf's novels, as we shall see. Leonard Woolf once said that Clive Bell had a "fat little mind" and called Keynes "an effete and rotten old lecher."[19] Fry thought that G. E. Moore's *Principia Ethica* was "sheer nonsense," and Forster said he'd never read it. Although critics and historians have been fond of seeing Moore's philosophy as the fountainhead of all Bloomsbury theory and wisdom, in fact the only member of the Group who unmistakably shows in his own writings that he read Moore carefully is Keynes – and he rejects part of Moore's system of thought. Keynes analyzes Moore's philosophy in *Two Memoirs* (1949). Keynes says here[20] that while many of the young Cambridge men of the time accepted Moore's idea that, in religion, "nothing mattered except states of mind" – one's attitude toward one's self – most of them rejected his moral system as too idealistic. This was because, according to Keynes, it placed undue emphasis on the question of the rightness or wrongness of one's actions and conduct. Thus while they accepted the idea that awareness of one's inner nature was important, the "Bloomsburies" rejected the idea that one must always be using this awareness to analyze the moral quality of everything one did. My own impression is that G. E. Moore had as much or as little influence on the Bloomsbury Group as any other philosopher and aesthetician of the time, and that he had much less impact upon it than either Roger Fry or Samuel Butler.

Virginia Woolf represents much of what is both good and bad

about Bloomsbury, and a lot of what is most interesting and contradictory about it. She is its most important – and I think she will be its longest-lasting – voice; and she demonstrates, in her life and in her work, what seems to me most typical of Bloomsbury: its brilliant creative energy on the one hand and its paucity of warmth, of human feeling, on the other. No rule decrees that great artists must also be great men and women, and indeed the reverse is often the case. As a diplomat, Chaucer was not fastidious about the services he was paid for rendering. Marlowe, a professional spy with a passion for practical jokes, must often have stretched to the limit the forbearance of his friends. Surely Milton was tiresome to have around the house. Johnson rarely bathed. I should not have liked Jane Austen to know me too well. I am happy that Dickens was not my father, or Beethoven my friend. Henry James cast off his friends if their names got into the newspapers. Thomas Hardy was one of the meanest men who ever lived. The Russian novelists, amongst them, seem to have been prey to every known form of psychosis. A list of literary dope-addicts and alcoholics would be quite long. Not every great writer can radiate the warmth and the sympathy of a George Eliot.

There are factors mitigating Virginia Woolf's obvious unpleasantness. Leslie Stephen was sexually repressed and in many ways maladjusted, and his children suffered under the reign of meanness and puritanism of his household in its later years. Indeed, the portrait of him we get in *To the Lighthouse* shows how the strain of having such a man as patriarch of a family might very well, as Quentin Bell suggests, have driven three of his four children mad.[21] Certainly Virginia Woolf – despite some recent efforts, rather feeble, to prove otherwise – was periodically insane, and so it may not be fair to subject her to the sort of prying judgments to which we often subject the great and famous. Still, there she is, and we may judge her if we wish. In recent years many have so wished. The torrent of volumes about Virginia Woolf – biographies, critical studies, new editions of her obscurest works, publication of letters, diaries, recollections, and so on – invites judgment.

It is clear that the most dangerous relationship one could have with her was that of friendship. Her letters and diaries mercilessly attack her friends behind their backs, making one very glad indeed never to have known her. She thought that Duncan Grant should have gone into the Army, Strachey into the Anglo-Indian Civil Service, and Clive Bell into law. She believed that if T. S. Eliot had stayed where he belonged – in banking – he would have ended up where he belonged: as a branch-manager. Married to a Jew, she was virulently anti-Semitic, as several of her novels, especially *The Waves*, make clear. She was arrogant and snobbish. No one, she said, could be an artist who hadn't £500 a year to live on and a room of his or her own. George Gissing, who said no one could be an artist who hadn't starved, was attacked by Virginia Woolf in a silly essay for writing about money so much. It is just what one expects of working-class writers, sneered Mrs. Woolf, who never had to worry about starving. She was paranoid, and her persecution complex led her to assume, if you praised her latest book, that you disliked its predecessor. When someone remarked to her that it must be hard for her sister Vanessa to stand for long hours and paint, Virginia immediately went out and bought a tall desk and insisted on standing up to write. When the Germans bombed London, she calculated the serious damage in terms of decreased book sales.[22]

Bitterly jealous of everyone she knew, especially successful artists, Virginia Woolf has also been described as "malicious" – the word keeps recurring – by Alix Strachey, Nigel Nicolson, Barbara Bagenal, Raymond Mortimer, and Christopher Isherwood. "The greater the intimacy the greater the danger of sudden outbursts of scathing criticism," Duncan Grant remarked about his friendship with Mrs. Woolf. "I have the impression that no one had much encouragement [from her] for anything they produced."[23] "She was consumed with . . . neurotic jealousies of other writers," Raymond Mortimer has said.[24] Nigel Nicolson reports that she was kind to people to their faces but not behind their backs.[25] The weight of the evidence, however, is against Mr. Nicolson; that is, most of Virginia Woolf's acquaintances were perfectly used to her rudeness face to face. On one infamous occasion, Mrs. Woolf remarked to Molly MacCarthy (Mrs. Desmond MacCarthy) in a loud voice, "Molly, you are dull. DULL, Molly, you are DULL, aren't you?" But Molly, who wrote *A Pier and a Band* and *A Nineteenth Century Childhood* and founded the Memoir Club, in which Mrs. Woolf herself took so much delight, was not dull at all, according to Mrs. Ralph Partridge,[26] which may well be why she was attacked in this fashion by Virginia Woolf.

Alix Strachey's opinion of Mrs. Woolf is in many ways typical of that of most of her contemporaries: "She was not angelic in any way, in fact quite the opposite . . . she had a rather mocking spirit. Her laugh could be . . . malicious too, but unlike other members of the Bloomsbury Group she was malicous not [only] behind one's back but to one's face." And, "the sensibility which was evident in all her writing was not really present in her daily life." Whereas Lytton Strachey was rude to people on purpose to annoy them, Virginia Woolf did it neither knowing nor caring how they would react: "To her, people were rather like cardboard figures; she did not expect them to mind at all."[27] This fits with Stephen Spender's opinion that Mrs. Woolf regarded anyone outside the Bloomsbury Group as merely a two-dimensional figure, and with David Cecil's feeling that she was "out of touch with the warmth of common humanity."[28] William Plomer says, "I wouldn't single her out as a woman with an exceptional power for putting everybody at their ease and keeping them there."[29] She "enjoyed the embarrassment and discomfiture of a victim" of her sarcasm, according to Rosamond Lehmann.[30] Angelica Garnett recalls that Virginia Woolf enjoyed conversationally demolishing the defenseless.[31] Arrogant, conscious of being part of an intellectual dynasty, the Stephen girls "were very much born in the . . . purple and keenly aware of it," Raymond Mortimer remarks.[32] Angus Davidson thinks that if Virginia Woolf had been unfortunate enough to have children, they would have suffered. She probably would not have disliked them, he says, whenever she happened to remember their existence.[33] Plomer says Mrs. Woolf was overly confident in her own judgment, and others found her dogmatic. She wished, said Clive Bell, to be treated by people less as an equal than "as a superior."[34]

Almost everyone who knew her agreed that she disliked the younger generation, especially those in it who were aspiring artists and writers. She did help some (Eliot and Isherwood) and made a point of insulting others (Lawrence and Joyce; her rejection of *Ulysses* for the Hogarth Press was not even polite). If she happened, despite precautions, to find herself in a room with young people, she preferred them to be smart and frivolous rather than dowdy and intellectual, according to Mrs. Partridge. She called the next generation "the smarties" and thought the new poets (Auden, Spender, and others) both too introverted and too ambitious, too desirous of getting into print. She disliked "my generation," remarks John Lehmann.[35] Rebecca West says that Virginia Woolf was no judge of contemporary writers, especially Joyce, of whom, says Dame Rebecca, she "wrote . . . in an astonishing, almost stupid way."[36] The younger generation on the whole reciprocated her feelings. "This afternoon is sad brilliant autumn sunshine," Isherwood wrote to Spender in 1932, "the sort of afternoon . . . on which Virginia Woolf looks out of her window and suddenly decides to write a novel about the hopeless love of a Pekingese dog for a very beautiful maidenhair fern."[37]

Nor did Isherwood and his friends mistake Mrs. Woolf and her circle for avant-garde bohemians. "The Woolfs," said Isherwood – others sometimes called them "the Woolves" – "The Woolfs belonged to the previous generation, and their press, despite its appearance of chic modernity, tended to represent the writing of the twenties and the teens, even the tens."[38] In all fairness – when one remembers that Isherwood was happy to let the Hogarth Press bring out six of his books, including *The Memorial*, his second novel, which no other publisher would touch – one has difficulty seeing this as a particularly devastating attack on the taste of "The Woolfs."

There is a famous scene in James's *The Spoils of Poynton* in which, during an intense conversation between two people having tea, a biscuit falls on the floor and a third party, intruding unexpectedly, deduces all sorts of information about the intimacy of the situation from the fact that neither of the others has stirred to pick the biscuit up. Duncan Grant tells the story of the first visit of Lady Strachey to Virginia Woolf, in the course of which Virginia's dog Hans relieved himself on the rug of the drawing-room. Neither lady alluded to it, or even indicated that anything amiss had occurred.[39] This sounds a very Victorian scene. It also suggests that Virginia Woolf must have been a fastidious woman, but, as so often when one deals with her, one is surprised to find something else quite unexpected. For it appears that, despite the elegant photographs of a well-groomed woman with which we are all familiar, she was not, in terms of clothes and cleanliness, fastidious at all. Beautiful, delicate-featured, distinguished-looking, yes: clean, no. She looked, remarked Henry James after seeing her in 1908, "as if she had rolled in a duck pond." According to Rebecca West, she usually appeared as if she'd "been drawn through a hedge backwards . . . Virginia was not well turned out."[40] Madge Garland says her first impression of Virginia Woolf was that of a "beautiful and distinguished woman wearing an upturned wastepaper basket on her head."[41]

We may ask how a woman so obviously indifferent both to humanity and to individual human beings could write such brilliant fiction, especially fiction in which the relationships between people are so fully, so carefully, so skillfully defined. The answer may be this. Like Keats, whom she admired, Virginia Woolf had the capacity to enter into her creations body and soul, a capacity for a sort of negative capability, a sort of androgyny in relation to the world around her. Something of the same thing may be found in James. She lived fully in her art; apparently there was very little of her left over for the population of her real life. So, as a person who had finished her daily stint of writing, she was naked, sharp, almost defenseless against the world's irritations; unlike her contemporary Edith Wharton, she was unable to organize a personal life outside of her study. "I find the climax immensely exaggerated," she admitted.[42]

Moreover, she was writing a particular sort of literature, a literature in which what was important was sequence, cause and effect, the relationship of the parts to one another; a type of literature, in short, indifferent to the fate of *real* human beings in its single-minded devotedness to the fates of its fictional people. Like Trollope, she cared less about real people than about the people in her novels, less about the real world than the world of her novels. Ortega says that "realistic" fiction has to abolish "outer reality" in order to establish the autonomous "reality" of its own inner world; Virginia Woolf's fiction is the best example I know of fiction that is "realistic" and "autonomous" in this way. *To the Lighthouse*, whose last section is actually *about* its first section, is as perfect an illustration as there is of Fry's concept, much more influential upon Bloomsbury than anything G. E. Moore said or wrote, of "significant form": it is a novel *about itself*, self-referring and self-sustaining.

This is not to say that some of the characters in *To the Lighthouse* cannot also be based upon real people, or at least people known to the author; for of course some of them are, especially the Ramsays. In *A Writer's Diary* Virginia Woolf describes the novel as an act of exorcism, an attempt to see her parents more clearly by surrounding them and herself with scenes from her childhood, especially their summer house in St. Ives in Cornwall. (This is the actual setting – not the Hebrides, as the novel suggests; her flora and fauna are wrong for the Hebrides.) Mrs. Woolf says in the *Diary*, "the centre is father's character, sitting in a boat, reciting 'We perish each alone,' while he crushes a dying mackerel."

Forster observes in *Aspects of the Novel* that each of us feels there is always something, a secret life of some sort, behind every life we see revealing itself in action.[43] *To the Lighthouse* provides an example of this. It reveals Virginia Woolf's interest *as an artist* in her family and in other people, and it shows, by contrast, how little of this interest and warmth was translated into her real life, her relationships with other people. All life, the novel tells us, is equally important – or, conversely, equally unimportant.

In revealing a brilliant mind and a sophisticated artistry on the one hand and, on the other, the failure of these things to be part of the writer's life, *To the Lighthouse* (1925) becomes for me the perfect Bloomsbury novel. It is evidence at once of Bloomsbury's genius and of its heartlessness, the heat of its creative originality and the damp soul of its self-absorption. Bloomsbury's appeal is to the brain rather than the heart. It doesn't care, as the Victorians did, for us as readers; it cares only for itself and its own creations. Carlyle described Mill's *Autobiography* as "the autobiography of a steam-engine." I would describe much of the art produced by the Bloomsbury Group as being very much in the same tradition: self-interested, self-referring, oblivious to its reader's feelings, just as Virginia Woolf, according to most accounts, was oblivious to people's feelings most of the time.

This need not prevent *To the Lighthouse*, of which I wish to say a little more, from being a great novel, one of the very best English novels ever written. It is a brilliant expression of the isolation of the individual human spirit and at the same time a reaffirmation of the power of art to bring everything together, to find meaning in chaos, to bring coherence out of seeming disorder. Unlike *Howards End*, where the same things are attempted, *To the Lighthouse* lucidly achieves these objectives. Almost everything initiated at the beginning of the novel is completed or understood by the end, though some of the characters have to disappear to bring this about. Mrs. Ramsay's influence on her surroundings goes on long after her death; her real significance is only seen posthumously. Like her *boeuf en daube*, which to Mrs. Ramsay "seemed always to have been, only was shown now, and so being struck everything into stability," Mrs. Ramsay's impact on others can be measured only retrospectively, at the end of the book, when James has at last reached the lighthouse; when he and his sister have finally made peace with their father; when Lily Briscoe has been able to complete her painting, which in section I depicted Mrs. Ramsay as only "a triangular purple shape."

Lily, in section III, goes on asking herself Mrs. Ramsay's favorite question, "What does it all mean?" The answer comes to her at the end. It is that each of us has his or her own vision of things, and that vision, for each of us, is reality. "With a sudden intensity, as if she saw it clear for a second, she drew a line there, in the centre. It was done; it was finished. Yes, she thought, laying down her brush in extreme fatigue, I have had my vision."

And yet vision, reality, is a constantly shifting, constantly changing phenomenon, different for everyone in every situation, never static. At the end of the description of the dinner party – one of the greatest pieces of narrative ever written; Virginia Woolf always thought it her own best bit of work – Mrs. Ramsay turns, goes out of the room, and then looks back for a moment. The scene she sees, we are told, actually becomes the past as she looks at it – becomes, that is, internalized, part of the mind rather than part of objective reality. The scene she reviews, the dinner party itself, still in progress as she thinks of it, illustrates the general plan of the novel by exposing us to multiple consciousnesses, moving from one place at the table to another in order to show us how each of us is imprisoned within his own subjectivity no matter how close, physically, he may be to others. Nonetheless, as the novel also shows us, through our consciousness of others we are attached to them, inseparable, no matter how physically distant we may be from them – even from the dead, as in the case of Mrs. Ramsay, whose spirit and memory give the third section of the novel its peculiar resonance and illumination.

In a famous passage in her essay "Modern Fiction" (1919), Virginia Woolf says,

Life is not a series of gig lamps symmetrically arranged; but a luminous halo, a semi-transparent envelope surrounding us from the beginning of consciousness to the end. Is it not the task of the novelist to convey this varying, this unknown and uncircumscribed spirit, whatever aberration or complexity it may display, with as little mixture of the alien and external as possible?[44]

It is this quality of life, of consciousness, Mrs. Woolf wants to describe and convey to us in *To the Lighthouse*. The characters in section III exist largely in relation to themselves and others, as they did in section I. So Virginia Woolf, in her novel, writes in middle age of her parents and her life when she was a little girl; the action of the novel begins in 1893, when Virginia was eleven, and ends in 1903, the year before her father's death. Mrs. Ramsay is Julia Duckworth Stephen, Mr. Ramsay is Leslie Stephen – his children used to call him "the cold bath," and this aspect of his personality comes through to us very directly indeed from the novel's opening scene onward – and the house, as I have said, is the Stephens' summer home in Cornwall, from which the St. Ives lighthouse is visible in the distance, the house standing on a hill and having no obstacles to vision in front of it. *To the Lighthouse* is a record of Mrs. Woolf's consciousness not only of others but of her own past, her childhood, her nostalgia for her loving mother.

As one might imagine, Virginia Woolf's fiction brings textualists of all stripes galloping out of the closet, the chief result being that more rubbish has been written about her work than that of any other twentieth-century writer, with the possible exception of Joyce, who in my opinion deserves his critics. The post-structuralists on Virginia Woolf may felicitously be ignored; but it might be interesting to conclude by looking briefly at what her Bloomsbury colleague E. M. Forster has to say of her work.

Forster wrote two major essays on Mrs. Woolf. The first, called "The Early Novels of Virginia Woolf," was composed in 1925 and first published in *Abinger Harvest* in 1936. This essay begins as follows: "It is profoundly characteristic of the art of Virginia Woolf that when I decided to write about it and had planned a suitable opening paragraph, my fountain pen should disappear." At her worst, says Forster, Mrs. Woolf's novels give no sense of exterior reality, being merely bad reproductions of the traditional English novel: "an inspired breathlessness, a beautiful droning or gasping, which trusts to luck, and can never express human relationships or the structure of society." At her best, Forster declares, she *sees* beautifully, and is especially good at showing how a human brain works: "to convey the actual process of thinking is a creative feat, and I know of no one except Virginia Woolf who has accomplished it" – though he suspects that Joyce may be trying to do some of the same things. For Forster, Mrs. Woolf's chief contribution to the English novel (as of 1925) was the attempt to advance the novelist's art by solving the problem of how to render character in fiction.

Forster goes on in this piece to admire Virginia Woolf for, as he perceives it, her theme of bridging gaps and bringing people together – of, no doubt he thought, "connecting." And certainly this is an important part of Mrs. Woolf's work, as it is of Forster's (it is interesting to note how singularly unsuccessful both were at achieving "connection" in their private lives; perhaps this is why they wrote about it so much). *Mrs Dalloway* is about the need for communication, for bringing people together out of their disparateness. Again we encounter the seeming contradiction, the interesting question: Why should someone so personally aloof and cold as Virginia Woolf be so concerned with bringing people together and bridging gaps? Because, perhaps, she wished she could do these things herself.

In his other major essay on Virginia Woolf – actually a memorial lecture given at Cambridge in 1941 and published ten years later in *Two Cheers for Democracy* – Forster says that Virginia Woolf never really tells a story or creates a memorable character. He is, as so often, wrong; for if Mrs. Ramsay isn't a memorable character then there is no such thing as a memorable character in literature. Of course Mrs. Ramsay in a sense is not a "character" at all but a real person. Julia Stephen, however, died when Virginia was thirteen; for the novelist the portrait of her mother was partly a product of memory and partly a brilliant act of creation, or rather of re-creation. If Virginia Woolf's genius lies anywhere, beyond her brilliance as a stylist, it lies in her portraiture, which is almost always in sharp focus. One can say this of very few novelists, and Forster is not one of them. He goes on, somewhat more charitably, "she reminds us of the importance of sensation in an age which practises brutality and recommends ideals." He criticizes her for not doing justice to "the Auden–Isherwood generation," especially to its experiments in technique, even though she herself was an innovator. She remained detached from public events, committees, appeals, and so on, says Forster, because she felt women should ignore a world made and controlled by men; but her withdrawal, he observes, may also be explained by her snobbery: "This detachment from the working classes and labour reinforces the detachment caused by her feminism, and her attitude toward society was in consequence aloof and angular." Here, it seems to me, he is on firmer ground. But surely it is ironic that Virginia Woolf liked his novels more than he liked hers when she was so clearly the better novelist.

"Her going," said Rose Macaulay, "seemed symbolic of the end of an age."[45] Miss Macaulay does not name the age, but clearly she does not mean the modern age. Virginia Woolf, a child of the Victorians, a grandchild of the Clapham Sect, and a hater of the contemporary, always looked more to the past than to the present, and her literary subject-matter reflects this choice. Whatever one may think of her as a personality, one may conclude with no more eloquent praise of her as an artist than that grudgingly given by Forster at the end of his memorial essay. "Virginia Woolf," he says here, "got through an immense amount of work, she gave acute pleasure in new ways, she pushed the light of the English language a little further against the darkness. Those," Forster admits, "are facts."

NOTES

1. Adrian Stephen, *The Dreadnought Hoax* (London, 1936), pp. 10–11.
2. Quentin Bell, *Virginia Woolf: A Biography*, I (London, 1972), 170.
3. Quentin Bell, *Bloomsbury* (London, 1968), p. 45.
4. Quentin Bell, *Bloomsbury*, p. 46.
5. Michael Holroyd, *Lytton Strachey and the Bloomsbury Group* (London, 1971), pp. 41–2.
6. Holroyd, *Strachey*, p. 38.
7. Sir John Rothenstein, *Modern English Painters* (London, 1956), p. 14.
8. See Holroyd, *Strachey*, p. 38.
9. Quentin Bell, *Virginia Woolf*, I, 98.
10. Quentin Bell, *Bloomsbury*, p. 46.
11. Holroyd, *Strachey*, pp. 40 and 51.
12. Holroyd, *Strachey*, p. 39.
13. See T. S. Eliot, "The Bloomsbury Group," *Horizon*, 3, no. 17 (May 1941).
14. Noel Annan, *Leslie Stephen* (London, 1952), p. 126.
15. Quoted in Quentin Bell, *Bloomsbury*, p. 41.
16. Clive Bell, *Old Friends* (New York, 1957), p. 131.
17. Leonard Woolf, *Sowing* (London, 1961), p. 132.
18. Leonard Woolf, *Beginning Again* (London, 1964), pp. 22–3.
19. See Leon Edel, *Bloomsbury: A House of Lions* (Philadelphia and New York, 1979), pp. 212, 219, and 234, respectively.
20. J. M. Keynes, *Two Memoirs* (New York, 1949), pp. 83 and 98, *passim*.

21. See Quentin Bell, *Virginia Woolf*, I, ch. 3.
22. Holroyd, *Strachey*, p. 28.
23. *Recollections of Virginia Woolf*, ed. Joan Russell Noble (London, 1972), p. 29.
24. *Recollections*, p. 207.
25. *Recollections*, p. 158.
26. *Recollections*, p. 95.
27. *Recollections*, pp. 137–8.
28. *Recollections*, p. 222.
29. *Recollections*, p. 120.
30. *Recollections*, p. 71.
31. *Recollections*, p. 103.
32. *Recollections*, p. 205.
33. *Recollections*, p. 71.
34. *Recollections*, p. 89.
35. *Recollections*, p. 46.
36. *Recollections*, p. 112.
37. See Christopher Isherwood, *Christopher and His Kind* (New York, 1976), p. 113. The letter quoted is dated 14 November 1932.
38. Isherwood, *Christopher and His Kind*, p. 97.
39. *Recollections*, p. 26.
40. *Recollections*, p. 110.
41. *Recollections*, p. 208.
42. Edel, *Bloomsbury*, p. 198.
43. See E. M. Forster, *Aspects of the Novel* (London, 1927), ch. 3.
44. See Virginia Woolf, *The Common Reader* (London, 1925), p. 154.
45. *Recollections*, p. 202.

12

Elizabeth Bowen and Henry James

In the 1940s Elizabeth Bowen had occasion to wonder if her prose style was beginning to resemble Henry James's. Her editors complained to her that sections of *The Heat of the Day* (1949) were "more Jacobean than James." Asked in 1959 about his influence upon her work, she replied, "you can't say it's like catching the measles, because it's a splendid style, but it's a dangerous style." She disliked, she said, the very late James: "I really belong to *The Portrait of a Lady*." Her friend Virginia Woolf warned her in the thirties to beware the influence of James, Bowen reported: "she foresaw him as a danger to me."[1] From this time on, Bowen asked her editors to scrutinize her manuscripts carefully and watch out for double negatives, for sentences which placed the adverb before the verb on the "To whom do you beautifully belong?" model, for grammatical inversions and stylistic tricks in general. She was very much aware of the Jamesian "measles," and somewhat apprehensive about catching them.

Despite her vigilance, her style resembles James's in many particulars. Harrison says to Stella in *The Heat of the Day*, "You, I mean to say, have got along on the assumption that things don't happen; I, on the other hand, have taken it that things happen rather than not. Therefore, what you see is what I've seen all along" (p. 25). "You're great; it's that that I've felt in you," one character tells another in "Aunt Tatty." In "The Inherited Clock" Clara says to Paul, "Have you *no* idea that I've no idea what you mean?" (*Collected Short Stories*, pp. 271 and 636).

But there is much more here than merely a stylistic resemblance. The two novelists shared many assumptions about what fiction should do and how it should do it. The echoes of James one hears everywhere in Bowen's work, from her first novel to her last and all through the stories, are the products more of a temperamental affinity as artists than of conscious or unconscious mimicry.

James is mentioned twice by name in Bowen's fiction. Of a

character in her last novel, *Eva Trout* (1968), it is said, "This mannered manner of his was not quite the thing: no. Yet the ambiguities had one sort of merit, or promise – one was at least on the verge of the Henry James country" (p. 28). In *The Last September* (1929) Laurence, home from Oxford for the holidays, remarks, "Last term I dropped a cigarette case into the [river]. . . . It was a gold one, left over from an uncle, flat and thin and curved, for a not excessive smoker. It was from the days when they wore opera cloaks and masked, and killed ladies. It was very period, very original; I called it Henry James; I loved it" (p. 47).

But we do not need such clues to detect James's ghostly presence everywhere in Bowen. The community of interests they shared as writers is striking. Fascination by the magical moment of psychological insight, of sudden vision, is common to the work of both. Both deal in their fiction with highly intelligent people; on the one occasion when Bowen departed from this practice, she self-consciously made fun of herself and her subject by calling the story "The Dolt's Tale." Her dialogue, like James's, is less naturalistic than expressive. Uninterested in politics, and believing in any case that art and politics must not mix, like James she was so certain of the value of civilized behavior that to articulate this belief directly in her work would have seemed to her inept. An instinctive artist, with an instinctive sense of form, she shared James's interest in what she called "the art of exclusion" in writing; "shape is possibly *the* important thing" in fiction, she observed.[2] She, too, declared that the French novelists had influenced her more than the English – and said, "I am fully intelligent only when I write."[3] "Art is the only thing that can go on mattering," Stella's son Roderick reminds us in *The Heat of the Day*.

In the works of both novelists the tiny gesture may be all-expressive, with apparently small actions carefully discriminated and people's motives minutely scrutinized. In *The Last September* Lady Naylor remarks of Lois and Gerald, who are too innocent to know that they are in love, "Of course, naturally, *they* haven't thought of it – if they had, don't you see, they'd be much more careful to make it appear they hadn't" (p. 68). Subsequently, going to a meeting with her niece's fiancé, Lady Naylor has an unpleasant surprise of the sort that may be epoch-making in a James story: "Lady Naylor, coming into Fogarty's soon after four, was annoyed to find Gerald there before her. She had now, instead of being discovered, to manoeuvre more or less openly for position" (p. 221).

But there is much more even than this. Bowen was a writer, as Victoria Glendinning has observed, whose atmospheric descriptions of place and whose other-worldly perceptions, hyperaesthetic responses to shifts of mood, light, pace, and mass, may allow one to characterize her as a literary impressionist – an artist, that is, of the same school as James.[4] "It seems to me," Bowen said of herself in 1947, "that often when I write I am trying to make words do the work of line and colour. I have the painter's sensitivity to light. Much (and perhaps the best) of my writing is verbal painting."[5] Certainly the language of sensory perception is everywhere in her work. Like James, she often took as her subject something only half glimpsed or understood, and thus suggestive. A watcher, a dedicated recorder of what she saw, Bowen described her prose fiction as "transformed biography,"[6] feeling that the novelist should tell stories that are "true." Like James, she thought of her characters as persons in "real" life, and of the novelist as historian–recorder of that life. The underpinnings of her realism cannot be separated from the importance to her of "things" – *things* "are what we mean by civilization," she once observed.[7] Sounding like Madame Merle in her favorite novel by James – or any one of several characters in the *The Spoils of Poynton* – Bowen writes in *The Death of the Heart* (1938) of the "solicitude for *things*. One's relation to them, the daily seeing or touching, begins to become love, and to lay one open to pain" (p. 179). Her interest in "things," especially English "things," must have been generated in part by their romantic strangeness to her – for England was no more her native land than it was Henry James's.

It hardly needs saying that Bowen's chief interest was in manners: the texture by which society is bound together, if at all. She was fascinated by what underlay social behavior in personal life at its most intense. Both Bowen and James pay great attention to *place* and the atmosphere it generates. Both write of houses as of personalities; the furnishings declare their owners. Both are fond of architectonic images, and use them everywhere; there is, for example, this, in *The Last September*: "In this world, affections were rare and square – four-square – occurring like houses in a landscape, unrelated and positive, though with sometimes a large bright looming – as of the sunned west face of Danielstown [the house; modelled on Bowen's Court] over the tennis courts"

(p. 45). And both employ the international theme to help express their interest in comparative manners. Bowen's first novel, *The Hotel* (1927), set on the Italian Riviera, is a book about the English abroad, a subject she was to mine again and again. Bowen perhaps makes fun both of James and herself in her story called "Shoes: An International Episode," in which a young Englishwoman becomes hysterical because the shoes she left outside her door to be cleaned in a French hotel are mixed up with somebody else's. She and her husband spend much of their time on their honeymoon worrying about local customs. "How," asks the heroine, "can we possibly eat peaches in a cathedral?" (*Collected Short Stories*, p. 244).

On the subject of passion Bowen, like her great predecessor, has the art of saying both everything and nothing, so that we may be unsure how well we know the characters' feelings – appropriately, since often enough the characters do not know their own feelings. The illusions people have about one another are as central to her stories as they are to James's; people *study* each other carefully in the works of both, and often draw the wrong conclusions. The way people see or avoid seeing one another is always a central theme in her books, as it is in James's.

Bowen's novel *Friends and Relations* (1931) is most eloquent on this subject. As in *The Golden Bowl* the focus is on two couples closely connected. One of the women is in love with her sister's husband, and he with her. Both marriages, as well as the ostensibly intimate four-sided relationship, are beset with un-nameable flaws and secrets. We are never certain whether or not the would-be adulterers consummate their relationship (probably not). Each of the ladies has a confidante, in good Jamesian fashion. All four are seen through the eyes of a young girl, whose ignorance of the world leaves much unsaid, much to be guessed or misunderstood, but who winds up understanding more about everything than she bargained for. In at least one instance the observations of the adolescent Theodora in *Friends and Relations* strike a Jamesian note:

> There were moments – Edward's handwriting on an envelope, his name casually in Janet's talk – when Theodora, exasperated, sighted a large possibility of destruction; when Janet's composure became something precariously but calmly held, some very delicate glass or a dish piled high with fruit that balanced curve

on curve just not tottering. To splinter the vase, to knock the dish out of Janet's hand, Theodora had only to cry: 'You still love him.'   (p. 97)

As in *The Golden Bowl*, with its similar imagery, the weaker, more innocent spouses triumph over the others in keeping their flawed marriages intact, and ultimately bring the relationships nearly back to their original standing. It is the victory of convention over love, a theme equally dear to James. What Janet Egleson Dunleavy has noted in Bowen's work may be said with equal justice of James's: "even when dialogue is witty and relationships sophisticated, a contrasting melancholy just beneath the surface . . . is barely perceptible in what the principal characters think and feel but never reveal to others."[8]

Many of Bowen's stories are "ghost" stories of one variety or another, in which the "ghosts" seem more real to the characters than "real" people. As James did, Bowen felt the thinness of the barrier between the living and the dead. What has been called James's "vampire" theme – the preponderance in his stories of people living in various ways off of others, drawing sustenance and the life-blood out of them in the process – may be found everywhere in Bowen's fiction, in which few human relationships are balanced or mutually satisfying. Among James's many fictions it is difficult to find any relationships between adults which are equally satisfying or fruitful for both partners. His is always a tragic vision of needs unfulfilled – or fulfilled at a terrible price. Bowen and James both populate their tales with characters who lead lives of frustration and emptiness, hoping for something wonderful to happen and being frustrated in this desire; one thinks of Bowen's story "The Secession," her version of James's "The Beast in the Jungle."

On the other hand Bowen's fiction, like James's, is replete with characters who know one another's minds so well that talk is unnecessary – and when it does become necessary they often interrupt and finish each other's sentences.

Living is a complicated business, and contented people are not always interesting subjects for the novelist. Bowen and James both believed, and show in their work, that the tragic complexity rather than the success of interpersonal relationships could be the writer's ideal subject. In this they differ markedly from most of their Victorian predecessors. Their characters, stultified or trapped,

tend to bring disaster to others in the act of trying to free
themselves.

The sympathetic understanding of both sexes makes for a kind
of androgyny in both writers; the sex of the author becomes
irrelevant, and other people's lives are seen with the novelist's
sexual antennae unplugged.

Partly for this reason, perhaps, children who have not yet
reached sexual awareness play a large part in the fiction of both.
Each was fascinated by human innocence and the havoc it could
bring, by virtue of its very ignorance, into the lives of the more
worldly. In the stories of Bowen and James, children are often
palmed off on relatives or others, become acutely conscious of
their unfamiliar surroundings, and are plunged into the corrupting
maelstrom of the dance of desire going on around them. Such
prodigies tend to grow precociously observant. James's Maisie is
only one of many such characters. The tightrope between
innocence and knowledge may be found hanging somewhere in
all of Bowen's best novels; the confrontation of innocence with
evil is everywhere in her books, as it is in James's. Often the
theme finds life in her novels in the consciousness of adolescent
girls surrounded by a corrupt adult world they are resolutely
engaged in spying upon. "It is not only our fate but our business
to lose innocence," Bowen once remarked.[9]

But innocence can be inadvertently cruel in its ignorance, and
it is this understanding and this theme which draw Bowen and
James most closely together. We have seen how impotent
knowledge can be when confronted with innocence in Bowen's
Friends and Relations. In *Eva Trout* "innocence" actually kills; the
child with the gun illustrates the lethal potential of innocence. In
Bowen's *To the North* (1932) innocence, in the form of the heroine
Emmeline – chronologically adult but emotionally childish – is
single-minded, immoderate, and ultimately murderous. "Innocence always calls mutely for protection," Graham Greene
reminds us in *The Quiet American* (1955), "when we would be so
much wiser to guard ourselves against it; innocence is like a dumb
leper who has lost his bell, wandering the world meaning no
harm."

We may best be able to see the confluence of many of these
themes in *The Death of the Heart*, Bowen's masterpiece. Coming
into contact with the others in the book, young Portia is robbed of
her genial innocence, a gradual but inexorable process. Most of

the action of the novel is seen through her eyes. All the personal relationships in *The Death of the Heart* prove unsatisfactory and disillusioning; betrayal is the rule rather than the exception. As so often in James's novels, the focus here is on a civilization too frivolous and unfeeling and predisposed to falseness to be serious. There is a striking passage, in this novel, about the cruelty of innocence:

> Innocence so constantly finds itself in a false position that inwardly innocent people learn to be disingenuous. Finding no language in which to speak in their own terms, they resign themselves to being translated imperfectly. They exist alone; when they try to enter into relations they compromise falsifyingly – through desire to impart and to feel warmth. The system of our affections is too corrupt for them. They are bound to blunder, then to be told they cheat. In love, the sweetness and violence they have to offer involves a thousand betrayals for the less innocent. Incurable strangers to the world, they never cease to exact a heroic happiness. Their singleness, their ruthlessness, their one continuous wish makes them bound to be cruel, and to suffer cruelty. The innocent are so few that two of them seldom meet – when they do meet, their victims lie strewn all round.   (p. 133)

The need for illusion to preserve sanity – a radical theme of *The Ambassadors*, to take just one example from James, and a radical theme as well of one work after another by James's devoted disciple Joseph Conrad – is articulated bluntly in *The Death of the Heart* (pp. 327, 333, and 409) when the writer St. Quentin tells Portia, "If one didn't let oneself swallow some few lies, I don't know how one would ever carry the past." Portia wonders if perhaps "it's better" after all "to know." "No, truly it is not," St. Quentin replies. His final words to her express most eloquently Elizabeth Bowen's great debt to Henry James. After all, says St. Quentin, "society" is people "making little signs to each other."

NOTES

Page references for quotations from Elizabeth Bowen's novels and short stories are given in the text. The novels are quoted from the original editions (dates as specified on first mention); the short stories from *Collected Short Stories* (New York, 1982).

1. See Victoria Glendinning, *Elizabeth Bowen: Portrait of a Writer* (London, 1977), pp. 153 and 99.
2. *Why Do I Write? An Exchange of Views between Elizabeth Bowen, Graham Greene, and V. S. Pritchett* (London, 1948; Folcroft, PA, 1969).
3. See Glendinning, *Bowen*, pp. 165 and 16.
4. Glendinning, *Bowen*, p. 98.
5. See Glendinning, *Bowen*, p. 242n.
6. Janet Egleson Dunleavy, "Elizabeth Bowen," *Dictionary of Literary Biography*, XV (1983), 38.
7. See Glendinning, *Bowen*, p. 131.
8. Janet Egleson Dunleavy, "The Subtle Satire of Elizabeth Bowen and Mary Lavin," *Tulsa Studies in Women's Literature*, 2, no. 1 (Spring 1983), 81.
9. See Elizabeth Bowen, "Out of a Book," in *Orion II* (1946); repr. in *Collected Impressions* (London and New York, 1950).

13

Barbara Pym
and the War of the Sexes

*Perhaps the time will come when one may be permitted to do
research into the lives of ordinary people.*

– No Fond Return of Love

"What a good thing there is no marriage or giving in marriage in
the after-life," remarks Jane Cleveland in *Jane and Prudence* (1953);
"it will certainly help to smooth things out" (p. 214). The war of
the sexes goes on continually in Barbara Pym's novels, with men
apparently winning it at some moments, women at others. "As an
anthropologist," Rupert Stonebird in *An Unsuitable Attachment*
(1982) knows "that men and women may observe each other as
warily as wild animals hidden in long grass" (opening paragraph,
p. 13).

Pym has sometimes, unfairly, been compared to Jane Austen,
and readers coming to her for the first time have been heard to
proclaim their disappointment upon finding out that her work is
not at all like Austen's. Of course this is not Pym's fault; indeed,
given her own reverence for Austen, she would have been the
first to find the comparison inappropriate. Like the books of all
great novelists, hers are unique: no one is like her, she is like no
one else. A convenient comparison one could make, and that by
way of a sort of thematic shortcut only, might be to say that her
novels resemble Henry James's in containing amongst them
virtually no relationship between the sexes which is entirely
satisfactory. In the works of both authors – and in the works of
each the balance of power keeps shifting – we see men victimized
or taken advantage of by women, and women victimized or taken
advantage of by men. What has been called James's "vampire"
theme – one human being living off of and gaining sustenance
from another, and depriving him or her of life in the process – is
ubiquitous in Pym's novels as well.

201

This essay will focus on four of Pym's novels: *Jane and Prudence*, *Less than Angels* (1955), *A Glass of Blessings* (1958), and *The Sweet Dove Died* (1978; written in the 1960s). But brief reference to several other sources may help to set the scene of conflict under scrutiny here. Pym's closest friend and literary executrix Hazel Holt has observed, "Do you remember, in *A Very Private Eye* she says: 'With the years men get more bumbling and vague, but women get sharper.' There is no doubt that she thought women the stronger sex" (letter to the present writer, 14 January 1985). In *A Very Private Eye: The Diaries, Letters and Notebooks of Barbara Pym* (1984) we find her remarking in a letter to Philip Larkin in 1977 that her "treatment of men characters suggested [to some readers] that I had a low opinion of the sex" (p. 303) – a suggestion with which she disagreed but which, by her own admission, she found herself unable to refute. Mildred and Mrs. Morris in *Excellent Women* (1952), "a couple of women against the whole race of men" (pp. 23–4), are among dozens of female characters in Pym's novels who sometimes see themselves as fighting a lonely battle against superior odds – the power, the impregnability, and the callousness to the other sex of men.

Equally to the point are two other passages in *A Very Private Eye*. "Women have never been more terrifying than they are now," Pym wrote in her diary in 1955; "no wonder men turn to other men sometimes" (p. 197). And in 1963, corresponding with her friend Bob Smith, Pym inquired, "Why is it that *men* find my books so sad? Women don't particularly" (p. 223). If men find her books "sad" perhaps it is because, in them, men are so often portrayed on the one hand as overbearing and egotistical and on the other as weak and incompetent, dependent for their survival from day to day upon the unselfish and untiring support of exhausted and harassed – and, yes, "excellent" – women.

There is a battle going on all right in Pym's novels, but the most interesting thing about it is that no one is winning.

Jane and Prudence, arguably Pym's best novel, depicts women as victims of men, of their selfishness and brutality. Some nastiness on the distaff side is also visible, but *Jane and Prudence* remains the most sustained attack on men among Pym's novels.

The small case against women here may be quickly summarized. The novel argues that men evade marriage when they can, but often are trapped into it by women; the latter "take precedence" in marriage, and "husbands exist only in relation to" them (p. 8). A husband, Jane observes, is "someone to tell one's silly jokes to, to carry suitcases and do the tipping at hotels" (pp. 10–11). Jessie Morrow, the intrepid husband-hunter in *Jane and Prudence*, declares that "women are very powerful – perhaps they are always triumphant in the end" (p. 110): she means in their relationships with men. We have seen that Pym believed this herself. In *Jane and Prudence* Jessie overpowers the elusive widower Fabian Driver and makes him marry her. Driver's first wife, Jessie learns, had typed his manuscripts for him: "Oh, then he had to marry her . . . that kind of devotion is worse than blackmail – a man has no escape from that" (p. 126) – and she formulates her matrimonial plans accordingly. For Fabian, finally, "it was as if a net had closed round him" (p. 199); the wild animal hidden in the long grass is brought down by the huntress. Jane remarks that women "are getting so much bigger and taller and men are getting smaller" (p. 161) – and, since "Victorian times," the relation between the sexes has been reversed. The women are in charge now, the men are exhausted (p. 172). Jane looks upon the first sex with pity: "men are such children in many ways" (p. 150).

But the primary animus in *Jane and Prudence* is against men; and if male readers do find Pym's books sad, this novel must be one of the saddest. What Pym dwells on here, perhaps more single-mindedly than anywhere else, is the *heartlessness* of men. On two occasions Fabian is said to be *eating* hearts – both times *en casserole* (pp. 33 and 46). Indeed, the eating-habits of men are a sort of moral index here. "A man must have meat," declares Mrs. Mayhew (p. 30). "A man needs eggs!" says Mrs. Crampton (p. 51). "A man needs a cooked breakfast," observes Miss Doggett (p. 90). "Man needs bird," Jane thinks: "Just the very best, that is what man needs" (p. 52). While Arthur Grampian, Prudence Bates's boss, eats smoked salmon for dinner at his club, Prudence, we learn, has to choose between shepherd's pie and stuffed marrow in a restaurant (p. 41). When Jane and her husband lunch at Mrs. Crampton's restaurant, Jane is given bacon, one egg, and some potatoes, while Nicholas is presented "with *two* eggs and rather more potatoes. . . . Nicholas accepted his two eggs and bacon with the implication that his needs were more important than his wife's with a certain amount of complacency" (p. 51). In this novel men are consumers, women providers.

In Jane's words, men "expect women to do quite everything for them" (p. 189). They expect in fact to rule, while the women seem resigned and reduced to serving them. This carries over into the arena of interpersonal relations. Thus Grampian is pleased to see that Prudence is in love with him, though he has no plans to do anything about it: "the tears in Miss Bates's eyes proved that he still retained his old power over women," he reflects with satisfaction (p. 197). The death of Fabian's wife, we learn, "came as a great shock to him – he had almost forgotten her existence"; he retaliates for this selfish act of his late wife by carrying to her grave flowers said to be not "her favourites" (p. 28).

> He had been unprepared for her death and outraged by it, for it had happened suddenly, without a long illness to prepare him, when he had been deeply involved in one of the little romantic affairs which he seemed to need, either to bolster up his self-respect or for some more obvious reason.   (p. 57)

And, on the relationship of Grampian and his wife:

> it was splendid the things women were doing for men all the time . . . Making them feel, perhaps sometimes by no more than a casual glance, that men were loved and admired and desired when they were worthy of none of these things – enabling them to preen themselves and puff out their plumage like birds and bask in the sunshine of love, real or imagined, it didn't matter which.   (p. 75)

The operative clause here is "when they were worthy of none of these things."

Both Jane and Prudence are asked again and again to prop men up in various ways, to massage their egos – and without much reward, for the men in the novel are clammily selfish. Thus the relation of the sexes in *Jane and Prudence*. Men, it is said, require love and attention, while it is left to women to type their theses, correct their proofs, put their sheets sides-to-middle, bring up their children, and balance their housekeeping budgets (p. 127). "Oh, the strange and wonderful things that men could make women do!" Jane thinks (p. 158). When Prudence loses Fabian to Jessie, she (Prudence) observes that men prefer "restful and neutral" women (p. 193) to those less passive; men need to dominate. Inconstant and promiscuous themselves, men require steady women waiting at home (p. 213). In the war of the sexes "husbands take friends away" from their wives (p. 83), "ridicule" and "soon dispose of" women's views (p. 134), and, by withholding their "sympathy" for women, reduce them to dependence on "the sympathy of other women" (p. 200). Men think women should be satisfied with their own company (p. 205), while inducing in their wives "the blankness and boredom of indifference": thus do women "suffer" for their attachments to men (p. 198).

The truth, *Jane and Prudence* suggests, is that men are more "limited" than women (p. 165). A woman's love can transform a man; without a woman's love a man would be a cipher. Having lost Fabian, Prudence finds herself stuck with the colorless Geoffrey. "What object could Fate possibly have," Prudence wonders at the end of the novel. "But of course, she remembered, that was why women were so wonderful: it was their love and imagination that transformed these unremarkable beings. For most men . . . were undistinguished to look at, if not positively ugly."

So much for men.

Less than Angels is more even-handed in its approach to the sexes, perhaps because its central subject lies elsewhere. Still, in it one gets glimpses of Pym's characteristic views on the differences between men and women.

Again we see here women victimized in various ways by men.

> Some of them had been fortunate enough to win the love of devoted women – women who might one day become their wives, but who, if they were thrown aside, would accept their fate cheerfully and without bitterness. They had learned early in life what it is to bear love's burdens, listening patiently to their men's troubles and ever ready at their typewriters. (p. 46)

Tom Mallow, meeting Deirdre Swan, "in her eyes . . . had read the unspoken question, that was so often in women's eyes, 'When shall I see you again?' His first impulse had been to ask, 'Are you any good at typing?' " (p. 64). The novel refers to "the universal concern of women for men" (p. 193), but not to any reciprocal feeling on the part of men. In one of the most moving sections of *Less than Angels*, Elaine, Tom's first and now forgotten love, remembers Anne Elliot's famous words in *Persuasion* on the nature and the quality of feminine and masculine feelings:

> 'We certainly do not forget you so soon as you forget us. It is, perhaps, our fate rather than our merit. We cannot help ourselves. We live at home, quiet, confined, and our feelings prey upon us. You are forced on exertion. You have always business of some sort or other to take you back into the world immediately, and continual occupation and change soon weaken impressions.'   (p. 183)

That word "fate" keeps cropping up in Pym's novels, whether used by herself or quoted from elsewhere. She shared with Jane Austen a deep sympathy for the hapless fate of the undowried, unmarried woman. This theme is articulated everywhere in Pym's novels. Women are stronger than men, yes; but, by needing women and playing on their sympathies, men *use* them to their own advantage: it is their *fate* to be used. Thus, at the end of *Less than Angels*, Alaric Lydgate needs Catherine Oliphant, discarded by Tom, to put his life in order: "Like so many men, he needed a woman stronger than himself" (p. 238).

But the novel also gives the other side of the case. "What seems wrong with so many relationships now," Catherine observes, is "the women feeling that *they* are the strong ones and that men couldn't get on without them" (p. 111). It may be true, but it is tactless and self-destructive of women to operate openly on this basis, which so many do. (In *Northanger Abbey*, we may recall, Jane Austen observes that a woman, should she wish to marry, must never let a man see how clever she is.) "Women do think the worst of each other, perhaps because only they can know what they are capable of. Men are regarded as being not quite responsible for their actions" (p. 132), Pym's Catherine observes. In *Less than Angels* women take advantage of men by "intimidating" them and "often leading them captive in marriage" (p. 37). The stronger of the animals in the long grass is the female, but she does not always exercise her power with discretion and gentleness. Catherine sometimes employs analogies similar to Rupert Stonebird's memorable one in *An Unsuitable Attachment*. We catch her, in *Less than Angels*, thinking this:

Men appeared to be so unsubtle, but perhaps it was only by contrast with the tortuous delicacy of women, who smothered their men under a cloud of sentimental associations – *our* song, *our* poem, *our* restaurant – till at last they struggled to break free, like birds trapped under the heavy black meshes of the strawberry net.   (p. 107)

Being the stronger sex does not necessarily make women happy; Catherine feels "the general uselessness of women if they cannot understand or reverence a man's work, or even if they can" (p. 102).

The unwinnable war goes on in *A Glass of Blessings*. As in *Jane and Prudence*, men are given an especially low valuation here.

In the opening chapter we are presented with an account of a woman civil servant "discovered preparing Brussels sprouts behind a filing cabinet" in her office; "poor thing, I suppose she felt it would save a precious ten minutes when she got home" (p. 11), Sybil, Wilmet Forsyth's mother-in-law, observes. A woman cowering behind a filing cabinet while she gets a head start on her husband's dinner is appropriately emblematic of the story *A Glass of Blessings* tells. The ladies discussing this event agree that when it comes to food, men look upon every meal "as no more than was due to them. . . . Women are prepared to take trouble . . . whereas men . . . hardly think it worth while" (pp. 13–14). Wilmet's friend Rowena Talbot, a good cook who would like to experiment at home with unusual menus, is prevented from doing so by the "tyranny" of her husband and children (p. 37). Rowena's husband Rodney "complacently" agrees that his wife "does have a good deal to put up with" (p. 138), but has no plans to alter his pleasant life. So it is not surprising to find that Rowena envies "really *wicked* women, or even despised spinsters" – because, as she says, they may continue to "have their dreams," whereas the married woman knows "that there's absolutely no hope of their coming true . . . the despised spinster," at least, is "*free!*" (p. 149).

In fact in *Crampton Hodnet*, the novel Pym put aside in 1939, and only recently published (1985), we come face to face with just such a person – a "despised spinster" who appears to be "*free!*" –

or so it seems to another unhappy wife who notices, while
lunching out, that her neighbor's hands are "ringless."

> Then, presumably, she hadn't got a husband. She was a
> comfortable spinster with nobody but herself to consider. Living
> in a tidy house not far from London, making nice little supper
> dishes for one, a place for everything and everything in its
> place, no husband hanging resentfully around the sitting-room,
> no husband one moment [paring] gooseberries and the next
> declaring that he had fallen in love with a young woman. [She]
> sighed a sigh of envy. No husband.   (p. 172)

Here are enumerated by Barbara Pym some of the advantages of
spouselessness apparent to an independent-minded Oxford
graduate in her early twenties. There is relief as well as "envy" in
the resounding refrain of this passage, "no husband." Pym's
failure to marry became more galling to her in later life, as some
of the subsequent novels plainly demonstrate.

But in *A Glass of Blessings* marriage is still portrayed as a dead
end. Wilmet, who believes that her clerical friend Father Thames
"went about cajoling or bullying women into being the answer to
prayer" (p. 27), is also unhappily married. She falls in love with
Piers Longridge, who turns out to be living with a male model.
Wilmet's husband James, we discover late in the novel, is having
an affair with our old friend Prudence Bates. And so it goes: the
women in *A Glass of Blessings* are cabined, cribbed, and confined,
their morale "tottering" (p. 151), while the men do as they
please. "Men are so narrow-minded and catty" (p. 215), Rowena
complains.

But the "tyranny" of men is perceived here, once again, as
unnatural, since they remain the weaker vessels. While Wilmet
admits that "women especially . . . want to be needed," she also
observes that "our advice and strength" are "sometimes greater
than theirs" (p. 165). Despite Rodney's career at public school and
university, in the war and in the Civil Service, Wilmet sees "that I
with my sheltered life was in some ways more fitted to deal with
certain things" than her best friend's husband (p. 201). Men are
like bees seeking a queen: when they find her "they will follow
her to the hive" (p. 233).

This queenliness is broadly criticized in *A Glass of Blessings*.
"Women are so terrifying these days and seem to expect so much,

really far more than one could possibly give," the homosexual Piers declares (p. 8). We may recall Pym's 1955 diary entry (*A Glass of Blessings* was written in 1955–6): "Women have never been more terrifying than they are now . . . no wonder men turn to other men sometimes." In *A Glass of Blessings* the men wear themselves out in work, the women remain unchanged – and thus, ultimately, stronger. "Women nearly always outlive men," as Sybil remarks (p. 118). When Wilmet and her friend Mary Beamish go out to lunch one day they observe in their midst "a rather uncomfortable-looking husband with his wife's parcels piled on his knee. 'That poor man looks so miserable,'" Mary comments. "At that moment a young clergyman with an elderly woman, presumably his mother, came in. The two men looked at each other as specimens in a zoo might, each commiserating with the other in his unhappy situation." Wilmet merely observes that many men "let themselves be led by their women" (pp. 81–2), and the subject is dropped. But the image of the two caged specimens – once, perhaps, wild animals hidden in the long grass who have been definitively captured – lingers on. "One never knows what men are *feeling*," Wilmet muses (p. 213), but in the restaurant scene it is clear that they are feeling caught.

A final observation on *A Glass of Blessings*. In it the relation of the sexes seems to inspire in some women a modest sadism. The usually sensible Wilmet agrees that refusing a man in marriage brings with it "a kind of triumph" (p. 24). And her mother-in-law declares that "Women like to see men doing domestic things, especially if they are not done very well – if the tea is too weak or too strong, or the toast burnt" (p. 188). The perverse pleasure of seeing men founder outweighs the inconvenience of bad tea or burnt toast.

The Sweet Dove Died is perhaps Pym's most complex treatment of the war of the sexes. In addition to the struggle between men and women for control of their lives, this novel also tells the story of a battle between a middle-aged woman (Leonora) and a younger man (Ned) for the heart, soul, and body of another young man (James). Peripherally, there is the abbreviated contest between uncle (Humphrey) and nephew (James) for Leonora, and that (equally abbreviated) between Leonora and Phoebe for James. *The Sweet Dove Died* may be the most even-handed among this group in its account of the foibles, the strengths and the weaknesses, of both sexes. Though no one is winning it, the battle rages on in this novel with a ferocity unmatched in its predecessors.

The very first sentence serves notice that again Pym's view of men will not be complimentary: "'The sale room is no place for a woman,' declared Humprey Boyce" (p. 7). He thinks of women as hopelessly ignorant when it comes to the buying and selling of antique books. Humphrey's further thoughts on the matter are given to us:

> A *book* sale was certainly no place for a woman; had it been a sale of pictures or porcelain, fetching the sort of inflated prices that made headline news, or an evening sale – perhaps being televised – to which a woman could be escorted after being suitably wined and dined – that might have been another matter altogether. (pp. 8–9)

Women are pronounced satisfactory cooks for men, and indeed spend much of their time trying, for the most part unsuccessfully, to capture them with culinary temptations – having, it seems, few other weapons at their disposal. But the many meals Leonora serves up to James and Humphrey and others gain her little ground (she forgets which of them likes chocolate mousse).

Ned sees his defeat of Leonora in his contest for the possession of James as reducing her to "a wounded animal crawling away to die" (p. 159) – another extension of the metaphor of the wild animal hidden in the long grass – and comments complacently, "Life is cruel, and we do *terrible* things to each other" (p. 160). Here he is the zookeeper with the net. Women's chief function and virtue, according to Ned, is to forgive men: "That was what women should do and even did, in his experience; they overlooked things, they took people back, above all they forgave" (p. 199). Not all the women in this novel are so malleable, however. Leonora's friend Liz "now loved cats more than people" because her "husband had 'behaved so appallingly'" that forgiveness is out of the question (p. 26). Women's susceptibilities to handsome men are used cunningly by Humphrey in his antique business: "James's good looks and pleasing manners were a definite advantage in attracting customers to the shop and persuading difficult American women to buy" (p. 11).

On the other hand, women in this novel – especially Leonora –

are described in predatory terms: they wish to entrap, capture, imprison men. Leonora ejects an old lady from her lodgings in order to move James into them; once there he feels as trapped as any animal in any zoo, and his departure from Leonora's house to join Ned is described as a sort of prison break-out. Leonora tries to recapture James; Pym's language is significant: "wooing James" back is compared to "an animal being enticed back into its cage" (p. 207). Again the wild animal in the long grass is overtaken by the hunter, the would-be zookeeper. It is not coincidental that in *The Sweet Dove Died* there is actually a visit to a cat show during which James finds himself identifying sympathetically with the confined animals:

> They had stopped in front of a cage where a cat-like shape shrouded in a cloth lay fast asleep. How much wiser to contract out altogether, James felt, as this creature had evidently done. Or to sit stolidly in one's earth tray, unmoved by the comments of passers-by. Yet too often, like some of the more exotic breeds, one prowled uneasily around one's cage uttering loud plaintive cries.   (p. 68)

The word "one" signals the movement from the animal to the human world.

That women wish to "trap" men is made clear again and again in *The Sweet Dove Died*. "Just when you think they're close they suddenly go off," complains Miss Culver (p. 118). Leonora "did sometimes feel slightly uneasy when James was out of her sight" (p. 119). No wonder James, in Pym's words, fancies himself "fenced in" (p. 129) by Leonora. His response once again is that of the wild animal with its escape route cut off: "He had a sudden impulse to run down and bury himself in . . . leaves, covering over his head and body in an extravagant gesture of conceal-ment. . . . There was no escape. . . . [Leonora] would arrange or adapt him to her satisfaction" (p. 149).

As in the other books, battles for the affections of men are described in terms of triumph and defeat: thus Leonora thinks of James's former mistress Phoebe "as her vanquished rival" (p. 126). The women in this novel treat each other badly in their contest to become the one Eve to present "Adam with the apple" (p. 39). "Leonora had little use for . . . women friends, but regarded them rather as a foil for herself, particularly if . . . they were less

attractive and elegant than she was" (p. 153). Nor does she want
a man to be conscious for a second of other women when he is
with her. When Humphrey takes Leonora out to tea and remarks
that he and his late wife sometimes used to meet in the very café
they are sitting in, Leonora responds in a "tone reverent to
conceal her boredom. She considered it a slight error of taste that
he should be able to think of another woman, even one long
dead, when he was with her" (p. 38).

Pym's verdict here is that women are more petty than men.
"Only a woman could think of a trivial thing like stopping the
milk when one was in the middle of an affair," we are told
(p. 171). It is indicative that Leonora "had always cared as much
for inanimate objects as for people" (p. 182). Like Gilbert Osmond
and Madame Merle in James's *The Portrait of a Lady*, Leonora has a
great regard for *things*, and collects people largely to supplement
the inventory of her possessions.

Hazel Holt has remarked that Barbara Pym "saw all the faults and
weaknesses [of men] very clearly, but with the eye of love . . . she
always [had] great affection, even for those who had hurt her"
(letter to the present writer, 14 January 1985). *A Very Private Eye*,
along with other testimony, suggests that Pym – who, like Jane
Austen, wished to marry but never did, due to a long series of
near-misses and absurd anti-climaxes – regarded men with
affection, yes, but also with wariness, cynicism, and some
contempt. Their selfish treatment of women in her novels may
have in part a biographical source. Like her character Dulcie
Mainwaring in *No Fond Return of Love* (1961), Pym for many years
at the International African Institute found herself, instead of
getting an early start behind a filing cabinet on the family dinner,
"making indexes and doing little bits of research for people"
(p. 50). She would have preferred to work on the Brussels sprouts.
Certainly many of the men she knew disappointed her in one
way or another. And yet Pym understood her own gender well
enough to know that the war of the sexes was not entirely of
man's making, as no war can be fought without an opponent –
thus the long line of "terrifying" females in her books. Her
women are not always "excellent." Indeed, they are often
overbearing, vindictive, trivial – and sometimes cruel. They do
not use their superior strength magnanimously. Men, though

potentially tyrannical by nature, forcing women to become slaves
or ignoring them, do not always win the war of the sexes because
they too misuse the superiority of their status, or because, when
they come home at the end of the day, they are subject to a
tyranny and tenacity stronger than their worn-out wills. And so the
sexes remain at knife-edge, with neither gaining a clear victory –
something like the deadly stalemate in France during the Great
War, with each side making sorties from time to time and then
returning to its trenches to lick wounds and plan the next
campaign.

As Barbara Brothers has written, Pym's fiction carefully avoids
"portraying an idealized version of love . . . while Pym . . .
mocks women's naivety and their romantic susceptibilities," she
also "exposes male pretentiousness, men's pompous acceptance
of their own importance, and their vain belief in the myth they
have created."[1] Perhaps the only peaceful solution to this
impossible situation, thinks one of the characters in *Crampton
Hodnet*, is platonic love: "the most beautiful relationship between
a man and a woman was one in which they were in perfect
spiritual harmony" (p. 186; Pym's emphasis). In any case,
"beautiful" relationships of other kinds do not work in Barbara
Pym's novels.

Though hers is primarily a comic *genre*, her comedy, like all
great comedy, is essentially serious, focusing as it does on
psychological aberration, especially that of mental cruelty. Those
who regard her work as trivial or light or cosy have perhaps failed
to perceive the hard edge of the laughter in it. The protagonist of
Anita Brookner's *Hotel du Lac* (1984) comments that she knows
women too well to regard them complacently, and the same may
be said of Barbara Pym. She knows that one partner in a
relationship may be weaker than the other, but that, as in many
of James's stories, strength is often defeated by weakness. Such
unnatural relations give her comedies of manners tragic overtones.
Her books are funny, but no one in them is very happy.

All conflict is tragic. Pym's novels deserve to be read with
greater attention paid to their tragic theme: the pathos, the
ultimate failure, of human relations.

NOTES

Page numbers for quotations from Barbara Pym's novels and *A Very Private Eye* are given in the text and refer to the original editions (dates as specified on first mention).

1. Barbara Brothers, "Women Victimized by Fiction," in *Twentieth-Century Women Novelists*, ed. Thomas F. Staley (London, 1982), pp. 69 and 71.

14

Between Two Worlds:
The Novels of John le Carré

*One spy in the right place is worth
twenty thousand men in the field*

– Napoleon

I

The vogue of books about espionage is so ubiquitous these days
that the spy ranks as one of the most potent and familiar images
of modern life. Surely a reason for this is that so many British
writers of the twentieth century have worked for clandestine
organizations – the list would include John Buchan, Compton
Mackenzie, T. E. Lawrence, Somerset Maugham, Graham Greene,
Malcolm Muggeridge, Dennis Wheatley, Ian Fleming, Lawrence
Durrell, C. P. Snow, possibly Rudyard Kipling. Still another
would be David Cornwell, who spent five years in the British
Foreign Service and started writing novels in the early 1960s
under the pen-name of John le Carré.

John le Carré is the only writer of espionage "thrillers" today
who is also a writer of literature (the feeble efforts of the later
Graham Greene may be gauged by a reading of *The Human
Factor*). Few writers of thrillers have been as skillful as le Carré in
placing their stories in a world recognizable as our own and yet
stamped with a character that makes it unique. Not the least
interesting aspect of le Carré's stories – which seem so tuned to the
present, the modern note – is that they are in many ways old-
fashioned, even Victorian, in cast, set as all of them are in the
recent past and in a world as atmospherically familiar from book
to book as one created and populated by George Eliot or Trollope
or Conrad.[1] The "literary" quality of le Carré's work resides
largely in this familiarity of texture and atmosphere, and in the
repetition of themes and characters as in a saga by Galsworthy or

Arnold Bennett. Indeed, le Carré's novels provide the sort of critical analysis of modern life and values that Matthew Arnold and Camus and T. S. Eliot undoubtedly would have found congenial, and embody a pathology of contemporary existence instantly recognizable to, say, the scholar-gypsy, Sisyphus, or Prufrock. The absurdist, waste-land quality of modern international politics is le Carré's subject; the world he describes is as deeply divided by allegiance to the past, distaste for the present, and inability to fathom the future as the visitor to the Carthusian monastery in Arnold's "Stanzas from the Grande Chartreuse," who saw modern man as "Wandering between two worlds, one dead, / The other powerless to be born."

The "two worlds" of le Carré's novels are East and West as often as past and present; and the relation between the "two worlds" of fact and fiction is also a relevant concern, as we shall see. It is no accident that Kipling's *Kim*, an early – perhaps the first – spy novel, whose very subject is the bifurcation of East and West, is quoted copiously throughout le Carré's work. *Kim* articulates a theme, contained in a verse by Kipling, that most of le Carré's books are written around:

> Something I owe to the soil that grew –
> More to the life that fed –
> But most to Allah, who gave me two
> Separate sides to my head.

The last chapter of le Carré's first novel, *Call for the Dead*, is entitled "Between Two Worlds." In the book's final paragraph the hero, embroiled in rivalry with an old-friend-turned-enemy-agent, glimpses an "eternity between two worlds." Leo Harting, the elusive hero of *A Small Town in Germany*, is ultimately "crushed . . . between . . . worlds" which cannot be reconciled. Many of le Carré's fictional agents are split personalities, having "separate sides to [their] heads" and being subject to arrested development in the matter of political loyalties. In the novel in which this problem is most minutely scrutinized – *Tinker, Tailor, Soldier, Spy* – the central character is based on a real spy who himself was named after Kipling's hero. Like Kipling's Kim, le Carré's spies, in book after book, see themselves as players in "The Great Game."

II

The deglamorization of espionage in le Carré's novels is in part the result of a monolithic cynicism which sees espionage itself as an endlessly self-serving game played with varying degrees of competence by an ineffective, class-bound, non-ideological, politically naive Civil Service establishment. That the protagonist– hero of most of these stories should be a man who is apparently ordinary, even physically repulsive, is thematically appropriate. "The byways of espionage are not populated by the brash and colourful adventurers of fiction," le Carré tells us (*A Murder of Quality*). George Smiley is introduced, in *Call for the Dead*, as short, fat, and quiet, a man whose clothes "hung about his squat frame like skin on a shrunken toad" (his brother-in-law calls him "a bull-frog in a sou'wester"). The same sort of imagery is carried on in *A Murder of Quality*, the next book, in which it is said that Smiley "looks like a frog" and "dresses like a bookie"; he is described in this novel by Miss Brimley as "the most forgettable man she had ever met." In *The Spy Who Came in from the Cold* he has only a walk-on, but he is fixed in the reader's vision long enough to appear as "a small, frog-like figure in glasses." In *The Looking Glass War* he plays once more a minor role – yet again comes into focus as "a small, distracted man with plump fingers and a shadowy, blinking way with him." He does not appear in the flesh either in *A Small Town in Germany* or *The Naive and Sentimental Lover*, le Carré's one foray outside the espionage *genre*. But in the next two books Smiley bounces back to reassume the leading role. Mendel in *Tinker, Tailor, Soldier, Spy* compares him to a hedgehog: "You thought, to look at him, that he couldn't cross the road alone." In *The Honourable Schoolboy* Smiley is "A podgy ill-sighted little body in very round spectacles"; he is "tubby and in small ways hopelessly unassertive." Whenever he takes off his glasses and polishes them on the fat end of his tie, a characteristic habit, his face is left "so disconcertingly naked" that the secretaries in his office want to jump up and "shelter him from the impossible task he seemed determined to perform." What task? The task of a spy.

"It is sheer vanity to believe that one fat middle-aged spy is the only person capable of holding the world together," Smiley says to himself in *Tinker, Tailor*, but it is something he nevertheless longs to do. The unprepossessing appearance is a sort of ultimate "cover"; it is typical of the sordid world he inhabits that, in order to do his work, Smiley must shroud his brilliance in the protective mantle of mediocrity. Both *The Looking Glass War* and *A Small Town in Germany* use the phrase "dream factory" to describe the espionage establishment as it was before it became hostage to cynical international politics – an earlier era in which Smiley came of age in his profession. That he still lives by old ideals makes him in these novels both appealing to us and vulnerable to his enemies – the problem being, as *A Small Town* reminds us, that for many old-fashioned men such as Smiley "the dreams have quite replaced reality." But in his unique humanity Smiley becomes the embodiment of a plea for feeling and sense in a world in which political systems have gone mad with self-interest.

In *Call for the Dead* Smiley is labeled "The Head Eunuch," a phrase which describes the moral poverty and ineptitude of the political establishment that has placed him near the top of its intelligence-gathering apparatus. What makes him more interesting than his milieu is his unwillingness to capitulate to its amoral forces. *A Murder of Quality* sums up this aspect of Smiley:

> It was a peculiarity of Smiley's character that throughout the whole of his clandestine work he had never managed to reconcile the means to the end. A stringent critic of his own motives, he had discovered after long observation that he tended to be less a creature of intellect than his tastes and habits might suggest; once in the war he had been described by his superiors as possessing the cunning of Satan and the conscience of a virgin.

A sense of moral responsibility in a world without one can make a man a eunuch.

The moral chaos and the moral ambiguity of this world reflect the international political situation, a situation in which no one seems to know which "side" anyone else is really on, in which some men have difficulty answering this question about themselves, in which lifetime loyalties may be discarded in a second for no logical reason. If, as some have said, le Carré is "difficult," one reason may be that the world he describes, which has few steadfast moral rules, is a difficult place in which to live, and men's places in it are difficult to discern. "Cheats, liars, and criminals may resist every blandishment, while respectable gentlemen have been moved to appalling treasons by watery cabbage in a Departmental canteen," says le Carré in *The Spy Who Came in from the Cold*. "I knew a man once who sold his birthright because he couldn't get a seat on the underground," says Turner in *A Small Town in Germany*. *A Murder of Quality* refers to "the obscurity of motive in human action." "We just don't know what people are like, we can never tell; there isn't any truth about human beings," says one character in this novel, while Smiley makes a bold declaration of his unfaith in human nature: "I don't believe . . . that we can ever entirely know what makes anyone do anything." In *The Looking Glass War* Haldane despairingly asks the same question: Why do people "do anything? Why do any of us?" "Who believes in *motive* these days?" snarls di Salis in *The Honourable Schoolboy*. As Leamas says in *The Spy Who Came in from the Cold*, "All cats are alike in the dark." It is this "darkness" that represents the apparent "difficulty" in le Carré's novels.

If le Carré's fiction ultimately places the reader "between two worlds," he cares little which side he comes down on – like Leamas in the final scene of *The Spy Who Came in from the Cold*, perched atop the Berlin Wall and despising both sides. Why? Because the British political establishment is seen as thoroughly rotten, not worth saving from destruction within or from its enemies without. The protagonist of *A Perfect Spy*, who cannot do without "the mystery, the privacy of another side of life," finds that being an Englishman is not enough: "He needed to be able to close the door on his Englishness . . . and carve a new name somewhere fresh."

In *The Spy Who Came in from the Cold* the chief of the secret service admits that, "since the war, our methods . . . and those of the opposition . . . have become much the same." In *A Small Town in Germany* it is no coincidence that the British embassy building in Bonn embodies "an indefinable hint of Nazi architecture." As to the different "sides" here, Bradfield touches upon a major theme of the novel when he declares, "There are no absolutes. It is all doubt. All mist. There are no distinctions." "You can't distinguish the good from the bad," says Meadowes, in the same novel. "I don't know what I'm defending. Or what I'm representing. Who does?" asks de Lisle in *A Small Town*. "The poor world dreams we have a book bound in gold with POLICY written on the cover . . . God, if only they knew." In *Tinker, Tailor, Soldier, Spy* Smiley asks Karla, later head of the Soviet secret service, if it isn't "time to recognise that there is as little worth on your side as there is on mine?" Karla's favorite dictum, once he gets to the top of his profession, emphasizes the constantly shifting alignments in the political dance: "Spy on your friends today, they're certain to be your enemies tomorrow." At the end of *The Honourable Schoolboy* Westerby, betrayed like Leamas by his own "side," finds his loyalties equally hard to locate: he "had no position any more, this side or that side. He didn't know what the sides were." Indeed, it is le Carré's point that "sides" cease to exist when governments, like squabbling boys, give way entirely to self-interest.

Another thing that makes the various "sides" so hard to distinguish from one another is the universal intelligence muddle. In le Carré's novels the muddle the secret services make of everything is both a reflection and an extension of the government muddle: the paralytic incompetence of politicians and bureaucrats. Neither "side," le Carré tells us, is more efficient – or more moral, or more feeling – than the other: "feelings are hard to trace among so many corridors" (*The Honourable Schoolboy*). Democracy is seen by the novelist as having no edge on Communism, moral or otherwise. "Democracy is like Christ," says a character in *A Small Town in Germany*: "there is nothing you cannot do in the name of democracy."

The manifold connections between governments and the spies they employ are emphasized in all of the novels. The "secret services [are] the only measure of a nation's political health, the only real expression of its subconscious," muses Haydon in *Tinker, Tailor, Soldier, Spy*. "The British secret services . . . are . . . microcosms of the British condition, of our social attitudes and vanities," le Carré himself has said. Spies dissemble: lying is their profession; the intelligence world by definition is full of deluded and deluding people. For le Carré, the world of double-dealing, the world in which illusions are bought and sold and traded, the world in which faith is bartered rather than felt, is the real world, no imaginary place. His "secret" world is a paradigm of the "real" world; between these "two worlds," as between East and West, there is little difference. At every opportunity le Carré shows us how the subterranean, grubby, amoral world of espionage, populated largely by international mercenaries, is merely a reflection of that other, more respectable world – the world of politics and government, which has set the "secret" world going.

"No secret service can be more clear-headed than its government," le Carré has said.[2]

Each of the novels comments in some way upon the political establishment of which espionage departments are the creatures and playthings. In *The Spy Who Came in from the Cold* the British secret-service chief ("Control") and the murderous German gangster Mundt, a double-agent, work together to protect Mundt's secret relationship with the British, who eliminate a number of their own agents along the way to keep their unsavory ally secure. Leamas ultimately sees that his mission has been little more than "a filthy, lousy operation" to save a Nazi animal who has sold out his country. At the end of the book Liz tells Leamas, "You're all the same," and she is right; neither "world" is any better than the other, and indeed in its willingness to sell its own agents down the river for so little reason, the perfidious British seem even more diabolical than the East Germans they are spying upon – thus Leamas's disinclination to climb down on the "free" side of the Wall at the final moment.

The Looking Glass War is largely an indictment of interdepartmental rivalries within the clandestine services; the "looking glass" element lies in the battle being fought by Civil Service departments against one another instead of against a foreign enemy. In this novel an agent in East Germany is abandoned in mid-mission by the secret service as part of the process by which it seeks to humiliate would-be competitors within its own jurisdiction. In le Carré's world, agents in the field are often left hanging for political reasons, cold-bloodedly viewed by political administrators as always expendable. For Leclerc, head of the little military-defense bureau seeking a larger slice of the secret-service pie, the "enemy" here is his superiors in the bureaucracy rather than the East Germans; "the forgers all went over to [Control]," Leclerc complains at one point. Surely he is right to see Control as his enemy; for Control himself ultimately alerts the East Germans to the mission of Leclerc's agent, thus making sure he will be caught and killed.

A Small Town in Germany, perhaps le Carré's finest novel, is based largely on his experiences as a secretary at the British embassy in Bonn. The primary targets are the diplomatic corps and diplomacy itself as a profession of supposedly civilized men. In this novel the British are depicted as being more interested in friendly relations with their allies than in moral questions; once again the good guys have enough blood on their hands to make any moral preferences irrelevant. Indeed, the British are portrayed here as willing to do or to be anything – *anything* – to advance their own interests. "Know what counts in politics?" the treacherous Praschko asks. "Cash. Selling. Everything else is a load of crap. Treaties, policies, alliances: crap."

Diplomacy, that purveyor of pleasant illusions, is variously defined in *A Small Town in Germany* as "a poker game," "a system without a mind," and a meaningless "verbal battle for something nobody wants. A constant, sterile cacophony of claim and protest." "The cold war's over for everyone except the fucking diplomats!" says the journalist Allerton. By the end of the novel we see how completely out of touch with reality these diplomats are. Bradfield, head-of-mission in Bonn, acknowledges that the pressures brought to bear on diplomats by the system they serve, that "system without a mind," often blunt moral distinctions. "I have spent half my life learning not to look, and the other half learning not to feel," he admits sadly. "Only appearances matter. . . . What else is there when the underneath is rotten?" He goes on to state the diplomat's creed: "I'm a great believer in hypocrisy. It's the nearest we ever get to virtue. It's a statement of what we ought to be. . . . I serve the appearance of things. . . . That is my profession, and that is my philosophy." It is appropriate that in a novel in which men serve only "the appearance of things" the world is painted in the drab colors of a waste land. In *A Small Town in Germany*, as in Dickens's *Our Mutual Friend* – one of the inspirations of Eliot's poem – the misty city is full of wind-blown paper, the metaphorical refuse of a people given over to the pursuit of garbage. The novel's atmospheric texture is just right for a world in which "only appearances matter" and "hypocrisy [is] the nearest we ever get to virtue." The rich brilliance of the writing is sustained longer here than in any of le Carré's other novels.

In *Tinker, Tailor, Soldier, Spy* the secret service is depicted as so shot through with disloyalty and subversion as to be an unwitting tool of England's enemies. "Difficult to know what one's aims *are*, specially if you're British," says a character here. The atmosphere of political ambivalence and cloudy loyalties permeates every corner of the story. Politicians are perceived as largely irrelevant bunglers: the minister who has direct responsibility for the secret service is described as being "without a single redeeming feature."

This aspect of *Tinker, Tailor* is an extension of le Carré's assault upon the "ruling class" begun in *A Murder of Quality* and carried on in subsequent books. *A Murder of Quality* is set at Eton; in the opening chapters of *Tinker, Tailor* the venue is an unnamed public school. The earlier novel attacks class pride and blind snobbishness, and tells us that the "ruling class . . . is distinguished by neither talent, culture, nor wit"; that it "grows old without growing wise"; that it hasn't "had an original idea . . . for the last fifty years"; that it is suffering from "a gradual putrefaction of . . . intellectual extremities" and from spirits that "atrophy and rot." *A Murder of Quality* articulates le Carré's disdain for those "born to rule," those he shows in one novel after another running governments. In *Tinker, Tailor*, as in *A Murder of Quality*, the villain gets away with his crimes for so long because he is socially impeccable and therefore above suspicion. But le Carré sees through the varnish. "Smiley was not opposed to social distinctions," he writes in *A Murder of Quality*, "but he liked to make his own."

The Honourable Schoolboy also takes pot shots at contemporary politics and diplomacy. Connie Sachs's cynicism reflects le Carré's: "There'll be no war . . . but in the struggle for peace not a single stone will be left standing." Here, as in *A Small Town in Germany*, diplomacy is seen as "a mad world [in which] you keep the fiction going." The novelist's idea of diplomacy's role in a world already torn by war may be gauged by his description of the lobby of the British embassy in Cambodia, in the midst of which, "with the spine-breaking irrelevance which only diplomats can quite achieve, a big partitioned poster recommended 'British High Performance Cars' to a city parched of fuel, and supplied cheerful photographs of several unavailable models."

No matter who is in charge of espionage, the nature of the beast remains unchanged. The pessimism of le Carré's novels, their waste-land quality, grows directly out of his conception of what spying is. Espionage not only terrifies the man engaged in it; it is also dehumanizing, a cauterization of the feelings. In espionage work "the mind becomes separated from the body; it thinks without reality, rules a paper kingdom and devises without emotion the ruin of its paper victims," Elsa Fennan remarks in *Call for the Dead*. Dieter, the master spy of this novel, "cared nothing for human life: dreamed only of armies of faceless men bound by their lowest common denominators; he wanted to shape the world as if it were a tree, cutting off what did not fit the regular image; for this he fashioned blank, soulless automatons like Mundt."

Dieter's creature Mundt, a nerveless assassin in the earlier novel, becomes in *The Spy Who Came in from the Cold* the ally of the British. Espionage, the novel tells us, consists of different kinds of treachery dressed up as something else. "Intelligence work has one moral law – it is justified by results." So le Carré declares at the beginning of the novel, and the rest of it is a gloss of this text. When men operate by and under only "one moral law," and the law is that of expediency, they are likely to come out looking more or less identical. "We're all the same, you know," Fiedler says. It is one of le Carré's constant themes: "sides" don't matter when all men conduct themselves like animals in a jungle. Indeed, the repression demanded by espionage of ordinary humane instincts is seen by the novelist as a primary source of moral erosion in the individual. He comments on this in *The Spy Who Came in from the Cold*:

> A man who lives a part, not to others but alone, is exposed to obvious psychological dangers. In itself, the practice of deception is not particularly exacting; it is a matter of experience, of professional expertise, it is a facility most of us can acquire. But while a confidence trickster, a play-actor or a gambler can return from his performance to the ranks of his admirers, the secret agent enjoys no such relief. For him, deception is first a matter of self-defence. He must protect himself not only from without but from within, and against the most natural of impulses . . . though he be an affectionate husband and father, he must under all circumstances withhold himself from those in whom he should naturally confide.

It is the protecting of oneself "from within" that is most difficult, and also, potentially, the most morally damaging. Leamas, forced to play such a part as le Carré outlines here, finds himself unable to stop "caring about little things," to give up altogether his "faith in ordinary life; that simplicity that made you break up a bit of bread in a paper bag, walk down to the beach and throw it to the gulls." This aspect of Leamas – his inability to depersonalize himself – allows him to retain his humanity, but makes him a poor spy. To feel, in his world, is to be weak. Liz thinks the

British are "more wicked" than the other side for playing on these human weaknesses. "It's far more terrible, what they are doing: to find the humanity in people . . . and use it to hurt and kill." Leamas's reply is le Carré's most quoted passage: "What do you think spies are: priests, saints and martyrs? They're a squalid procession of vain fools, traitors too, yes: pansies, sadists and drunkards, people who play cowboys and Indians to brighten their rotten lives. Do you think they sit like monks in London balancing the rights and wrongs?"

The Looking Glass War continues this theme, providing its own "depressing miscellany of rogues, double agents and lunatics" who spy on one another for pay. The book defines intelligence work as largely "luck and speculation" – and love as "whatever you can still betray. We ourselves live without it in our profession," says Haldane.

The picture is no rosier in succeeding books. *Tinker, Tailor, Soldier, Spy*, in which the intelligence establishment has been demoralized by Britain's fall from world power, describes the head of the secret service as a man who "would sell his mother for a knighthood and this service for a seat in the House of Lords." He has made his reputation in South America with a network of spies to whom he "preached loyalty . . . paid them next to nothing, and – when it suited him – sold them down the river." The chair he sits in during meetings is called "the megalomaniac's throne." Lederer speaks of espionage this way in *A Perfect Spy*: "We're licensed crooks. . . . our racket . . . is to place our larcenous natures at the service of the state."

The Honourable Schoolboy tells the story of how two men, Westerby and Smiley, are betrayed and defeated by their addiction to faiths and feelings. Westerby, like Leamas, ultimately prefers death to escaping with his life and going back to his "side," so shabbily has it treated him. But the focus here is primarily on Smiley, whose mission to clean up the secret service and start scoring points against his opposite number in Russia is characterized as his "black grail" – a witty description of the idealism of the man and the worthlessness of his brief. Smiley has always believed in being "inhuman in defence of . . . humanity" and "harsh in defence of compassion." But it is his lingering belief in humanity that finally undoes him: for "survival," the novel tells us, requires "an infinite capacity for suspicion," and Smiley does not possess this. At the end of the book, having been defeated by a

combination of "friends" and real enemies, Smiley muses on the
pass to which he has come:

> *So far as I can ever remember of my youth, I chose the secret road
> because it seemed to lead straightest and furthest toward my country's
> goal. The enemy in those days was someone we could point at and read
> about in the papers. Today all I know is that I have learned to interpret
> the whole of life in terms of conspiracy. That is the sword I have lived
> by and . . . I see it is the sword I shall die by as well. These people
> terrify me but I am one of them. If they stab me in the back, then . . .
> that is the judgment of my own peers.* (Author's emphasis.)

The enemy is more difficult to spot, perhaps, because the
process of identifying him has become more subjective. Like
Kurtz in Conrad's *Heart of Darkness*, Smiley has ultimately been
eaten up and assimilated by the "horror" he has fought against so
valiantly: humanity's inner emptiness. Forces are strong; men are
weak. In *Call for the Dead* and *A Murder of Quality*, published in
1961 and 1962, Smiley could do battle against the amoral forces of
his milieu and remain separated from them; the search for the
grail was still worthwhile. By the time of *The Honourable Schoolboy*,
published in 1977, it is apparently no longer possible for Smiley to
do and to be these things. The grail has turned black; and he has
become at last "one of them." "The Smiley of the first book was
not the Smiley of [the later books]," le Carré is quoted as saying
in the *Sunday Telegraph Magazine*. "Years later . . . both Smiley and
I were seeing the world in a rather different way. . . . There were
even moments," says the novelist, when he "wondered . . .
whether" he himself might one day have betrayed his country.[3]

III

No discussion of le Carré's work would be complete without an
account of the historical origins of some of his stories: the extent
to which he draws on actual events, people, and places in his
studies of the "two worlds." All of his novels bear some relation
to his own experiences as well as to his knowledge of the inner
workings of the intelligence establishment; and one of them, as
we shall see, is based closely on a famous British espionage case.

The novelist draws on his own past in the use of Eton in *A*

Murder of Quality and the unnamed public school in *Tinker, Tailor, Soldier, Spy*. Avery in *The Looking Glass War*, Prideaux in *Tinker Tailor*, Pym in *A Perfect Spy*, and Smiley are all linguists; like them all, le Carré read modern languages at Oxford. *A Small Town in Germany* grew out of the novelist's five-year sojourn in the British Foreign Service, spent mostly in Bonn. The locations in his novels are often based on actual ones. Sarratt, "the nursery" of *Tinker, Tailor*, is probably the British spy school at Gosport. The "Circus" is shorthand for headquarters of the Secret Intelligence Service, or MI6; the Security Service, responsible for monitoring counterespionage within the United Kingdom and thus theoretically only defensive in its activities, is called MI5. SIS, or MI6, is charged with conducting global espionage: it is an offensive, information-gathering organization. This is an important distinction; the two services, which may roughly be compared to the U.S. Central Intelligence Agency and Federal Bureau of Investigation, are often in conflict and competition. The Circus is so called because its headquarters are said to be located in London's Cambridge Circus – though they aren't. For years they were near the St. James's Park underground station, later on in Westminster Bridge Road, and later still in Lambeth; now they are housed in a building near Waterloo Station. The Director of MI6 from its earliest days traditionally occupied the top floor of a block of flats reached only through a tortuous series of architectural barriers, called himself "C" – either for "chief" or "control," or because the first director of MI6 was named Cumming – and wrote all of his memoranda in green ink. The rivalry of MI6 and MI5 has always been a feature of life in the British clandestine services: they distrust each other's security and rarely exchange information. Between them the Foreign Office has often mediated and also attempted on occasion to take over for itself the operation of secret intelligence operations. The SIS is responsible to the Prime Minister via the Permanent Under-Secretary at the Foreign Office, the Foreign Office adviser, and the Foreign Secretary himself.

Readers of le Carré's novels will not need to be told that this is the world his books describe, down to the last detail. Smiley uses "the traditional green ink of his office" when he takes over the Circus. His conference room is at the top of a building which gives "on to nothing but orange night sky and a coppice of rusted radio aerials." The path to his inner sanctum is described thus in

The Honourable Schoolboy: "The corridor turned left, then right again, then rose by a few narrow steps . . . steps again, two up, three down," and so on. The path to Cumming's old headquarters is recalled by a former associate as "a maze of rabbit-burrow-like passages, corridors, nooks and alcoves, piled higgledy-piggledy on the roof."[4] The rivalry between the services is insisted upon in all of the novels – most emphatically, perhaps, in *The Looking Glass War* – and Foreign Office people such as Maston and Lacon are always trying to squeeze in and take over. The head of the service is called Control through all of the novels except the last two, by which time he has been forced to give way to a successor addressed by his real name.

By far the most sustained and detailed reconstruction of history in le Carré's books is the painstaking re-creation of the Kim Philby story in *Tinker, Tailor, Soldier, Spy*, carried over into early chapters of *The Honourable Schoolboy*. The resemblance between Philby and le Carré's master spy Bill Haydon in *Tinker, Tailor* is unmistakable.

Philby's father, St. John Philby, was a famous Arabist who lived in Mecca, dressed as an Arab, ate camel meat, and had a "bodyguard" of four huge Abyssinian baboons. A successful businessman and dedicated believer in Empire – he worshipped Kipling and T. E. Lawrence – the elder Philby seems to have bred in his inimical son the same sort of mystical impulse to destroy British power and its most tangible manifestation, the Empire, as existed in Kipling's *Kim*. The younger Philby was fond of quoting the novel: he and Kipling's hero shared a profession as well as a nickname. Kim Philby's impeccable family background, his upper-class, boyish charm, his capacity for scholarship, and his prodigious memory combined to make him a conspicuous social and academic success at Cambridge, where he was a year ahead of Guy Burgess. Thick-set, untidy, a lover of liquor and of classical music, and a first-rate linguist, Philby was an avowed Communist in the early 1930s. No one took him seriously; radical politics were fashionable then. After his recruitment at Cambridge by Anthony Blunt, an art-history don who also recruited Burgess and Donald Maclean for the Russians – and, up to the moment of his unmasking in 1979, served as Keeper of the Queen's Pictures – Philby adopted right-wing views as a cover. He worked as a journalist in Spain during the Civil War, had an affair there with a married woman, Lady Lindsay-Hogg, and joined MI6 in 1940. Within a year this Soviet agent was working in the anti-Soviet department of SIS. His job placed him in the central citadel of the intelligence world. A man from Trinity College and a member of the Athenaeum and Reform Clubs could hardly be a spy. Philby exploited his social acceptability and British class-bound snobbery, and by 1944 had managed to get himself put in charge of MI6's anti-Soviet section.

For years Philby was protected from discovery by the naivety of his colleagues, most of whom thought Marxism was a stage of puberty, like acne. "The inbred philistinism of the English élite," remark the authors of *Philby*, "had always prevented any serious study of Marxism: it was assumed to be some sort of rather funny rubbish got up by a foreigner."[5] Entrance requirements for the secret service, unlike those for the Civil Service or the diplomatic corps, were not rigorous. Since jobs couldn't be advertised, most recruitment was done through personal recommendation and introduction, associations at schools or clubs, and so on. The old-boy network kept the service inbred and insular. After the war it became a haven for eccentrics and mediocrities. Malcolm Muggeridge has said that it would be impossible to overestimate the stupidity of the secret service in these days; le Carré himself observes, "Every government department . . . carries its fair share of . . . idiots. There has never been any reason to suppose that the secret service should be absolved from this responsibility."[6]

In 1939 much publicity was given to a celebrated failure of MI6. Two of its agents going, so they thought, to meet and interrogate an anti-Nazi German general who wished to co-operate with Germany's enemies, were instead trapped and interrogated by the Abwehr, the German CIA. This became known as the Venlo incident.

In the general reorganization that took place in 1940–1, Philby was made head of the anti-Soviet section, as we have seen. This marked the beginning of a series of battles within the secret services for their control, a battle in which Philby himself was very much involved; at one time he was actually in the running for the directorship. His job in counter-intelligence was to set up espionage networks in Eastern European countries for anti-Soviet operations – that is, to plan subversion in Communist satellite countries. His career prospered in the 1940s. He got on well with everybody, and was considered tough. He was allowed to visit Russia, an unusual privilege.

A well-known event of this period was the Volkov incident. In

1945 the head of Russian intelligence in Turkey offered to defect and sell information to the British, including the names of Russian agents in the Foreign Office and the secret service. The offer was sent by diplomatic bag to London. There was no answer for three weeks, despite repeated queries. Finally Philby himself came out. Volkov disappeared; later a heavily bandaged man was taken aboard a Soviet plane and flown to Russia.

In the late 1940s Philby was involved in an MI6 plot to subvert the government of Albania; the Albanians were tipped off in advance, and hundreds of would-be revolutionaries were killed. Another such incident occurred in the Ukraine; scores of dissidents were betrayed at the eleventh hour and massacred. And so on. Through it all Philby was considered a model MI6 employee. He was an able administrator, good at paperwork, had a clear mind, even wrote reports without first drafts. He would often work late at night over his files. For a time he was allowed to pose as a double agent, passing what was supposedly "chicken-feed" to the Russians in exchange for the genuine article; needless to say, the information passed back and forth in this way was reversed in terms of importance. In 1949, when he went to Washington as first secretary of the British embassy there, Philby ran the liaison between MI6 and the CIA, and so had even more material than before to send to Russia. He hated America, but of course the position he occupied there was the perfect one for him.

In 1950–1 the leakages finally began to be noticed and investigated, but it was some years more before the chief culprit was unmasked. "In the final analysis," the authors of *Philby* remark, "a spy has no protection but the faith of his friends, who must believe that no matter how far he has gone with the enemy he remains in the end loyal."[7] In fact it is impossible to tell which side a really skillful double agent is on until you count up your gains and losses at the end. Philby fooled so many for so long largely because his apolitical colleagues never saw that beneath his affected nonchalance he was an idealogue and an idealist. As late as 1954 a former Abwehr agent was kidnapped and subjected to lengthy interrogation by the KGB solely to determine whether Philby was in fact a double agent betraying the Russians to the British.[8]

At this point Guy Burgess and Donald Maclean[9] come into the picture. Burgess, the son of a British Naval officer born in Aden, had a brilliant school career, read history at Cambridge, was openly homosexual and a prodigious drinker. A large, apparently careless man with a gruff, gravelly voice, he alternately told people he was a fascist and a Communist agent: no one took him seriously – again, because of his background. Early on he got a job in "Section D" of MI6, responsible for sabotage and subversion in enemy countries; later he switched over to the Foreign Office. For years his apparent honesty and guilelessness were his protection, and he continued to be promoted. In 1949 he boasted he was a Marxist; nothing happened. In 1950 he was sent to Washington along with Philby, in whose house he lived while posted there. By this time he was a hopeless alcoholic. Still immune, because of his background and his class, from doubts about his loyalty, he would soon be under suspicion.

Maclean's background was more narrowly diplomatic. The son of a baronet who eventually became a Cabinet minister, Maclean, a bisexual, also worked for the Foreign Office; his posts included Washington – he too hated America – and Cairo. His chief accomplishment was to give to the Soviets all the United States atomic secrets he could lay his hands on. Later he became head of the American desk at the Foreign Office. From here he passed details of American troop-movements in Korea to the Russians, who gave them to the Chinese: Russia and China were allies once upon a time. Also an alcoholic, Maclean nonetheless worked hard, keeping especially late hours over his files wherever he happened to be posted. He too announced to all of his friends that he was working for Russia; but he too came from the right background, and so they laughed and kept him on.

Maclean was the first of the trio to be suspected. MI5 started investigating him in 1950. Philby, assuming that his own career would soon be over, redoubled his efforts on behalf of his masters, working later and later into the night as the requests for his files increased ominously. Philby and Blunt – the "Fourth Man" – gave Burgess ample warning that the security net was closing in on Maclean. On a Friday in May 1951 Maclean was asked by M15 to make himself available for questioning on the following Monday. Weekends being sacrosanct in Whitehall, it was assumed that he would do nothing in the intervening two days – or perhaps it was a warning to get out before the inevitable public trial could damage the secret services. In any case, the delay allowed Maclean and Burgess to escape together to Russia, and it saved Philby's career for another thirteen years.

The defection of his two friends tainted Philby, and he was recalled from Washington. Until this time he was powerful in MI6; afterwards his power was diminished, but he still worked at the anti-Soviet desk and continued to find plenty of secrets to pass along to the Russians. He was briefly and quietly investigated by MI5 in 1951 and again in 1952, and both times exonerated. MI6 did not cooperate in either investigation. They could not believe him guilty; it would have meant that they had been outrageously betrayed. In the mid-1950s Philby worked for several years as a minor field agent in anti-Soviet areas of the Middle East. In 1955 he was investigated again and cleared again. Throughout the late fifties he was stationed in Beirut, supposedly as a newspaper correspondent. Finally, late in 1963, a KGB defector gave his name away in no uncertain terms. Philby was allowed to escape to Russia by a British government that did not wish to go through a long debriefing and public scandal; in fact the announcement of his defection was not made by the British until 1967. So to Russia he went. Burgess had just died there, but Maclean and his wife were then very much alive; Maclean was working in the Soviet Foreign Office. Having nothing else to do, Philby took Maclean's wife away from him and set up house with her[10] – the situation of Alan Bennett's hit West End play of the 1977–8 season about Philby in Russia, *The Old Country*. Maclean died only a few years ago.

So ended Philby's thirty-year career as a closet Communist and twenty years of subversion of the British secret service. Between 1941 and 1951 Philby single-handedly destroyed the entire Western intelligence effort, providing among other things a good lesson for the political establishment in the dangers of accepting social background as a qualification for government service when competing with an aggressive ideological enemy.

That Philby and his cohorts Burgess and Maclean were ever caught at all was due largely to the efforts over a number of years of one man – Dick White, who reformed MI5 and later took over as chief of all the secret services. He had always suspected Philby and was instrumental in getting him moved out of his central position of power in London in the 1950s. After Philby's defection White supervised the thorough dismantling, house-cleaning, and rebuilding of the secret service that had to take place.

In an essay on Philby written in 1968 – around the time he was beginning work on *Tinker, Tailor, Soldier, Spy* – le Carré attacks the apoliticism of the British intelligence agencies, their ignorance of political doctrine, their "political incompetence" and naivety. He describes Philby as a man dependent on the people he deceived – dependent on their admiration of him, and on their stupidity. He says Philby was an enthusiastic wife-stealer but sexually "ambivalent" and that he often used his wide choice of sexual partners to pay off old scores. He notes that Philby cold-heartedly sent many agents to their deaths. For a decade, says le Carré, the British secret service was useless because of him and didn't know it.

Tinker, Tailor, Soldier, Spy and early sections of *The Honourable Schoolboy* are consecutive history, a careful reconstruction of the last month's of Philby's career in the anti-Soviet department of MI6 and of the climate there after his fall and during the coming to power in SIS of the man who caught and toppled him. Haydon is Philby in these books, and Smiley is Dick White, with something of the late Sir Maurice Oldfield thrown in. Formerly head of SIS and subsequently security co-ordinator for the British in Northern Ireland, Sir Maurice was described on 7 October 1979 by the *Sunday Telegraph* in a speculative profile as "a short, stocky man," "heavy [and] stolid," with "thick-rimmed glasses and heavy jowls," and an astounding memory.

Haydon's unmasking by Smiley and Smiley's appointment as caretaker chief of the service is translated, in *The Honourable Schoolboy*, into "*before the fall* and *after* it" in "Circus history." In an article describing the post-Philby MI6, Craw the journalist writes in this novel of a Russian "mole inside the Circus's London headquarters . . . [who] had compromised every Anglo-American clandestine operation worth a dime for the last twenty years." Where is he now? asks Craw. "*Is Kim the boy spy vanished for good . . . from the legends of the East?*" (le Carré's emphasis). *The Honourable Schoolboy* goes on to tell the story of a different intelligence caper, and the account of Philby's career in le Carré's fiction ends here.

At first glance, *Tinker, Tailor, Soldier, Spy* seems simply to carry on some of the motifs and themes le Carré had been concerned with in earlier novels. As in *A Murder of Quality* and *The Spy Who Came in from the Cold*, there is in *Tinker, Tailor* some unsubtle criticism of the ruling classes, in which homosexuality plays a part, and the danger of accepting social background as a qualification for office is stressed. As in *The Looking Glass War*, inaccurate "information" is bought and sold largely for private motives and gain. But soon enough we perceive a difference. Within the confines of MI6 there can be perfidies deeper even than these: there can be treason.

The "mole" theme is familiar to readers of le Carré: Mundt in *The Spy Who Came in from the Cold* is England's "mole" in East Germany; Nelson Ko in *The Honourable Schoolboy* is Russia's in China. In *Tinker, Tailor, Soldier, Spy* there is a Russian "mole" inside MI6 – British agents are being betrayed and shot, clandestine campaigns are being undermined, secrets are being passed. The British are slow to recognize that "one of them" is a double agent, but the recognition ultimately comes. Perceiving that MI6 cannot investigate itself – indeed, that it will not even cooperate in any investigation – the Foreign Office brings in its own man to investigate, as Dick White was brought into the Philby affair. The investigator is Smiley, formerly of MI6, now retired. What he finds is the story the novel tells. It is the story of Kim Philby.

Haydon's career as le Carré outlines it in the book follows Philby's closely. Like Philby, Haydon grew up under an "authoritarian father"; his "Marxism [made] up for his . . . loveless childhood." The father of Haydon, like Philby's father, was "a passionate Empire man"; so was the man who recruited Haydon at Oxford for MI6 – an Arabist whose habit it was "to put on Arab costume and go down to the Bazaars, there to sit among the great unwashed and give ear to the word of their prophets." Haydon evolved into "a romantic and a snob," seeing himself "standing at the middle of a secret stage, playing world against world" (the language recalls that of *Kim*). An "ambitious man born to the big canvas, brought up to rule, divide, and conquer, whose visions and vanities were all fixed . . . upon the world's game," Haydon in the 1930s became disillusioned with democracy and, like Philby at Cambridge, posed as a right-winger at Oxford while he moved closer and closer to the Communist side. At Oxford, Haydon was a year ahead of Jim Prideaux, as Philby was a year ahead of Guy Burgess at Cambridge: Haydon later helped recruit Prideaux for MI6 and became his close friend, which also repeats the relationship of Philby and Burgess. Like Burgess, Prideaux is a linguist, a heavy drinker, a large, apparently guileless man with a deep, gruff voice; like Burgess, he is from the right social background, and sexually ambivalent; later he comes to work for Haydon in MI6, as Burgess did for Philby.

While playing within MI6 the role of "torch-bearer of a certain
kind of antiquated romanticism, a notion of English calling,"
Haydon is secretly working for the Russians. His social background
as it is described in *Tinker, Tailor*, like Philby's, puts him above
suspicion.

> He was of that pre-war set that seemed to have vanished for
> good, which managed to be disreputable and high-minded at
> the same time. . . . At Oxford he favoured the unfashionable
> right rather than the fashionable left. . . . He had connections
> in every embassy and consulate across the Middle East and he
> used them ruthlessly. He took up remote languages with ease,
> and when 1939 came, the Circus snapped him up. . . . He was
> ubiquitous and charming; he was unorthodox and occasionally
> outrageous. He was probably heroic. The comparison with
> [T. E.] Lawrence was inevitable.

Haydon exhibits the same fascination with the East and the
same mystical impulse to destroy Western power that moved
Philby. Like Philby too, Haydon has great charm, a talent for
scholarship, an aptitude for languages, a prodigious memory, and
a capacity for hard work. Like Philby, Haydon is thick-set, untidy,
a great drinker, genial but considered tough. Philby loved classical
music; Haydon loves art. Like Philby, Haydon sometimes uses
sexual liaisons to pay off old scores. He sleeps with a married
woman (Ann Smiley) to humiliate her husband, who for some
time is his rival in the department; and he sleeps with men. After
school he joins MI6 and goes to work immediately in their anti-
Soviet bureau, quickly making himself indispensable there,
eventually becoming a candidate for director of the service. Like
Philby's, his job in SIS is to undermine the Soviets in Eastern-bloc
countries by setting up espionage networks there and stimulating
subversion. A few of his capers succeed, but the most critical ones
are uncovered by the Russians and defeated, with many agents
butchered in the process. "His operational life," someone says of
Haydon, "has been spent weaving and ducking round the Eastern
markets" – a characterization that could easily be applied to
Philby's career.

For years Haydon is protected by the naivety of his colleagues.
He uses mercilessly his admirers' image of him, living "through
them to complete himself . . . disguising the fact that he was less

. . . than the sum of his apparent qualities." Like Philby's, none of Haydon's peers is politically sophisticated, none can detect passionate idealism behind his façade of nonchalant cynicism. They always think of him as being one "of [their] own kind," also an important part of Philby's protection. Haydon is allowed to visit Russia, as Philby was. He does a stint in America, supposedly coordinating United States and British intelligence and hating America all the while; this too recapitulates an aspect of Philby's career. A good administrator, clever with paperwork, Haydon spends many evenings in his office supposedly working over his files but in fact preparing material for the Soviets: again, Philby.

At the time he is caught, Haydon is described as having spent ten years giving British secrets away to the Russians. Toward the end of his career as a double agent he had finally begun to be suspected by his colleagues: "all of them had tacitly shared that unexpressed half-knowledge which like an illness they hoped would go away if it were never . . . diagnosed." After all, Haydon was one of them; if he was betraying Britain, he was also betraying them, which they found it even more difficult to accept. This too is reminiscent of Philby's last years in SIS. In the wake of Haydon's exposure, the British authorities prefer shipping him quietly to Russia to a grisly public trial. The plan is to send him back secretly and announce it several years later – exactly what was done in the Philby case, as we know. Haydon, however, is assassinated before he can return to Russia – an equally effective way of avoiding publicity. After Haydon's removal the SIS is taken over by the man who exposed him (Smiley), which duplicates the role played by Dick White in Philby's story.

The plot of *Tinker, Tailor, Soldier, Spy* centers on operations engineered and undermined by Haydon/Philby as head of anti-Soviet activities within MI6. The novel begins with a version of the Volkov incident. In le Carré's account a potential Russian defector who knows the name of the Soviet "mole" inside the British secret service is betrayed by the London office of MI6 into Soviet hands under virtually the same circumstances. The offer of defection comes by diplomatic bag; a long delay, and silence from London; finally Haydon himself appears upon the scene, the would-be defector vanishes, a heavily bandaged figure is put aboard a Soviet plane, and so on. Later in the novel a Czechoslovakian general offers to defect with Warsaw Pact military secrets, British agents are sent in to escort him out, the operation is blown, and much of the Eastern-bloc espionage network is rolled up by the Russians along with a number of liberal Czech revolutionaries. This may recall the Venlo incident as well as some of Philby's exploits in the Ukraine and the Balkans; in each case, clusters of British agents and Western sympathizers were sold down the river. The subsequent investigation in the novel of the Czech debacle recalls the various investigations of Philby by his superiors in the 1950s: only perfunctory questions are asked; everybody is quickly exonerated of wrongdoing.

Most important of all, Haydon, like Philby, is "posing" as a double agent, supposedly giving "chicken-feed" to the Russians in exchange for hard and valuable information, while in fact he is handing the Soviets "the crown jewels and getting Russian chicken-feed in return." The British prefer to think that though Haydon has been playing along with the enemy he has remained loyal to the West. That it can only be determined for certain after the gains and losses are totalled up which side a clever double agent is really on is as true in Haydon's case as in Philby's. As the net begins to close around Haydon, and his colleagues find it increasingly difficult to believe in him, he works more and more furiously over his files, as Philby did during his last months in London. Like Philby, Haydon must depend on the people he has been deceiving – until they finally cease to believe in him altogether.

IV

The Philby story is a prime example of how the "two worlds" theme operates in le Carré's fiction. The novelist sees Philby (Haydon) as in effect straddling the worlds of East and West – his pose as a double agent being itself a pose, as surely a metaphor as Alec Leamas's ultimate balancing act is tragically literal. With a foot in each world, the double agent becomes an emblem for the ambivalent loyalties, the inevitable treacheries, the moral schizophrenia that ensue whenever a man's allegiance is sought by competing forces. In using Philby's story as a model for the one he tells in *Tinker, Tailor, Soldier, Spy*, le Carré illuminates a present reality known to him at first hand – that is, the recent history of MI6 – through the narration of what are in fact past events. The "two worlds" of past and present are as closely linked here as those of fact and fiction in any work of literary realism; such verisimilitude is an important ingredient of the peculiar spell le Carré's novels cast over their readers. His is a unique world in which love and loyalty may count for nothing in the headlong scramble to betray – may indeed become the only things left to betray in a world without God.

"Jesus Christ only had twelve, you know, and one of them was a double."[11] Kim Philby is alive and well and living in Russia.

NOTES

1. Sometimes le Carré sounds like Conrad. Much is made in *The Looking Glass War* of the fact that the agent Leiser, a Pole, "is not one of us." Smiley, "telling a long story" in *Tinker, Tailor, Soldier, Spy*, continually drinks from a bottle and at one point interjects, "I tell you . . . no one has any business to apologise for what I did." Westerby in *The Honourable Schoolboy* saturates himself in Conrad during his travels through the Far East. Brotherhood in *A Perfect Spy* uses the pseudonym "Marlow."
2. Bruce Page, David Leitch, and Phillip Knightley, *Philby: The Spy Who Betrayed a Generation*; introduction by John le Carré (London, 1968), pp. 33, 400.
3. John le Carré, quoted in *Sunday Telegraph Magazine* (21 October 1979), pp. 108, 114.
4. Page *et al.*, *Philby*, p. 38. My summary of Philby's career and of MI6's past is adapted from this book.
5. Page *et al.*, *Philby*, p. 73.
6. Introduction to Page *et al.*, *Philby*, p. 34.
7. Page *et al.*, *Philby*, p. 173.
8. Andrew Boyle, *The Climate of Treason: Five Who Spied for Russia* (London, 1979), p. 407.
9. My account of the careers of Burgess and Maclean is based on that in *Philby*.
10. My account of the last years of Philby's career is taken from *Philby*.
11. John le Carré, *Tinker, Tailor, Soldier, Spy* (London, 1974), p. 180.

Index

Albert, Prince Consort, 51
All the Year Round (journal), 108, 113
Amis, Kingsley, 27
Anderson, Charles R., 121
Anderson, Quentin, 119
Annan, Noel, Baron, 179
Arnold, Matthew, 48, 81, 167, 216;
  "Rugby Chapel," 167–8; "Stanzas
  from the Grande Chartreuse," 216
Arnold, Thomas: Strachey on, 157, 159,
  161–8, 173; educational principles,
  162–6
Asquith, Herbert Henry, 1st Earl of
  Oxford and Asquith, 155
Athenaeum (club), 229
Athenaeum (journal), 87
Atlantic Monthly, 113
Auden, W. H., 184, 190
Austen, Caroline (Jane's niece), 10, 20
Austen, Cassandra (Jane's mother), 31–
  2
Austen, Cassandra (Jane's sister): and
  Jane's romantic life, 10–19, 23–4, 35;
  destroys Jane's letters, 16–17; death
  of fiancé, 17; on *Mansfield Park*, 19,
  35; declines E. Bridges' proposal, 21;
  relations with Jane, 30
Austen, Charles (Jane's brother), 30
Austen, Edward (Jane's brother), 16, 21
Austen, Eliza de Feuillide; Henry's
  wife, 40
Austen, Francis (Jane's brother), 30
Austen, Rev. George (Jane's father),
  14–15, 18
Austen, Henry (Jane's brother), 22, 24,
  40
Austen, Rev. James (Jane's brother),
  18, 32, 40
Austen, Jane: sex in, 7–8; romantic life
  and suitors, 8–12, 15–25; and Tom
  Lefroy, 9–11, 13, 17, 36; forges
  marriage entries, 11; and E. Taylor,
  12; and Samuel Blackall, 12–13; and
  Mr. Holder, 14–15; and H. F.
  Digweed, 15; and Mr. Evelyn, 16;
  letters destroyed, 16–17; lost lover,
  16–18; financial means, 18–19, 37;
  declines Bigg Wither, 18–20, 35–7, 45;
  declines E. Bridges, 21; and

Lushington, 21–2; and Mr. Seymour,
22; and Haden, 22–4; relations with
sister and mother, 30–2; love of
nature, 33–4; neurasthenia, 33–4; and
the Church, 40–1; love of theater,
41–4; character, 182; Barbara Pym
compared with, 201, 206; remains
unmarried, 212; *Emma*, 7–8, 22–3, 37,
72; *Mansfield Park*: singular nature, 5,
27–9, 35, 44; sex in, 7; marriage
refusal in, 19–20; revised, 21;
autobiographical elements in, 12, 27–
47; vice in, 27–8; on marriage, 36–7;
on materialism, 38; clergymen and
religion in, 40–1; theatricals in, 40–4;
ending, 44–6; somber mood, 46;
Northanger Abbey, 33, 206; *Persuasion*:
sex in, 7, 12; on women's love, 11; on
happiness delayed, 17, 46; E. Bridges
in, 21; bitterness in, 24; sibling rivalry
in, 30; on theater, 42–3; and Barbara
Pym's *Less than Angels*, 206; "Plan of
a Novel" (sketch), 23; *Pride and
Prejudice*: romance in, 7, 12; on
spinsterhood, 14; marriage in, 19;
drafted, 21, 29; publication, 21; on
values, 27; and *Mansfield Park*, 27, 29,
44; sibling rivalry in, 30;
autobiographical elements in, 39;
ending, 46; *Sense and Sensibility*:
romance in, 7; on marriage, 20;
publication, 21; sibling rivalry in, 30;
on landscape "improvements," 33;
on good reading, 44; somber mood,
46; "The Three Sisters," 30; "The
Watsons," 12
Austen, Mary (*née* Lloyd; James's wife),
14
Austen-Leigh, James Edward: *A
Memoir of Jane Austen*, 9, 24
Avery, Leopold, 86

Bagehot, Walter: *The English
Constitution*, 64–5
Bagenal, Barbara, 183
Bailey, J. O., 130
Banks, J. A., 76
Baring, Sir Evelyn (*later* 1st Earl of
Cromer), 169, 171–2

Volkov incident, 229–30, 236

Waldegrave, Frances, Dowager
  Countess (*later* Carlingford), 98
Waterford, John Henry de la Poer
  Beresford, 5th Marquess of, 96
Weber, Carl J., 130–1, 134
Wells, H. G., 118
Wescott, Glenway, 118
West, Dame Rebecca, 185
Westminster Review, 72
Wharton, Edith, 69, 186
Wheatley, Dennis, 215
White, Dick, 232–4, 236
Wilberforce, William, 78
Willey, Basil, 164
Williams, Eric, 80
Wilson, Edmund, 118, 143
Winters, Yvor, 118
Wolseley, Garnet Joseph, 169
women: Trollope's views on, 71–8;
  Dickens on, 76–8, 150–2; Gissing on,
  76, 149–52; American, 109–14

Woolf, Leonard, 156–7, 178, 180–1
Woolf, Virginia: on Hardy's portrait of
  Leslie Stephen, 134; on Strachey,
  155, 181, 183; in *Dreadnought* hoax,
  174; at Post-Impressionist exhibition,
  175; homosexuality, 176–7; resents
  lack of university education, 177;
  Forster on, 181, 189–91; on Duncan
  Grant, Clive Bell, and T. S. Eliot,
  182–3; character, 182–6; anti-
  Semitism, 183; attack on Gissing, 183;
  lives for art, 186; quality of fiction,
  186; warns Elizabeth Bowen of
  James's influence, 193; "The Art of
  Biography," 155, 181; "How It
  Strikes a Contemporary," 156; *Mrs
  Dalloway*, 190; "Modern Fiction,"
  188–9; *A Room of One's Own*, 176; *To
  the Lighthouse*, 182, 186–9; *The Waves*,
  183; *A Writer's Diary*, 186–7
Wordsworth, William, 51

Zabel, Morton, 119